Temagami
A Debate
on Wilderness

The town of Temagami. *Courtesy: Ontario Ministry of Natural Resources.*

Design and Production: JAQ
Editor: Curtis Fahey
Printing and Binding: Gagné Printing Ltd., Louiseville, Quebec, Canada

The editors acknowledge with gratitude the funding assistance of the **Social Sciences and Humanities Research Council** both for the 1989 conference and for help in preparing this manuscript for publication.

Dundurn Press wishes to acknowledge the generous assistance and ongoing support of **The Canada Council, The Book Publishing Industry Development Programme of the Department of Communications, The Ontario Arts Council,** and **The Ontario Heritage Foundation.**

Care has been taken to trace the ownership of copyright material used in the text, including the illustrations. The author and publisher welcome any information enabling them to rectify any reference or credit in subsequent editions.

J. Kirk Howard, Publisher

Canadian Cataloguing in Publication Data

Temagami : a debate on wilderness

Eleven papers presented at a conference held by
Laurentian University's Institute of Northern Ontario
Research and Development in October, 1989.
Includes bibliographical references and index.
ISBN 1-55002-086-2

1. Land use – Ontario – Temagami, Lake, Region – Congresses. 2. Temagami Forest Reserve (Ont.) – Congresses. 3. Algonquian Indians – Claims – Congresses. 4. Algonquian Indians – Land tenure – Congresses. 5. Natural resources – Ontario – Temagami, Lake, Region – Congresses. 6. Wilderness areas – Ontario – Temagami, Lake, Region – Congresses. I. Thomson, Ashley. II. Bray, Robert Matthew. III. Laurentian University of Sudbury. Institute of Northern Ontario Research and Development.

HD319.05T45   1990   333.3'09713'147   C90-095728-X

Dundurn Press Limited
2181 Queen Street East
Suite 301
Toronto, Canada
M4E 1E5

Dundurn Distribution
73 Lime Walk
Headington
Oxford, England
OX3 7AD

Temagami
A Debate
on Wilderness

Edited by
Matt Bray and
Ashley Thomson

Published with the assistance of the
Ontario Heritage Foundation,
Ministry of Culture and Communications

DUNDURN PRESS
Toronto and Oxford
1990

The Temagami issue is of great concern to southern as well as northern Ontarians. Here high school students march on the Legislative Assembly building at Queen's Park in 1989. *Courtesy: Temagami Wilderness Society.*

Table of Contents

SECTION II: ENVIRONMENTAL PERSPECTIVES

SECTION III: THE NATIVE DIMENSION

Contributors

BRIAN BACK is executive director of the Temagami Wilderness Society.

CRANDALL BENSON is an associate professor in the Department of Forestry, Lakehead University, and has done extensive research in the Temagami Area.

MATT BRAY is an associate professor of history and director of the Institute of Northern Ontario Research and Development at Laurentian University.

ROMAN BROZOWSKI is dean of arts at Nipissing University College, and currently chairs the Temagami Advisory Committee.

ROGER FRYER is owner and president of several lumber companies in northeastern Ontario, and former owner of the now-defunct William Milne and Sons of Temagami.

DIANA GORDON is a doctoral student in the Department of Anthropology, McMaster University.

TONY HALL, formerly with the University of Sudbury, Laurentian University, is now an associate professor in the Department of Native American Studies at the University of Lethbridge.

BRUCE HODGINS is a professor of history at Trent University and director of its Centre for Canadian Heritage and Development Studies. He is co-author of *The Temagami Experience: Recreation, Resources, and Aboriginal Rights in the Northern Ontario Wilderness* (Toronto, 1989). Since 1971 he has been the director-president of Camp Wanapitei Coed Camps Ltd., on Lake Temagami.

GERALD KILLAN is a professor in the Department of History, King's College in London. Author of the award-winning *David Boyle: From Artisan to Archaeologist* (Toronto, 1983), Killan has just completed a study of Ontario's provincial parks and is currently working on a history of Algonquin Park.

KENT MCNEIL is an assistant professor, Osgoode Hall Law School.

PETER QUINBY, formerly with the Department of Geography at Wilfrid Laurier University, is a contract researcher for the Temagami Wilderness Society.

JUDITH SKIDMORE is executive director of NORTHCARE (Northern Community Advocates for Resource Equity).

ASHLEY THOMSON is associate librarian at Laurentian University and co-editor of *The Bibliography of Ontario History, 1976-1986* (Toronto: Dundurn Press, 1989).

The debate over Temagami has generated wide interest. Here Bob Rae (then leader of the opposition in Ontario, now premier), joins the protest. He is later arrested with the other protesters.

Introduction

Matt Bray
and Ashley Thomson

Who owns the land of Temagami?
How should the land be used? Over the past two decades these deceptively simple questions have caused a debate of unparalleled intensity among the many interested parties. The conflict has numerous dimensions and levels of complexity. For the Teme-Augama Anishnabai, it is a question of their land, the N'Daki Menan, being under attack. For environmentalists, many of them from other parts of Ontario, it is a case of ecological preservation of a unique but fast disappearing wilderness from the destructiveness of resource extraction. For proponents of multiple-use in Temagami, many of them from the region and dependent for their livelihoods upon the resource sectors, it is a matter of economic survival, both for themselves as individuals and for their communities. While the debate is not uniformly a northern versus southern Ontario one, the strong overtones of this dimension politically complicate the issue.

Beyond the level of grand principles, there are also instances of conflicting self-interest at work in Temagami. For the forest and mining sectors, that self-interest is most patently evident and most frequently commented on. But many anglers and hunters also favour multiple-use because of the motorized access to remote areas that lum-

bering and mining roads afford them. Self-interest, however, is not restricted to multiple-use proponents. In opposing this option, wilderness canoe trippers, youth-camp operators, and cottagers are able to
cloak their own vested interests in the wraps of environmental preservation.

Laurentian University's direct association with the Temagami land-
use conflict is of relatively recent origin, dating from the autumn of
1987 when then President John S. Daniel was appointed chairman of
the Temagami Area Working Group (TAWG), a citizens' committee
created by the Ontario government. Reflecting the complexity of the
debate, TAWG was composed, in addition to Dr Daniel, of fifteen representatives of the various 'stakeholders,' including tourist-camp operators, naturalists, environmentalists, youth-camp operators, wilderness-
tour operators, cottagers and property owners (two), municipalities
(three), prospectors and developers, permanent residents, anglers and
hunters, lumber and sawmill workers, and the woods industry. Notably
absent were the Teme-Augama Anishnabai, who do not recognize provincial jurisdiction over the area in dispute.

The mandate of the group was broad: to "identify and review the
concerns raised about this area in recent months." Its constraints — to
recognize "that environmental values will be protected for present and
future generations; and that the natural resources of the Temagami
area will continue to support jobs for the residents of the region" —
were understandable, if, in retrospect, somewhat naive.[1]

Laurentian University's Institute of Northern Ontario Research and
Development (INORD) acted as a research secretariat to John Daniel,
and therefore had a unique opportunity to follow the debate among
the various TAWG members. With surprisingly few exceptions, a reflection of the chairman's firm-handed guidance, debate on even the
most contentious points was carried on cordially and with good hu-
mour. Because of the absence of the Teme-Augama Anishnabai, there
were two general groupings of members, dividing roughly into environmentalist and multiple-use camps, but this division did not consistently hold true as on specific issues individuals shifted alliances. The
strongest impression left with the independent observer was the sense

that all TAWG members were genuinely concerned about adopting policies in the best interests of Temagami; they fundamentally disagreed, however, about which interests must ultimately be served, and how.

On the surface, the outcome of the group's deliberations would appear to have been failure, since its members, with a single exception and for totally contradictory reasons, refused to endorse the report which John Daniel submitted to the minister of natural resources, Vince Kerrio, in the spring of 1988. On the other hand, the ministry has since acted upon the report's main recommendations, particularly by creating the Temagami Advisory Council, chaired in 1988-89 by John Daniel and subsequently by Roman Brozowski, a geographer and dean of arts at Nipissing University College in North Bay. As a step in an ongoing process designed to resolve the conflict, then, TAWG was far from unsuccessful.

Since the submission of the TAWG report, the issue has evolved in new directions. The Temagami Advisory Council has worked steadily to devise development strategies that will accommodate as wide a spectrum of the Temagami stakeholders as possible. On 23 April there was a new turn of events when, as reported in the Toronto *Globe and Mail*, the Ontario government announced that the Teme-Augama Anishnabai "will have a veto over an environmentally sensitive 40,000 hectare tract of the Temagami forest ... The land in question, comprising four townships recently opened to logging companies with the completion of the Red Squirrel road, will be controlled from now on by a joint stewardship council. Half of its members will be appointed by the provincial government, and half by the Teme-Augama Anishnabai, the Indian band in the area."[2]

The government announcement was evaluated as a disaster by Roger Fryer, president of the William Milne and Sons mill in Temagami, a lumber company destined to go out of business with a loss of seventy jobs. And while the announcement was greeted with applause both by environmentalists and by the Indian band, neither viewed the decision as final. Again according to the *Globe and Mail*, environmentalists are concerned that about "30 per cent of the old-growth red and white pine that had originally been scheduled for cutting in Temagami over the next two years will still be cut down." Meanwhile, the Bear Island band, while acknowledging that the arrangement is an historic first towards Native self-government, nonetheless "intends to proceed with a lawsuit against the provincial government in which it is seeking title to 10,000 square kilometres in Temagami." The case is scheduled to be heard soon before the Supreme Court of Canada.[3]

Adding a new and unexpected dimension to the Temagami debate, of course, was the victory of Bob Rae's New Democratic Party in the September 1990 provincial election in Ontario. This would seem to portend well for the environmentalist cause. After all, few are the interest groups that can point to a premier having been arrested on their behalf. On the other hand, the political reality is that six members of the new cabinet represent northern Ontario constituencies, a level of representation for the north higher than that of any other time in the province's history. All backed by labour and all representing areas that need new employment, these members may temper what appear to be the premier's own inclinations on the subject.

If the various issues in Temagami are complex and confused, so too is the geographical definition of the area (Figures 1 and 2). As one of our contributors, Bruce Hodgins, explains in his recent book *The Temagami Experience*, co-authored with Jamie Benidickson:

> Ontario has never maintained a geographical district that corresponds exactly with our understanding of the Temagami country. The area certainly includes much more than the heartland immediately adjacent to Lake Temagami itself and to what is now the Lady Evelyn-Smoothwater Wilderness Park. It is somewhat larger than the boundaries of the original Temagami Forest Reserve established in 1901 with the stated intention that sustained-yield pine forest management might be implemented there. The area ... is also larger than the administrative unit currently known to the Ontario Ministry of Natural Resources as the District of Temagami ... The boundaries of the Temagami country are also close to the N'Daki Menan, the aboriginal homeland of the Teme-Augama Anishnabai.[4]

In an attempt to bring some clarity to the issues swirling around Temagami, INORD, drawing upon its experience with the Temagami Area Working Group, invited participants in the debate, as well as academics who have studied the area, to its first annual conference. This conference was held on 20 and 21 October 1989 on the Laurentian campus. Not all of the presentations were appropriate for this volume, several being of a highly technical nature. Still, a sufficient number were of such moment that INORD felt it in the public interest to make them generally available through publication. Most of those not found here have been published by INORD as part of its Technical Papers series and may be obtained from the institute.[5] In both cases the views expressed in the articles are those of their authors and not those of either INORD or Laurentian University.

The articles fall naturally into three categories — "Aspects of Resource Development," "Environmental Perspectives," and "The Native Dimension." Section I, "Aspects of Resource Development," begins with Peter Quinby's "Self-replacement of White Pine in Old-growth Forests of Temagami, Ontario." In this piece Quinby, a researcher for the Temagami Wilderness Society and formerly at Wilfrid Laurier University, examines the "old growth" idea and explains, in his opinion, why the Temagami pine stands must be preserved. Crandall Benson, a member of Lakehead's School of Forestry, approaches the question from a rather different angle. Although he sympathizes with the preservationist argument, the thesis of his paper, "Theoretically, the Management of Multiple Resources *is* Simple," is that the harvesting of Temagami's forests must be brought into balance with its regeneration, something he believes has not been done over the past sixty years.

In contrast, Roger Fryer, owner of the ill-fated William Milne and Sons mill in Temagami, as well as of several other lumber companies in northeastern Ontario, defends the record of the forest industry and paints his environmentalist opponents as enthusiastic but misguided persons whose actions place the industry and its workers at risk. The forest industry and recreational tourism, he believes, can co-exist in the Temagami area in the future, just as they have in the past. Supporting Fryer, but from a broader community perspective, is Judith Skidmore, executive vice-president of NORTHCARE (Northern Community Advocates for Resource Equity), who also argues that the solution to the Temagami conundrum is to be found in the "multiple-use" of the land.

Rounding out this section is a paper by Roman Brozowski entitled "The Importance of Tourism in the Temagami Area." Looking more to the future, Brozowski spells out some of the economic options to be considered if natural-resource exploitation increasingly gives way to tourism and recreation as the economic base of the region.

Section II, "Environmental Perspectives," begins with a general analysis of political developments relating to Temagami during the past two decades by Gerald Killan, an historian at King's College, University of Western Ontario. In "The Development of a Wilderness Park System in Ontario, 1967-1988: Temagami in Context," Killan shows how the policies of successive provincial governments, Conservative to 1985 and Liberal thereafter, have been shaped by representations made by the affected groups, the views of various governmental departments, political expediency, and their own philosophical presuppositions. The paper also demonstrates the changing dilemmas facing the Ministry of Natural Resources, the arm of government chiefly responsible for administering policy in the area.

In "Contexts of the Temagami Predicament," Bruce Hodgins, an historian at Trent University as well as the director-president of Camp Wanapitei Coed Camps Ltd. on Lake Temagami, presents the recent conflicts from a dedicated environmentalist's perspective, and especially points his finger at the Ontario government for failing to address the Temagami issues with imagination. Brian Back, executive director of the Temagami Wilderness Society, expresses the same view in his article. His concerns, and those of the TWS, are primarily ecological, and directed towards preserving Temagami's old-growth forests for the enjoyment of future generations.

Setting the stage for Section III, "The Native Dimension" of the Temagami conflict, is a list of "Key Dates" prepared by the Teme-Augama Anishnabai, detailing their dealings with the governments of Canada and Ontario with respect to the N'Daki Menan over the past 115 years. Diana Gordon's "Prehistoric Occupations at Lake Temagami," which follows, presents an archaeological perspective on the Temagami region. Gordon, an archaeologist at McMaster University, notes that the Temagami area has been inhabited for more than 6,000 years. On the basis of her research at the Three Pines Site on Lake Temagami, she argues that the area has a rich archaeological heritage that "is worthy of consideration and protection in future land-use planning."

Gordon's findings lead naturally to a discussion of the Teme-Augama Anishnabai land claim. Kent McNeil's "The Temagami Indian Land Claim: Loosening the Judicial Strait-jacket" is a careful analysis of the legal thinking that underlay the Ontario courts' treatment of the Teme-Augama Anishnabai claims. He concludes that it is the task of the Supreme Court of Canada to "loosen even further the unjustifiable restraints ... placed on aboriginal title over a century ago." Tony Hall, formerly of the University of Sudbury, Laurentian University, and now with the Department of Native American Studies at the University of Lethbridge, agrees. In "Where Justice Lies: Aboriginal Rights and Wrongs in Temagami" Hall reviews the history of Native land claims in the Temagami area and concludes that "there is an undercurrent of polite brutality" in most of the court-room dramas in which Natives have been involved. Whatever the legal outcome, he argues, justice lies only in one direction. If Hall and McNeil are correct, the Supreme Court of Canada will be hard pressed not to overturn the decisions of the lower courts.

It will quickly become apparent to readers that the majority of authors contributing to this volume come down on the Teme-Augama Anishnabai/environmentalist side of the debate. That is by accident rather than by design, and, more than anything else, reflects the state of research on the subject at the present time within Ontario's academic community. It should not, therefore, be interpreted to mean that the multiple-use proponents are without arguments. Similarly, the case in defence of the policies and practices of successive Ontario governments and their agencies, such as the much-maligned Ministry of Natural Resources, remains to be documented. Like the land-use conflict itself, one suspects, the story of Temagami is only beginning to be written.

To assist readers, glossaries defining technical terms particular to their respective disciplines have been appended to the articles by Peter Quinby and Diana Gordon. No attempt has been made to adopt a sin-gle uniform endnote style; instead, authors were encouraged to use the system most appropriate to their discipline.

For their financial assistance to the publication of this volume, we would like especially to thank the Social Sciences and Humanities Research Council of Canada and the Ontario Heritage Foundation. Also to be thanked is Dr Paul Bator, the historical consultant at the Foundation who worked with the editors since the inception of the manuscript. Kirk Howard and Mark Fenton of Dundurn Press, along with Curtis Fahey, were particularly helpful in the final editing of the papers. We must also acknowledge the contributions made by Margaret Hogan, a student assistant, and Lucille Brisebois, INORD's secretary, both to the success of the 1989 conference and to the production of this book. Finally, much credit is due to Laurentian University for the support and encouragement it has given to the research activities of the Institute of Northern Ontario Research and Development, and to the members of INORD Council for their efforts on the institute's behalf.

Matt Bray

Ashley Thomson

---

[1] Ontario Ministry of Natural Resources, "Fact Sheet," November 1987.

[2] *Globe and Mail* 24 April 1990, 1.

[3] *Ibid.*, 2.

[4] Bruce Hodgins and Jamie Benidickson, *The Temagami Experience: Recreation, Resources, and Aboriginal Rights in the Northern Ontario Wilderness* (Toronto: University of Toronto Press, 1989), 3–4.

[5] J. Roger Pitblado, "Satellite Remote Sensing: Possibilities and Limitations in Aid of Temagami Planning"; R.J. Day and J.V. Carter, "The Temagami Forest: Based on a Photointerpretive Survey and Forest Resources Inventory of Temagami District"; E. Willauer and T. Ton-That, "The Economics of Forestry"; Robert A. Cameron, "The Mineral Potential of The Temagami Area."

FIGURE 1

**PROVINCIAL
AND REGIONAL
SETTING OF
TEMAGAMI
AREA**

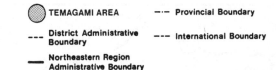

TEMAGAMI AREA

District Administrative Boundary

Northeastern Region Administrative Boundary

Provincial Boundary

International Boundary

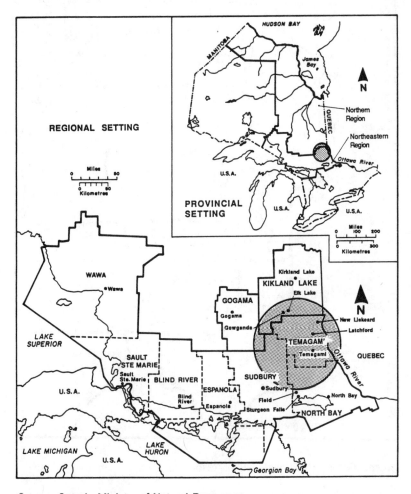

Source: Ontario Ministry of Natural Resources

FIGURE 2: The Temagami Area

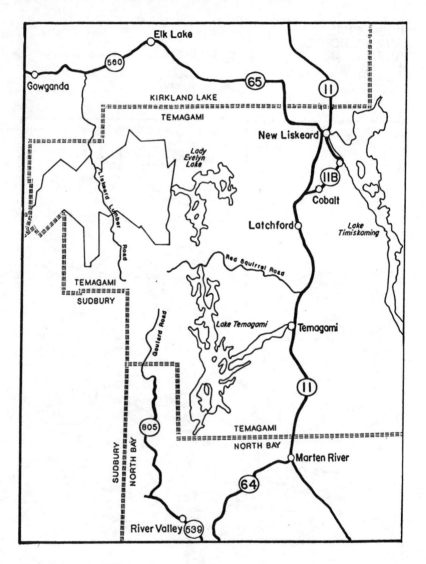

Source: Ontario Ministry of Natural Resources

Aspects of
Resource Development

At the heart of the conflict is the fate of Temagami's old-growth forest. Photo by Sean Sharpe. *Courtesy: Ontario Ministry of Natural Resources*

One

Self-replacement of White Pine in Old-growth Forests of Temagami, Ontario*

Peter Quinby

Catastrophic fire has generally been accepted as the facilitator of natural white pine regeneration (Maissurow 1935, Horton and Brown 1960, Frissell 1973, Ahlgren 1976). This ecological premise has spawned the theory in forestry that over-mature (also known as "old-growth") white pine (*Pinus strobus* L.) forests will simply fall apart in the absence of catastrophic fire, resulting in wasted fibre if not actively managed. Thus, the management strategy in many parts of Ontario including the Temagami region has been to clearcut old-growth white pine forest and maximize the number of rotations thereafter in order to obtain greatest fibre production (Ontario Ministry of Natural Resources 1983, Ontario Ministry of Natural Resources 1985, Stiell 1985).

Recent studies, however, have shown that continuous white-pine recruitment occurs within old-growth white-pine dominated stands,

* This research was conducted under contract to the Temagami Wilderness Society. Funding was provided by the Foster Hewitt Foundation, the Charles F. Fells Charitable Trust, and Mr. John Hackney. Those who provided direct contributions included but are not limited to Brian Back, Terry Carleton, Janet Childerhose, Laura Farkerson, Jim Garratt, Terry Graves, Bruce Hodgins, Ian Kennedy, Long Li, Elizabeth Macey, John McAndrews, George Meadows, Maryjka Mychajlowycz, Jennifer Purdon, the Teme-Augama Anishnabai, Hap Wilson, Trudy Wilson, and Teresa Zuniga.

many of which originate following catastrophic fire (Gilbert 1978, Holla and Knowles 1988, Quinby 1989). This continuous recruitment of white pine may take place for centuries in response to non-catastrophic disturbance, and results in at least a partial uneven-aged stand structure. Such local disturbances may include small patch fires, windthrown trees, and the death of large, individual trees through biological or other agents. In the old-growth coniferous forests of the Pacific northwestern United States, where fire rotations vary from 94 to 434 years, canopy gaps formed by non-catastrophic disturbances are also critical to successful regeneration of shade-tolerant as well as shade-intolerant tree species (Spies and Franklin 1989).

In theory, an uneven-aged stand structure implies the use of the selection system for harvesting trees. Despite the uneven-aged nature of some white-pine forests, however, the Ontario Ministry of Natural Resources (1983) has stated that white pine "must be managed under some form of even-aged management system; uneven-aged management by the selection system is not acceptable." Counter to this management strategy, Benson *et al.* (1989) suggest that natural regeneration facilitated through the use of the selection system of harvesting should be considered for white-pine forest in Temagami. Where the old-growth condition is desired, however, it is unlikely that logging is a viable strategy (Society of American Foresters 1984).

To date, studies of old-growth white-pine dynamics have focused only on the living tree component. As a result, descriptions of vegetation development have been limited to the number of years equivalent to the oldest trees in the stand, usually around 200 years (Gilbert 1978, Holla and Knowles 1988). By including dead vegetation as evidence of past forest composition, the successional sequence can be expanded by many years. The purpose of the present study was to examine self-replacement and its general features in old-growth white-pine forest. This was accomplished by reconstructing the composition and abundance of dead trees (Henry and Swan 1974, Oliver and Stephens 1977) and by sampling live overstory and understory trees in order to identify general successional trends. Implicit in the process of self-replacement in eastern North American forests unaffected by catastrophic disturbance is gap-phase regeneration, hitherto only associated with deciduous-dominated forests (Lorimer 1980, Runkle 1981, 1982).

STUDY AREA

The old-growth white-pine forest in the Wakimika Triangle Area of Temagami, Ontario, has been identified as the largest continuous stand of old-growth white-pine forest remaining in the province (Pinto 1989). The Wakimika Triangle Area is centrally located within the Temagami region and lies adjacent to the southeast corner of Lady Evelyn-Smoothwater Provincial Park (Figure 1). The study area included most of Shelburne Township, the northeastern portion of Delhi Township, and the extreme western portion of Canton Township. It is centred approximately at Latitude 47 degrees 10 minutes North, Longitude 80 degrees 20 minutes West.

General features of the climate in the Temagami region were provided by Brown *et al.* (1980). Mean daily temperature varies from 8 degrees F for January to 66 degrees F for July. Mean annual precipitation is approximately 32 in. The frost-free period is approximately 100 days, and the mean annual length of the growing season is approximately 180 days.

The terrain throughout much of the Wakimika Triangle Area is very rugged, featuring steep topography with many escarpments and elevations that range from 900 to 1,500 ft above sea level. The surficial geology is controlled mainly by the results of Wisconsin glacial activity and to a lesser extent by the underlying bedrock. There are many lakes both large and small with interconnecting systems of streams and rivers.

In upland areas the surficial geological material is dominated by glacial tills. These tills are composed mainly of dry to moist silty loams (Johnson 1988). Some upland areas, usually knolls, are characterized by exposed bedrock and bedrock with very shallow loamy tills, the result of scouring during glacial advance. Valley bottoms are often dominated by medium- to fine-grained sands of glaciofluvial origin (Johnson 1988). A small percentage of the area is covered with organic soils where drainage is impaired.

The forest vegetation of the Temagami region falls within the Laurentian Upland Section, Great Lakes–St. Lawrence Division, Hemlock-White pine-Northern Hardwoods Forest Region (Braun 1950). Rowe (1972) has described the forests of the area as typified by

> eastern white pine with scattered white birch and white spruce, although the spruce frequently rivals the pine in abundance. Another common though variable type is a mixture of the birch, pine and spruce, with balsam fir, trembling and largetooth aspens. Both red pine and jack pine are present, the former often prominent in bluffs along ridges, and the latter generally restricted to the driest sandy or rocky sites. The tolerant hardwoods, yellow birch and sugar maple, have only a scattered occurrence. The prevalent forest cover on the uplands is clearly a reflection of periodic past fires, and the sandy soils have provided conditions especially favourable for the propagation of eastern white pine, red pine and jack pine. On the lowlands, in poorly-drained depressions and in swamps, black spruce with tamarack or eastern white cedar, form well-marked communities.

In addition, McAndrews (1978) has shown that the centre of white-pine abundance in Ontario is located in the Temagami region.

METHODS

Forest succession was reconstructed using both live and dead vegetation to test the hypothesis that white-pine forest can be self-replacing. Logs were studied to determine the abundance and composition of the oldest forest. Snags, defined as dead standing trees, which are generally younger than logs, were sampled to represent the more recent forest. The abundance and composition of the present forest was obtained from the existing live trees. And the potential composition of the future forest was assessed by sampling tree regeneration in the understory.

The major weakness of this approach is that it does not incorporate the technique of cross-dating, which provides for the determination of the year in which an individual tree died, and thus allows for a precise chronology of events. The approach used could not account for the differential rate of decay between species or events in which a tree became a log without ever having been a snag. The state of decay (snag or log) is, therefore, not always directly related to age. For example, a tree toppled by windthrow would be classified as a log and accordingly would be misinterpreted as being older than members of its cohort, many of which may still be live trees. Recent windthrown trees were, however, seldom observed in the sample plots. Despite this weakness, the approach adopted here was useful for identifying general successional trends.

Old-growth forests are characterized by minimum amounts of old live trees, snags, and logs (Old-Growth Definition Task Group 1986). The major criterion used to select plots for this study was the presence of a minimum of two white or red pine, each at least 140 years old within a 50 x 20 m plot. The minimum of two old trees was based on quantitative vegetation survey results from the Big Crow Nature Reserve Zone in Algonquin Park, Ontario (Sheehey 1980), which is considered by the Ontario Ministry of Natural Resources to be one of the finest examples of old-growth white-pine forest in North America (Strickland and Ward 1987). Through his survey work in Algonquin's old-growth white-pine stands, Sheehey (1980) found that, at most, two old white-pine trees could be included within a circular plot of 1,256 m².

A total of 36 plots within the Wakimika Triangle Area (Figure 1) were established and permanently marked for future relocation. To sample the overstory, all trees 10 cm diameter at breast height (dbh) and greater within the plot were identified, measured for dbh, and numbered using plastic tags. All snags greater than 10 cm dbh and taller than 2 m within the plot were identified to the species level when possible and measured for dbh. Logs occurring within the plot having a minimum diameter of 15 cm at the larger end and a minimum length of 1 m were also inventoried. Log measurements included diameter at each end and total length. In the case of genus-level identification for both snags and logs, the proportion of species positively identified within that genus was used to allocate the unknown amount to the abundance of those species positively identified within that genus. Those logs that could not be identified to the genus level were excluded from the analysis.

Tree regeneration was defined as trees that were less than 10 cm dbh. A total of 11 2x1 m quadrats for estimating the per cent cover of tree regeneration were located at 5 m intervals along the first 50 m side of the plot. The 2 m side of the quadrat was positioned perpendicular to the 50 m side of the plot, and the 1 m ends of the quadrats ran parallel to the 50 m plot side at a distance of 1 m either side of the plot side line. For each individual tree and snag sampled, dbh values were converted to basal-area values expressed as m^2/ha. Log diameter and length measurements were used to produce log-biomass estimates. These basal-area and biomass estimates were then summed by species for each plot and for the study area as a whole. Tree regeneration cover for each species was estimated for each plot and for the entire study area.

A size-class analysis based on 8 plots within the largest old-growth white-pine stand in the study area was carried out. At each of the 36 plots, observations on fire and windthrow were also made. Nomenclature followed Fernald (1950).

RESULTS

A total of 12 tree species were found within the old-growth white-pine forest in the Wakimika Triangle Area (Table 1). All 12 occurred within the living overstory. Table 1 and Figure 2 show the absolute and relative abundance of trees, snags, logs, and regeneration. The most abundant species in the living overstory of these old-growth stands was white pine (19.5 m^2/ha) followed by red pine (3.7 m^2/ha) and white birch (3.4 m^2/ha). A total of 10 snag species were found in the study area. Of the 12 tree species, yellow birch and red oak were missing from the snag component. White pine dominated the snag component with a basal area of 4.1 m^2/ha followed by white birch (1.2 m^2/ha) and balsam fir (.7 m^2/ha). A total of 9 log species were identified in the log component. Of the 12 tree species, yellow birch, red oak, and red maple were absent from the log component. The most abundant species in the log component was white pine (35.5m³/ha), followed by white birch (8.3 m³/ha) and red pine (5.7 m³/ha).

A total of 10 tree species were present in the understory of the old-growth white-pine stands. Of the 12 tree species, both jack pine and red oak were absent. In contrast to the dominance of white pine in the overstory, snag, and log components, white pine (6.3 per cent cover) was only the fourth most abundant species within the understory behind balsam fir (19.4 per cent cover), black spruce (14.2 per cent cover) and red maple (13.4 per cent cover). The success of tree regeneration, however, depends on more than species abundance. Also important to successful regeneration are species-growth strategies and the availability of resources necessary for growth, the latter being controlled mainly by disturbance.

Figure 3 shows the size-class distribution for all overstory species sampled within the largest old-growth white-pine stand. The inverse "J"-shaped curve is typical of an uneven-aged forest where many stems are present in the smaller size classes and where there is a rapid decrease in stem number through the progression to the largest size classes. When the size-class distribution for white pine alone is plotted for this stand, a more variable curve emerges (Figure 4). The combination of some size classes (1, 2, 3, 7, 8, 14, 17, 18) fit the standard uneven-aged curve, whereas the peaks expressed by two other groups of size classes (4, 5, 6 and 9, 10, 11, 12, 13) are more characteristic of an even-aged size-class structure.

The species consistently of greatest abundance within the log, snag, and overstory tree component included white pine, white birch, black spruce, red pine, and balsam fir. Figure 5 shows the relative change in abundance over time for these five species. From this figure it can be seen that coincident with a decrease in white- and red-pine from the log component to the snag component was an increase in balsam fir, black spruce, and white birch. And with an increase in white- and red-pine abundance from the snag to the tree component there was a corresponding decrease in the other three species. This inverse relationship between changes in species abundances may reflect species growth-strategy responses to both disturbance and stand aging.

Evidence of windthrow was observed in or immediately adjacent to 26 of the 36 plots or at approximately 72 per cent of the plots. Evidence of fire in the form of fire scars on trees was observed in 22 of the 36 plots or at approximately 61 per cent of the plots.

DISCUSSION

General successional trends for old-growth pine forests in Temagami were examined using live and dead vegetation. Because data were not available for the rate of log decay of large white-pine trees, it was necessary to estimate the time period represented in these reconstructed successional trends using data available for Douglas-fir log decay. Douglas-fir logs between 40 and 60 cm dbh require up to 350 years to decompose (Harmon et al. 1986), and decomposition rates for Douglas-fir biomass may be more than twice that of white pine (data from Alway and Zon 1930, NOAA 1980, Cole and Rapp 1981, Vogt et al. 1986). If we extrapolate from this data, we can conclude that large white pine may require up to 700 years to completely decompose. Accordingly, keeping in mind that many logs in their final stages of decomposition were not included in the analysis, we may say that the successional trends represented by the dead-wood component in this study represent up to 500 years of vegetation development. With the addition of an approximate figure of 200 years to represent the live-tree component, successional trends in this study may represent up to 700 years of forest development.

The reconstructed forest-development trend for this period shows that white pine has been the dominant species within these old-growth forests. The dominance of white pine over the past several centuries was most likely maintained by continuous recruitment of white pine as shown in the results of the size-class analysis. Over the time period examined, the abundance of white pine also fluctuated less than any other species of major importance, including red pine, black spruce, balsam fir, and white birch. Except for white and red pine, all other species of major importance peaked in abundance mid way through the successional sequence. This peak may be evidence of a cyclical or alternating species co-dominance (Fox 1977) in response to conditions created by continuously occurring small-scale disturbances. For example, when non-catastrophic disturbance such as a surface fire occurs and large old-growth pine are left unharmed, early successional species such as white birch may colonize in abundance below the dominant overstory white pine. But, eventually, in the absence of further disturbance, early successional species will be outcompeted by the more shade-tolerant species such as balsam fir and black spruce, which may colonize exposed and non-exposed areas in smaller densities than early successional species. Non-catastrophic disturbance of sufficient severity initiates the cycle once again.

White pine is intermediate in shade tolerance (Baker 1949, Logan 1966), in contrast to shade-tolerant species such as balsam fir and black spruce and also to shade intolerant species such as red pine and white birch. Consequently, it can exploit a range of light conditions at the forest floor created by canopies ranging from open to closed and multilayered. Thus the limiting factor in the success of white-pine regeneration would not seem to be its performance under various light conditions, but rather its potential for seed dissemination and germination on exposed mineral soil or on a thin litter layer (Horton and Brown 1960, Methven 1973, Ahlgren 1976).

Disturbance patches created by windthrow and small surface fires are not large in area relative to areas normally affected by catastrophic fire. Yet they are characterized by exposed mineral soil and canopy openings representing sites of maximum resource availability, which in turn provide ideal conditions for white-pine regeneration. Throughout the mixed deciduous forests of North America, disturbed patches created by windthrow have often been colonized by white pine (Cline and Spurr 1942, Goodlett 1954).

Although white-pine regeneration in the study area was only the fourth most abundant, observations indicated that it was often most successful when associated with canopy gaps created by windthrow, small patch fire, and the death of large trees. These regenerating pine were sometimes seen in clusters of multiple stems where the peripheral saplings may act as buffers against competition, thereby maximizing the potential for the central or most competitive individual in the cluster to survive to maturity (Cline and Lockard 1925, Goodlett 1960, Hibbs 1982).

In addition, size- and age-class analyses indicating continuous recruitment of white pine within old-growth white-pine forest in the area observed in this study, in other parts of Temagami (Gilbert 1978), and in northeastern Ontario (Holla and Knowles 1988) provide indirect evidence that shifting, small-scale disturbances such as windthrow and small patch fires (Bormann and Likens 1979) create local sites for white-pine regeneration. In contrast, if these old-growth white-pine forests were solely dependent on catastrophic fire for regeneration, even-aged stands with little or no continuous recruitment would dominate.

Observations of natural disturbance in the study area indicated that windthrow occurred more frequently than fire, although the aerial extent of both disturbances is unknown and may not necessarily reflect this same relationship. For the study area, it is likely that the frequency of catastrophic fire was low, but detailed fire-frequency studies have not yet been conducted. During the interval between these infrequent catastrophic events, local disturbances caused by small fires, windthrow, and individual tree death most likely resulted in the renewed availability of resources required for tree establishment and growth. Because of its silvical characteristics, especially its ability to grow in a variety of light conditions and to produce high quantities of seed (Fowells 1965), white pine has been able to exploit successfully small patches of increased resource availability.

Although it is clear that old-growth white-pine forest in Temagami has been self-replacing over the last 700 years or so, it is not evident whether this process will continue in the future, especially in light of the current policy of fire suppression. Therefore, the extent and nature of small-disturbance patches and their associated white-pine regeneration will be an important focus for future studies. These studies should be long-term in nature through the use of permanent plots so that our understanding of forest development in old-growth white-pine forest is based on site-specific factual information.

FIGURE 1 — Location of study area and plots

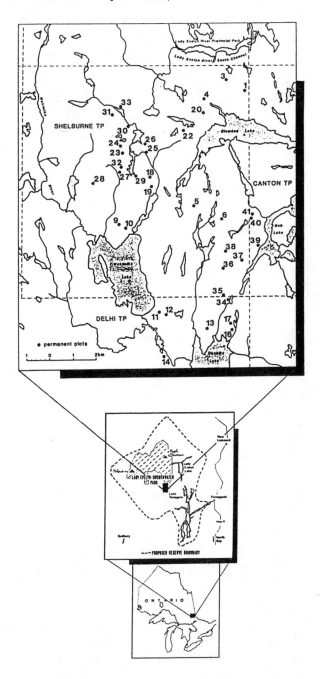

FIGURE 2 — Relative abundance of regeneration, trees, snags, and logs in old-growth white-pine stands

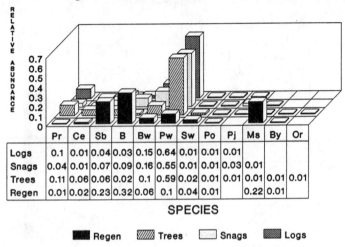

	Pr	Ce	Sb	B	Bw	Pw	Sw	Po	Pj	Ms	By	Or
Logs	0.1	0.01	0.04	0.03	0.15	0.64	0.01	0.01	0.01			
Snags	0.04	0.01	0.07	0.09	0.16	0.55	0.01	0.01	0.03	0.01		
Trees	0.11	0.06	0.06	0.02	0.1	0.59	0.02	0.01	0.01	0.01	0.01	0.01
Regen	0.01	0.02	0.23	0.32	0.06	0.1	0.04	0.01		0.22	0.01	

SPECIES

■ Regen   ▨ Trees   □ Snags   ▨ Logs

Key to species — Pr–red pine, Ce–white cedar, Sb–black spruce, B–balsam fir, Bw–white birch, Pw–white pine, Sw–white spruce, Po–poplar, Pj–jack pine, Ms–red maple, By–yellow birch, Or–red oak

FIGURE 3 — DBH size – class distribution for all species in old-growth white-pine stands

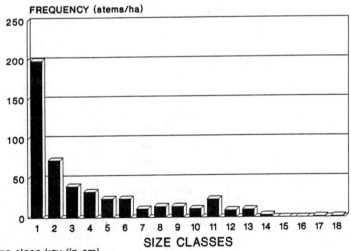

SIZE CLASSES

Size class key (in cm) —
1 (10.0-14.9), 2 (15.0-19.9), 3 (20.0-24.9), 4 (25.0-29.9), 5 (30.0-34.9), 6 35.0-39.9), 7 (40.0-44.9), 8 (45.0-49.9), 9 (50.0-54.9), 10 (55.0-59.9), 11 (60.0-64.9), 12 (65.0-69.9), 13 (70.0-74.9), 14 (75.0-79.9), 15 (80.0-84.9), 16 (85.0-89.9), 17 (90.0-94.5), 18 (95.0-100.0)

FIGURE 4 — DBH size-class distribution for white-pine in old-growth white pine stands

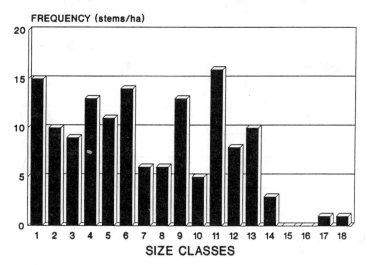

Size class key (in cm)
1 (10.0-14.9), 2 (15.0-19.9), 3 (20.0-24.9), 4 (25.0-29.9), 5 (30.0-34.9), 6
35.0-39.9), 7 (40.0-44.9), 8 (45.0-49.9), 9 (50.0-54.9), 10 (55.0-59.9), 11
(60.0-64.9), 12 (65.0-69.9), 13 (70.0-74.9), 14 (75.0-79.9), 15 (80.0-
84.9), 16 (85.0-89.9), 17 (90.0-94.5), 18 (95.0-100.0)

FIGURE 5 — Relative change in abundance for the five major tree species in a reconstructed old-growth white-pine successional sequence

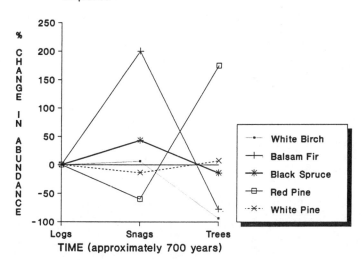

TABLE 1 — Summary of vegetation data for old-growth white pine stands

SPECIES	REGENERATION (% Cover)	TREES (m²/ha)	SNAGS (m²/ha)	LOGS (m³/ha)
Abies balsamifera	19.4	.6	.7	1.6
Picea mariana	14.2	2.1	.5	2.5
Acer rubrum	13.4	.2	.1	
Pinus strobus	6.3	19.5	4.1	35.5
Betula papyrifera	3.7	3.4	1.2	8.3
Picea glauca	2.6	.6	.1	.1
Thuja occidentalis	1.1	1.9	.1	.8
Betula lutea	.2	.1		
Populus spp.	.2	.2	.1	.7
Pinus resinosa	.1	3.7	.3	5.7
Pinus banksiana		.4	.2	.6
Quercus rubra		.1		

Glossary

Abies balsamifera: Balsam fir

Acer rubrum: Red maple

Basal area: Trunk cross-sectional area

Betula lutea: Yellow birch

Betula papyrifera: White birch

Coniferous: Bearing cones (normally referring to evergreens)

dbh: diameter at breast height

Deciduous: Tree that sheds its leaves at least every year

Escarpment: The abrupt face or cliff of a ridge or hill range

Hectare: In the metric system, one hectare equals 2.471 acres

m2/ha: Square metres per hectare

m3/ha: Cube metres per hectare (a volume measurement)

Overstory: Layer of vegetation formed by the tallest trees in a forest

Picea glauca: White spruce

Picea mariana: Black spruce

Pinus banksiana: Jack Pine

Pinus resinosa: Red pine

Pinus strobus: White pine

Populus: Poplar

Quercus rubra: Red oak

Silvical: Pertaining to the scientific study of the growth and life of forest trees

Thuja occidentalis: Eastern cedar

Understory: Layer of vegetation growing beneath the level of the tallest trees in a forest based on site-specific factual information

References

Ahlgren, C.E. 1976. "Regeneration of Red and White pine Following Wildfire and Logging in Northeastern Minnesota." *Journal of Forestry* 74:135-40.

Alway, F.J., and R. Zon. 1930. "Quantity and Nutrient Content of Pine Leaf Litter." *Journal of Forestry* 28:715-27.

Baker, F.S. 1949. "A Revised Tolerance Table." *Journal of Forestry* 47:179-81.

Benson, C.A., H. Cumming, H. Akervall and Willard Carmean. 1989. *The Need for a Land Stewardship, Holistic Resource Management Plan for N'Daki Menan.* School of Forestry, Lakehead University, Thunder Bay, Ontario.

Bormann, F.H., and G.E. Likens. 1979. *Pattern and Process in a Forested Ecosystem.* Springer-Verlag, New York.

Braun, E.L. 1950. *Deciduous Forests of Eastern North America.* Hafner Press, New York.

Brown, D.M., G.A. McKay and L.J. Chapman. 1980. *The Climate of Southern Ontario.* Environment Canada, Atmospheric Environment Service, Climate Studies No. 5, Canadian Government Publication Centre, Hull, Quebec.

Cline, A.C., and C.R. Lockard. 1925. *Mixed White pine and Hardwood.* Bulletin of the Harvard Forest No. 8.

Cline, A.C., and S. H. Spurr. 1942. *The Virgin Upland Forest of Central New England.* Bulletin of the Harvard Forest 21.

Cole, D.W., and M. Rapp. 1981. "Elemental Cycling in Forests." In D.E. Reichle, ed., *Dynamic Properties of Forest Ecosystems.* International Biological Program 23, Cambridge University Press, London. 341-409.

Fahey, T.J., and W.A. Reiners. 1981. *Fires in the Forests of Maine and New Hampshire.* Bulletin of the Torrey Botanical Club 108:362-73.

Fernald, M.L. 1950. *Gray's Manual of Botany.* American Book Co., New York.

Fowells, H.A. 1965. *Silvics of Forest Trees of the United States.* USDA Handbook. No. 271, Forest Service, Washington, DC.

Fox, J.F. 1977. "Alternation and Coexistance of Tree Species." *American Naturalist* 111:69-89.

Frissell, S.S. 1973. "The Importance of Fire as a Natural Ecological Factor in Itasca State Park, Minnesota." *Quaternary Research* 3:397-407.

Gilbert, B. 1978. Growth and Development of White Pine(*Pinus strobus* L.) at Lake Temagami. M.Sc.F. Thesis, University of Toronto, Ontario.

Goodlett, J.C. 1954. *Vegetation Adjacent to the Border of Wisconsin Drift in Potter County, Pennsylvania.* Bulletin of the Harvard Forest No. 25, 93.

Goodlett, J.C. 1960. *The Development of Site Concepts at the Harvard Forest and their Impact on Management Policy.* Bulletin of the Harvard Forest No. 28.

Harmon, M.E., J.F. Franklin, F.J. Swanson, P. Sollins, S.V. Gregory, J.D. Lattin, N.H. Anderson, S.P. Cline, N.G. Aumen, J.R. Sedell, G.W. Lienkaemper, K. Cromack, Jr., and K.W. Cummins. 1986. "Ecology of Coarse Woody Debris in Temperate Ecosystems." *Advances in Ecological Research* 15:133-302.

Henry, J.D., and J.M. Swan. 1974. "Reconstructing Forest History from Live and Dead Plant Material — An Approach to the Study of Forest Succession in Southwest New Hampshire." *Ecology* 55:772-83.

Hibbs, D.E. 1982. "White pine in the Transition Hardwood Forest." *Canadian Journal of Botany* 60:2046-53.

Holla, T.A., and P. Knowles. 1988. "Age Structure Analysis of a Virgin White Pine, *Pinus strobus*, Population." *Canadian Field Naturalist* 102:221-6.

Horton, K.W., and W.G.E. Brown. 1960. *Ecology of White and Red Pine in the Great Lakes-St. Lawrence Forest Region.* Canada Department of Northern Affairs and Natural Resources, Forestry Branch, Forest Reserve Division, Technical Note No. 88.

Johnson, J.A. 1988. *Map of Forest Land Productivity Survey, Forest Soil Management Units, Shelburne Township.* Ontario Ministry of Natural Resources, Toronto, Ontario.

Logan, K.T. 1966. *Growth of Tree Seedlings as Affected by Light Intensity. II. Red Pine, White Pine, Jack Pine and Eastern Larch.*Canada Department of Forestry, Ottawa, Ontario. Publication 1160.

Lorimer, C.G. 1980. "Age Structure and Disturbance History of a Southern Appalachian Virgin Forest." *Ecology* 61:1169-84.

Maissurow, D.K. 1935. "Fire as a Necessary Factor in the Perpetuation of White Pine." *Journal of Forestry* 33:373-8.

Maissurow, D.K. 1941. "The Role of Fire in the Perpetuation of Virgin Forests of Northern Wisconsin." *Journal of Forestry* 39:201-7.

McAndrews, J.H. 1978. *Forest Composition of Ontario in the Mid-Twentieth Century.* Royal Ontario Museum, Toronto, Ontario.

Methven, I.R. 1973. *Fire, Succession and Community Structure in a Red and White pine Stand.* Canadian Forestry Service Information Report PS-X-43. Petawawa Forestry Experimental Station, Chalk River, Ontario.

NOAA (National Oceanic and Atmospheric Administration). 1980. *Climates of the States: Narrative Summaries, Tables, and Maps for each State.* 2nd. ed., Vols. 1 and 2. Gale Research, Book Tower, Detroit, Michigan.

Old-Growth Definition Task Group. 1986. *Interim Definitions for Old-Growth Douglas-Fir and Mixed-Conifer Forests in the Pacific Northwest and California.* USDA, Forestry Service, PNW Research Station, Research Note PNW-447.

Oliver, C.D., and E.P. Stephens. 1977. "Reconstruction of a Mixed Species Forest in Central New England." *Ecology* 58:562-72.

Ontario Ministry of Natural Resources. 1983. *A Silvicultural Guide to the White pine Working Group.* Queen's Park, Toronto, Ontario.

Ontario Ministry of Natural Resources. 1985. *Timber Management Planning Manual.* Queen's Park, Toronto, Ontario.

Pinto, F. 1989. *White and Red Pine (121+ Years) Stand Data for Ontario.* Ministry of Natural Resources, Central Ontario Forest Technology Development Unit, North Bay.

Quinby, P.A. 1989. *Old Growth Forest Survey in Temagami's Wakimika Triangle.* Tall Pines Project, Research Report No. 2, Temagami Wilderness Society, Toronto, Ontario.

Rowe, J.S. 1972. *Forest Regions of Canada.* Department of Environment, Canadian Forestry Service, Publication No. 1300, Information Canada, Ottawa.

Runkle, J.R. 1981. "Gap Regeneration in Some Old-Growth Forests of the Eastern United States." *Ecology* 62:1041-51.

Runkle, J.R. 1982. "Patterns of Disturbance in Some Old-Growth Mesic Forests of Eastern North America." *Ecology* 63:1533-46.

Sheehey, G.W. 1980. White pine Nature Reserves in Algonquin Provincial Park. M.Sc.F. Thesis, Faculty of Forestry, University of Toronto.

Society of American Foresters. 1984. *Scheduling the Harvest of Old-Growth.* Society of American Foresters, Washington, DC.

Spies, T.A. and J.F. Franklin. 1989. "Gap Characteristics and Vegetation Response in Coniferous Forests of the Pacific Northwest." *Ecology* 70(3):543-5.

Stiell, W.M. 1985. "Silviculture of Eastern White pine." *Proceedings of the Entomological Society of Ontario* 116:95-107.

Strickland, D., and P. Ward (Ontario Ministry of Natural Resources). 1987. *Algonquin Provincial Park Canoe Routes.* The Friends of Algonquin Park, Whitney, Ontario.

Vogt, K.A., C.C. Grier and D.J. Vogt. 1986. "Production, Turnover, and Nutrient Dynamics of Above- and Below-Ground Detritus of World Forests." *Advances in Ecological Research* 15:303-77.

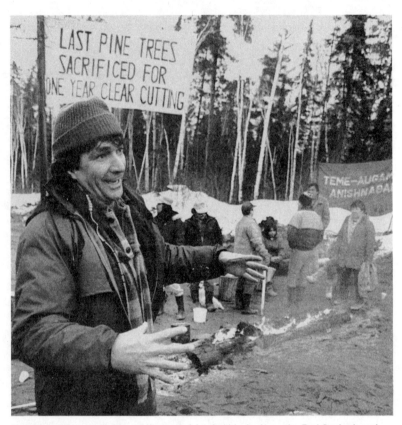

Chief Gary Potts at the Teme-Augama Anishnabai blockade on the Red Squirrel road.
Courtesy: North Bay Nugget.

Two

Theoretically, the Management of Multiple Resources is Simple

Crandall Benson

The conflict over resources in Temagami is typical of multiple demands for limited natural resources. For some of the resources of Temagami, the demand has deteriorated to a scrap over the remnants. Any area has a capacity to produce certain amounts of natural resources over time. In theory, the sustained management of these resources is simply a matter of allocating and using them within the limits of their productive capability. The two basic steps in the management of multiple resources are, first, determining the quantitative production limits for sustainable use, and, second, allocating the resources within those limits. These two steps are, in essence, what must occur at Temagami if sustainable development is to take place. The resource-users of the Temagami area are probably not deliberately overusing the resources, but are not aware of the limitations of resource production. A third step required is the recognition by forestry departments that the successful management of public lands in a democracy requires a public-participation approach in order to apply the type of management desired by the public. For private land, it requires the determination of the demands of landowners and the management of the land to meet their demands.

Throughout this paper, the assumption is made that the management of the resources is designed to provide for sustainable development; that is, the use of the resources is to be kept within the ecological capability of the area to produce them, and that the present-day use of the natural resources will not compromise the ability of future generations to use them.

THE THEORY

The theory of managing multiple resources may be demonstrated by the procedure used to allocate timber for the forest industry. If we think of the timber resource as a hot-water tank, the amount of hot water used should not exceed the amount of hot water produced (Figure 1). Two extreme situations may result in using the hot-water tank. First, if someone takes a long hot shower at a rate that exceeds the production of new hot water, the next person is going to get a cold shower. Second, if the heating element breaks down, the amount of hot water for one or more users will be reduced considerably. The forest responds in a similar fashion. If the resource is overused by one group, there is not enough for other users, and if the regeneration is not equal to the amount used, the amount of timber available for all users is reduced.

The theory becomes somewhat complicated when the use of other resources is considered. There are basically two categories of other uses. First, the production of these other resources may depend upon the nature of the timber tank; that is, the value of other resources will vary according to the state of the timber resource. In Figure 2 the thermometer measures the state of the timber resource in the timber hot-water tank and controls the production of the other resource. In this case, the other resource, moose, will have their numbers determined by the state of the actual forest.

Second, uses of other natural resources may be a drain on the timber-production area. For example, wilderness areas and reserves take some of the timber land and reduce the amount of timber available for industrial use (Figure 3). Both the forest and people develop dynamically; therefore, variations in the type of demand for these changing resources may be expected to occur over time. It may be a demand for more area to be used for timber production or it may be a realization that more protection of fragile sites or special features of the land is necessary.

Production of multiple resources consists of a number of tanks that are either a drain on the timber resource, or are governed by it (Figure 4). Management of multiple resources on a sustainable-yield basis requires an understanding of the quantitative links that control the flow of production of the various resources.

The production of natural resources becomes still more complicated when one considers that one species of the timber resource consists of a variety of age classes. Ideally, the age-class distribution would be uniform, with an equal area of forest in each age class (Figure 5). In this theoretical forest, the harvest areas would be fairly small and evenly distributed.

In such a forest, the amount of timber harvested per hectare on a sustainable basis will vary according to the harvest-rotation age. For example, the long-term sustainable yield is a simple mathematical calculation of the product of the Mean Annual Increment (MAI) at a selected rotation age, times the total productive area of the forest (Davis *et al.* 1987). The MAI at the rotation indicated in Figure 6 is merely the average volume produced per hectare up to a given age. The exact amount of the long-term sustainable yield varies according to the rotation age used; maximum production would be represented by using a rotation age where the MAI reaches the highest point in Figure 6. In Figure 6, this would be at 110 years for Gross Merchantable Volume (GMV). For studs and lumber, the rotation would be at least 150 years (Figure 6).

Production curves may be used for other resources that are governed by the state of the forest (Calish *et al.* 1978). Figure 7 represents a theoretical production curve for moose. To maximize the production of moose, a rotation age of 20 to 30 years would be used. On the other hand, to maximize aesthetic appeal would require a longer rotation of 200 years (Figure 8).

If a maximized GMV timber production with a rotation of 110

years were implemented, it would be to the detriment of maximum moose production and maximum aesthetic appeal. A rotation age of 100 years would produce moose, but not as many as would be produced at a rotation of 20 to 30 years. Similarly, the aesthetic production would be less with a rotation of 110 years than if a rotation of 200 years were used. Thus, it is not possible to maximize the use of all resources, but it is possible to produce resources for a number of different users at levels that may be less than the maximum-production level. Theoretically, all the resources can be produced on a sustainable basis for a number of different uses.

The difficulty of managing multiple forest resources is further compounded by the fact that the actual forest contains several different species of trees, lower vegetation, and wildlife, all living on a variety of sites. A number of more complex relationships than those shown in Figure 4 may exist, and there may be interactions among the various systems. For instance, there may be areas of predominantly white pine while other areas are predominantly poplar. Each area has its own inherent ability to support various uses, while some wildlife species may require the use of both areas.

THE REALITY

What is theoretically possible will not become a reality if the production levels are not determined and if the forest is not maintained and managed. The complex relationships of the living natural resources of the Temagami area are not sufficiently well known so as to be able to create precise production curves such as those shown in Figures 7 and 8. Documentation of the production level of the trees is better than that for the other resources (Figure 6), but this knowledge has not ensured the management of the timber resource on a sustainable basis. This may be illustrated by examining the past management of white pine in the Temagami area.

In Temagami the former forest consisted of large amounts of older pine that was able to regenerate naturally either after fires or blowdown. In the water-tank analogy, the tank was full of hot water (Figure 9).

Once harvesting started in the 1920s a problem arose, because the flow out exceeded the flow in (Figure 10). Harvesting methods did not produce the site conditions necessary for the pine to regenerate the way that it had before harvesting began. Much of the Temagami area was in the Temagami Forest Reserve. The intent of the forest reserve was to provide a continuous supply of red and white pine, even though problems of regenerating the forest were understood. Corrective measures and studies were recommended (Bureau of Forests 1904), but there is no evidence that such work was completed. By the 1950s management plans for Temagami (MNR 1964) aimed to regenerate the white pine and convert hardwood areas to pine. Yet the flow out still exceeded the flow in. Consequently, areas of white pine were lost to other species such as poplar, white birch, and balsam fir (MNR 1985a). The effect on the water tank was that the level of hot water (white pine) in the tank declined since the flow of regeneration was less than the flow out (Figure 10). We do not know how much area was lost to white-pine production by being converted to other competing species of trees. Management-unit boundaries have been changed by the Ontario Ministry of Natural Resources (MNR), making it difficult to determine what changes have occurred in a specific area (Benson 1989). A comparison of the 1959 forest inventory for the twenty-three townships of the old Temagami Crown Management Unit (1958-1978) and the 1980 forest inventory of the same townships provides some indication of the magnitude of the changes that have occurred (Table 1). The total area of the 1980 inventory is somewhat larger than the 1959 inventory as it includes an extra one-half township. The areas in four working groups — white, red and jack pine, and spruce — declined, while the area for the balsam-fir group increased. For the hardwoods, maple- and yellow-birch areas increased, but the areas of poplar and white birch declined. It appears that the pine area lost was converted to balsam fir, maple, and yellow birch rather than to poplar and white birch. In addition, 6.3 thousand hectares of the total forest land was lost to production. It must be noted that the data of Table 1 is based on inventory information that is only a rough estimate of the timber resources. Some error may have resulted from an inaccu-

TABLE 1 — Comparison of the 1959 Inventory to the 1980
Inventory for the Old Temagami Management Unit*

WORKING GROUP	1959 INVENTORY	1980 INVENTORY	1980–1959
White Pine	21,075	13,884	-7,191
Red Pine	5,495	5,382	-113
Jack Pine	17,755	17,398	-358
Spruce	36,876	35,914	-963
Balsam Fir	4,690	9,610	-4,920
Other Conifer	8,079	8,078	-1
Maple	0	5,666	5,666
Yellow Birch	0	4,681	4,681
Poplar	11,493	10,465	-1,028
White Birch	39,881	38,525	-1,375
Other Hardwood	8,739	429	-8,310
Protection forest	11,883	18,217	6,334
Total	**165,970**	**168,249**	**2,279**

* Areas of working groups are in hectares. Calculations are by the author.

rate classification of the forest for either inventory.

Other natural resources dependent on the white-pine timber base have suffered an undetermined reduction in their production as a result of the loss of area of the white-pine forests (Figure 11).

The nature of the trees in the forest determines the production of the other resources. In the past, the forests around Temagami have been high-graded (MNR 1985b) and converted to less desirable species. The Latchford plan (MNR 1985a) states: "Most pine stands were partially cut, leaving behind poorly stocked stands, stands of different age classes, or stands with younger, intolerant hardwoods scattered throughout older, residual softwoods. This hodge-podge of scattered white and red pine, mixed with aging poplar, white birch and intolerant young hardwoods, generally supports an understory of unhealthy balsam fir. This also presents challenges for forest managers." The Temagami Management Plan (MNR 1985b) states: "This prolonged period of high-grading has left much of the forest with trees of very poor quality. Stands contain a variety of age classes and species, and reduced stocking." Unfortunately, present MNR procedures are not helping to stabilize or rectify the matter. Exacerbating the present problems are four main factors — MNR's non-sustainable allowable cut-calculations, the lack of successful regeneration of previous white-pine cutovers, the inclusion of the Temagami skyline reserve in the cut-calculations, and the low proportion of white pine remaining in the forest stands (Benson *et al.* 1989). The present age-class structure of the white-pine forest is indicated by Figure 12 for the Temagami Management Unit. A very noticeable gap occurs in the age classes 0-80 years as a result of unsuccessful past regeneration of cutovers. To ensure that the white-pine forest provides for the various resource-users in the future requires the stretching out of the utilization of the older stands until they are replaced with new ones. To stretch out the utilization requires that the amount of area harvested is no larger than the area regenerated, and that the harvest level can be sustained on the productive land base.

With the application of these two points the harvest level will have to be reduced (Figure 13). In Figure 13, the sustainable level of harvest is initially lower than that arrived at by the MNR method of calculating the allowable cut, but the sustainable method provides for a constant level of production of white-pine lumber. In addition, the level of the sustainable cut used in Figure 13 would allow an area to be maintained in old growth. Using the MNR method, the allowable cut of white-pine sawlogs would eventually be about 30 per cent of the initial level. This calculation, as well as existing allowable cut-calculations for the Temagami Management Unit, includes the skyline reserve area in the calculation. If this reserve area is not included in the white-pine land base, the sustainable allowable cut would be reduced by about a third. MNR contends that the reserve will be removed from the land area used in allowable cut-calculations in the 1990 management plan (Ontario 1989a).

Both of the allowable cuts shown in Figure 13 assume that the white-pine stands are composed mainly of white pine only. In reality, white pine forms a relatively small portion of the stands (Benson 1989). Moreover, the majority of the white pine is obtained as remnants from other working groups of trees. Figure 14 shows the predicted five-year allowable cut as calculated by the MNR method for the five working groups that contain most of the white pine in the Temagami Crown Management Unit. The assumption was made that the white pine was regenerated only in the white-pine working group. By this method of calculating the allowable cut of white pine, the future harvest declines to about 15 per cent of the highest level after 120 years. The estimates of Figure 14 also include the Temagami skyline reserve. Accurate estimates of the sustainable level of harvest of white pine and the other species of Temagami require more and better information on the extent of the productive land base that can be effectively managed.

In the water-tank analogy, the flow from the hot-water tank must be limited to retain the present levels of production of all resources. To determine the amount of the limitation requires knowledge of the amount of the flow into the tank and the amount in the tank at present.

If the intent of management is to increase the amount of all the resources that flow from or are dependent upon the white-pine forest, the white-pine water tank must be refilled as in Figure 1. This would require a large increase in the application of both artificial and natural regeneration methods. On the other hand, the amount of area in balsam fir, maple, and yellow birch has grown (Table 1). Resources that flow from or depend upon these hardwoods will also probably have increased.

Although the amount of the reduction that will occur in the harvest of white pine either by using MNR's method of allocating the resource or by applying a sustainable harvest is difficult to quantify, it is obvious that a reduction will occur. This is recognized by a forest industry that is satisfied with MNR's method of determining the allowable cut and wants the mills to determine when the reduction will occur. It states: "To suddenly reduce the volumes by half, as indicated for sustainable or normal yield, would also reduce the existing mills by half. Which ones will close? Who will decide this drastic fate of a community? But, with the MNR's method, there is time for the pine mills to adjust or close down by their own decision. This is happening right now." (Ontario 1989b). In fact, over the years many mills have closed in the Temagami area as the older-growth white pine was harvested. It has been stated that "regarding Milne and Sons, that sawmill is the last of 12 sawmills ... between North Bay and New Liskeard." (Ontario 1989c). To attain a sustainable development requires a recognition of the productive capability of the land, sustaining or improving that capability, and basing the number of mills on that capacity.

OPTIMUM USE

Even if the forest is maintained and managed, and production levels are set, the forest manager must determine the best or optimum level of production for each of the resources. How much of the area should be used for timber production, and how much should be preserved for wilderness area? When the demand level for the various resources is lower than the production capacity of the forest, attaining the optimum level is not difficult; however, in the Temagami area demands for white pine have not declined, they have increased. In particular, the demand for parks and reserves has placed an additional drain on the area of white pine available for timber production. The entrenched positions of the various interest groups have in effect converted the hot-water tank from a free-flow tank to a pressure tank. Traditionally, "rich democracies frequently give special treatment to groups (such as big farmers or logging companies) whose subsidized activities may cause environmental damage" (*The Economist* 1989). At present, the control of the flow of products appears to depend more on which flow valves the political process opens or closes than on the natural production levels (Figure 1). There is nothing intrinsically wrong with the political process determining how the land is to be managed, if the process adequately considers and evaluates the desires of the public. Successful resource management of public lands requires forestry departments in a democracy to take a public-participation approach to determine and then apply the type of management desired by the public (Mealey 1988). A recent survey of the public's perception of forestry revealed desires that vary considerably from the strategy of managing the forest solely for timber production (Place 1989). For example, 64 per cent favoured preservation of the forest and only 23 per cent considered the forest important for jobs; 60 per cent stated that the most important use for Canada's forests were for wildlife protection, wilderness preservation, and recreation, while a mere 12 per cent thought logging important; 71 per cent opposed the use of chemicals in the forest; and 70 per cent opposed clearcutting. To a politician, public perception eventually must become the reality. Unfortunately, neither the politicians nor forestry departments have responded fully to the public's perception of forest management.

The Temagami Advisory Council was formed to advise MNR on the management of the resources of the area. Although this group may provide an avenue for the public to express its demands, it is faced with the problem of not only providing equitable and rational solutions to the land-use conflicts, but of doing so without knowing the sustainable production levels of the resources. And if it does manage to determine the sustainable production levels, it will still need to decide how to weigh the demands of the various user-groups. In conflicts over limited public resources, satisfying the demands of all groups will be impossible. The best the council can expect is to present information and data to the public which indicate that the proposed management procedures are within the sustainable development limits of the natural resources.

Residents dependent for their livelihood on the Temagami area have a difficult personal decision to make. Do they support sustainable development for the future, or continued exploitation of the area to provide for jobs that will eventually disappear?

N'DAKI MENAN

The land claim of the Teme-Augama Anishnabai does not change the concepts stated above. With the resolution of the land claim in their favour, the Teme-Augama Anishnabai would become the land managers. They would then have to determine their needs as well as the production levels possible, and manage accordingly. They do not plan to exclude other users, but do intend to include them in a manner that would ensure that the area is holistically managed for sustainable development (Ontario 1989d). Dealing with a private landowner such as the Teme-Augama Anishnabai may well be easier than conducting transactions with a complex government bureaucracy. Regardless of the outcome of the Teme-Augama Anishnabai land claim, the managers of the forest must respond to the wishes of the users. To reach a rational solution requires recognition of the natural production limits of resources by both the public and the managers. In addition, sustainable production necessitates an attempt to attain the even distribution of age classes.

In summary, the theoretical and the real solution to the problems of resource allocation in Temagami requires the determination of the sustainable resource production levels, and the recognition and use of the resources within the limits of their production. For the theory to become a reality, all users must limit their use to the capabilities of the area to ensure sustainable development.

FIGURE 1 — Timber production represented as a hot-water tank. In a sustainable development situation, the use of trees for industrial use does not exceed the flow in, by natural or artificial means.

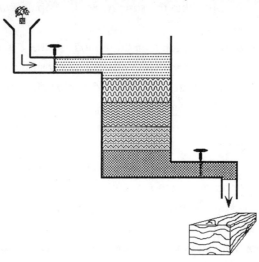

FIGURE 2 — The amount of moose produced depends upon the state of the forest. The thermometer in the top timber tank represents a measure of the state of the forest resource. This measure controls the input tap of moose in the lower tank.

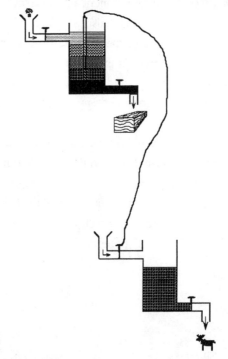

FIGURE 3 — The amount of forest area used for other uses, such as wilderness areas or reserves, drain land area from the timber-production tank.

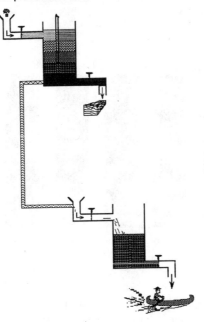

FIGURE 4 — Production of a number of resources consists of several resource tanks that either drain the timber-production tank or are controlled by it.

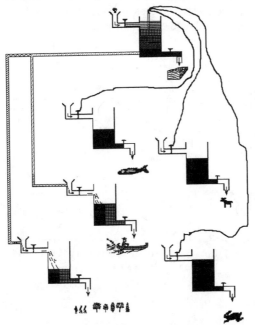

FIGURE 5 — Concept of a normal forest with a rotation of 120 years, and a total area of 18,000 hectares. An equal area would occur in each of the twenty-year age classes, for example, 1–20, 101–20.

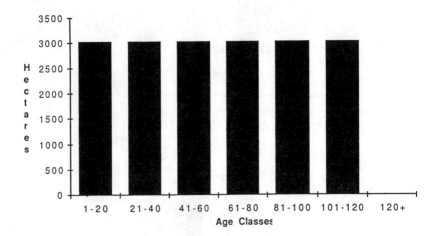

FIGURE 6 — Mean Annual Increment (MAI) at different ages for white pine in the northeastern region of the MNR (MNR n.d.). GTV is the gross total volume, while GMV is the gross merchantable volume. 'Studs' represents the MAI for smaller dimension timber, while 'Lumber' represents the MAI for producing lumber of different dimensions.

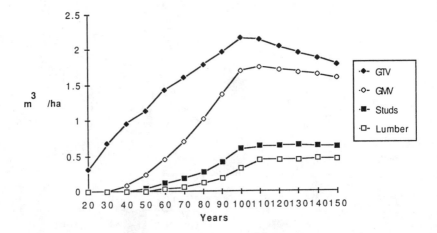

FIGURE 7 — Theoretical mean annual increment of moose production in a normal forest. Moose production for a given rotation would be calculated by multiplying the MAI of moose at that rotation age by the total productive area.

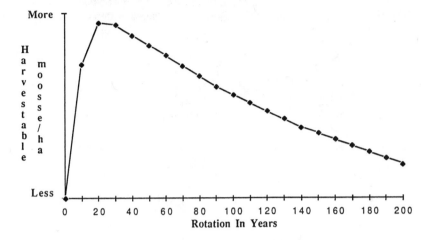

FIGURE 8 — Theoretical mean annual increment for aesthetics. Aesthetics was estimated using an index classification. At a given rotation age, the level of aesthetics can be determined by multiplying the index value at that rotation age by the total productive area.

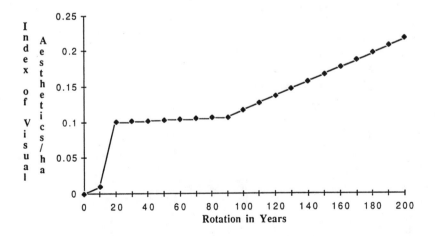

FIGURE 9 — The white-pine forests of Temagami as represented by a hot-water tank prior to the start of harvesting. Older age classes of white pine — the hot water — almost fill the tank. The forest, prior to the start of harvesting, regenerated and died naturally. Natural death could be the result of old age, suppression, disease, insects, fire, and windthrow.

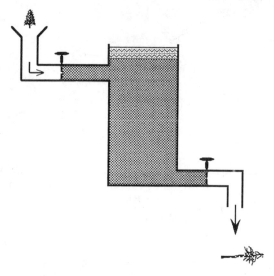

FIGURE 10 — The condition of white pine as represented by a hot-water tank after harvesting since the 1920s. The amount of older pine — the hot water — has been reduced. Harvested areas of white pine were not replaced by natural or artificial means in an amount equal to their use.

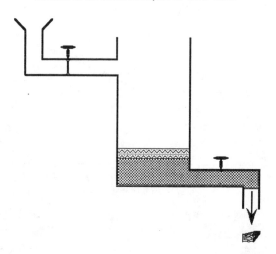

FIGURE 11 — The reduction of the white-pine land base can lead to a reduction in the production of other resources. Compare to Figure 4.

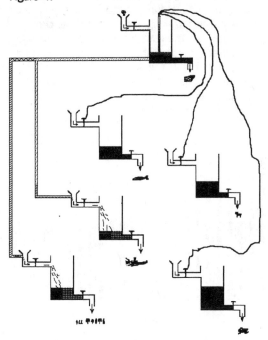

FIGURE 12 — Age-class structure of the Temagami Management Unit (MNR 1985b). Note the small amount of white-pine land in the younger age classes — the result of the lack of successful regeneration efforts in the past.

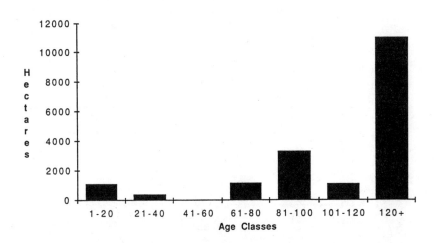

FIGURE 13 — Five-year allowable cuts of white-pine sawlogs from the white-pine working group for the Temagami Management Unit as calculated by the MNR method and a sustainable-yield method (Sust). Future predictions of allowable cuts by the MNR for white-pine sawlogs are about 30 per cent of what current levels would be. The sustainable method of calculating the allowable cut allows some of the white-pine forest to develop into older-growth forest. The Temagami skyline reserve was included in the calculations. If it were excluded, both allowable cuts would be reduced by about 33 per cent. The sustainable method is at a level that allows the retention of old-growth stands.

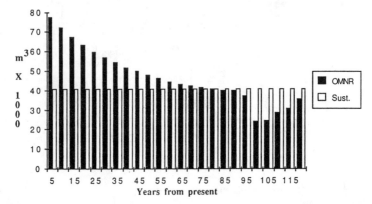

FIGURE 14 — Estimated five-year net merchantable volumes of white pine available from five working groups for the Temagami Management Plan if no regeneration of white pine occurs in working groups other than white pine. The first ten years allowable cut are from the 1980-2000, while the remaining years are estimated using the MNR method of calculating allowable cuts. The estimates of white pine in other working groups are based on the operational cruise data of the first ten-year allocation.

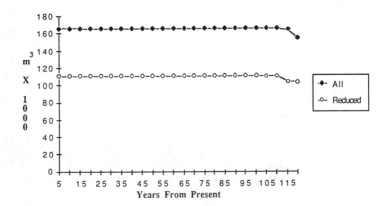

References

Benson, C.A., H. Cumming, H. Akervall and Willard Carmean. 1989. *The Need for a Land Stewardship, Holistic Resource Management Plan for N'Daki Menan*. Bear Island, Temagami.

Bureau of Forests. 1904. *Annual Report of the Bureau of Forests for the Province of Ontario*. King's Printer, Toronto.

Calish, S., R.D. Fight, and D.E. Teeguarden. 1978. "How Do Non-Timber Values Affect Douglas-Fir Rotations?" *Journal of Forestry*, April, 217.

Davis, L.S. and K.N. Johnson. 1987. *Forest Management*. McGraw-Hill, Toronto.

Mealey, S.P. 1988. "Democratizing Bureaucracy: Separate Enclosure in Managing North Central Forests for Non-timber Values." Society of American Forestry, Fourth Region, V Technical Conference, Duluth, Minnesota. 29 November 1988.

MNR. n.d. White Pine, Site Region 4200 (4E). Ontario Ministry of National Resources, Sudbury, Ontario.

MNR. 1964. Management Plan for Temagami Management Unit for the Period April 1, 1958 to March 31, 1978. Ontario Ministry of Natural Resources, Temagami, Ontario.

MNR. 1985a. Forest Management Plan for the Latchford Crown Management Unit, Ontario Ministry of Natural Resources, Temagami, Ontario.

MNR 1985b. Forest Management Plan for the Temagami Crown Management Unit, Ontario Ministry of Natural Resources, Temagami, Ontario.

Ontario 1989a. Legislative Assembly, *Hansard*. 20 November 1989. R-58.

Ontario 1989b. Legislative Assembly, Standing Committee on Resources Development, Temagami Forest Products Association, Submission to the Committee (Toronto: The Committee 1989).

Ontario 1989c. Legislative Assembly, *Hansard*. 23 November 1989. R-112.

Ontario 1989d. Legislative Assembly, *Hansard*, 22 November 1989. R-84.

Place, I.C.M. 1989. "Forestry Communicators's Forum: A Report." *Forestry Chronicle* 65: 170-2.

The Economist. 1989. "Costing the earth." 2 September.

The controversial Goulard lumber road. *Courtesy: Hap Wilson*

Three

Some Comments on Temagami Issues

Roger Fryer

Temagami, one of the most beautiful areas of Ontario and Canada, has been of great recreational value to my family for the last thirty years and, I expect, will continue to be so for the rest of our lives. Trapping, logging, and mining have established the infrastructure of the region, thereby allowing the tourism industry to develop, and all four sectors must remain viable if the community is to survive. Despite more than 130 years of logging, Temagami is still Ontario's leading recreational area. Perhaps logging is not the demon it is sometimes portrayed to be.

Ontario has large areas of old pine, many of which are in Temagami. Thirty per cent of the old pine is protected from cutting, but these trees too will die just as surely as will our grandparents, no matter how beautiful they are or were. Even without a disturbance such as fire or logging, old pine much past the ages of eighty to ninety years cannot reseed an area. Their seed is prevented from reaching the soil by the deep layer of organic material that builds up over the years.

I ask anyone to prove that the pine accessed by the Goulard and Red Squirrel roads are the only such trees in existence. If they are, what should we call the red and white pine that grow from Lake of the Woods through Ontario, Quebec, New Brunswick, and Maine, as well as in the mountains of Virginia? And what should we call the red and white pine in our large parks — Quetico, Lady Evelyn-Smoothwater, Killarney and Algonquin? Logging does not present the highest risk to these old pines. Fire, disease, insects, old age, and acid rain will cause the death of most of them. Acid rain, in particular, is greatly increasing their mortality rate; young pine can better withstand this type of pollution than old pine.

Why do we clearcut? Pine constitutes only 10 to 20 percent of most timber-rich areas, the balance being poplar and birch. A clearcut has proven to be the most successful way to regenerate conifer in these stands, with the results closely paralleling those of a natural fire. After a clearcut, genetically healthy stock is planted; regeneration does not depend on deformed and diseased trees. Clearcuts do not have to be large to achieve regeneration, and are not a cause of siltation and lower water quality. Compare water from Boatline Bay to water from Ferguson or Whitefish bays. Visibility is two to five ft. at Boatline Bay, depending on wave action, and thirty ft. at Ferguson or Whitefish bays, where water from the clearcut areas enters Lake Temagami. Clearly, it is not the logging industry that is putting a beautiful lake at risk.

When will preservationists abandon their obstruction and delay-at-any-cost wailings of doom and gloom, and come and plant trees alongside of industry? Let them do something positive for a change. They may even enjoy it once they get started. Let them put something back into the wilderness for a hundred years from now. Preserving the old pine as they are, in all areas, will leave them near extinction in fifty years. The alternative is replanting. We are able to grow 250 mature pine per acre compared to the existing stock of 2 to 20 per acre. Preservationists and the logging industry, with the help of government, should plant trees together. If we do, there will be many more pine growing in Temagami a century from now than there are at present.

The preservationists' actions have had serious consequences. Someone has driven large spikes in many trees, hoping, no doubt, to destroy machinery and forgetting that such spikes could injure or kill our workers. How many ten- and twelve ft. pieces of prime wood will be left on the forest floor with spikes inside them? Logging equipment has suffered more than $100,000 in damage; $38,000 of this was inflicted on one skidder operator alone. How long will it be before he will have a spare dollar for his family? How many extra trees will he have to cut to pay for his repairs?

The contract to build the Red Squirrel road extension likely increased in cost by many hundreds of thousands of dollars because of vandalism to Goulard machines and threats to stop construction — money that would have been better spent in the planting of trees. All this to halt the building of a road link-up through an area that was clearcut in 1946, not untouched forest land, as is so often claimed. Completion of the Red Squirrel road would allow closure of the Liskeard Lumber road, which runs almost through the middle of the Lady Evelyn-Smoothwater Park and is open to campers, hunters, and fishermen from 15 September to 15 June. The area is not an untouched ecosystem; it has been logged for the last twenty years and contains many miles of existing roads.

As for the Native land claim, I am not knowledgeable enough to judge this one way or another. But for all of us in the Temagami area, it needs to be resolved. The fact that some person in 1850 signed a paper with an "X" on behalf of his people, and that each Native as a result received one dollar or the equivalent in pound sterling, is beside the point — the settlement was surely unfair. Similarly, the provincial government's subsequent action in selling most of the Lake Temagami islands for a few dollars each does not free us from the responsibility to settle this in a prompt and equitable way. It would not have taken 140 years to settle a land claim against the city of Toronto. Temagami land has been tied up for sixteen years. No other area in Ontario has ever had to bear such a hardship.

What is wilderness? Is it a place where you are safe from city fumes and noise? Or is it a place where you may lose your life if you are not careful and wise in the ways of the forest? Both. The Temagami wilderness is certainly beautiful, but it also can be dangerous. Very little of the area more than 200 ft. from a cut trail or portage is ever walked on except by hunters, trappers, and loggers. In my opinion, 99 per cent of all land north of Highway 17 is wilderness and will remain so far into the future.

On the subject of Temagami, each of us needs to sort out the facts from the fantasy. It is unfortunate that the fanatics are able to sell their fairyland more easily than industry can communicate the facts, which are often more pleasant than our opponents would have people believe. If you care about Temagami and the environment, believe only what you see, and study that very carefully.

The closure of the Sherman Mine in 1989 devastated the local economy of Temagami.
Courtesy: The North Bay Nugget

Four

Canadian Values and Priorities: A Multiple-use Perspective

Judith Skidmore

The Temagami debate revolves around values which are central to the Canadian experience.

The issues at stake in Temagami are not environmental in nature. The Temagami forest has been logged for about 130 years. The area is riddled with bush roads. There has been no identification to date of significant ecological damage arising from the building or use of roads in the Temagami forest.

Nor are the issues economic. The village of Temagami enjoys a level of economic diversity that is the envy of other small northern Ontario towns. The district in which it is situated is a world-renowned tourist area. The local economy is further strengthened by forestry, mining, and trapping. As a result of all these factors, unemployment in Temagami has been negligible, which is all the more remarkable given that a land injunction has stifled development for about fifteen years.

The issues are not scientific either. Where are the scientists? Has David Suzuki, our self-proclaimed forestry expert, set up camp with others to study any of the old-growth or other parts of the forest? Where is the university or private-industry research data? Scientists who have been called to the area by government grants have not come to any specific conclusions. Sixty-five scientists asked for a moratorium on logging. When NORTHCARE (Northern Community Advocates for Resource Equity) contacted many of them, several indicated that they did not know where Temagami was. All of the others cited personal beliefs as a reason for their statements, but none had any hard data. In general, it is clear that, despite what some people claim, we don't know everything about the forest with absolute certainty.

How many times do we have to say that the Temagami forest is one of the most protected and regulated areas of Ontario? In terms of its productivity, real and potential, it is probably unrivalled.

No, the issues involve values other than environmental, economic, and scientific ones. Canada is sustained by its small community resource sector, and by the people who work there without the benefit of air-conditioned offices, university tenure, and travel grants to faraway places. In the Temagami area, one thinks of the Keevils and O'Connors (mining), the Goulards and the Fisets (lumber), the Grants and the Fryers (forestry), and of all the families who work with them. These people have built the communities that make up Canada. They also uphold the values, chief among which is a commitment to hard work and the land, that have made our country what it is.

Without the values of our resource people in the Temagami forest we wouldn't be able to provide the funds for the government office that is coordinating the study of development issues in Temagami. Without the values of the people in the Temagami forest and in forests across Canada we couldn't afford universities and hospitals. These values represent our basic Canadian heritage. So do the values of the prospector, who has been responsible for much of the importance of the Temagami forest, and of the trapper.

In recent years the values of people in all the resource sectors — forestry, mining, and trapping — have been effectively ignored, and they continue to be ignored. In the Temagami area, they are now banned from huge areas of our forest even though, without them, there would be not a Tall Pines Project, a Wilderness Society, or a canoe-vacation company. But make no mistake: these values hold much of the hope for the future of Temagami.

Have our values changed? Canada is still sustained by forestry, mining, agriculture, and fishing. Half of the world's lumber is Canadian. Canada is the world's largest producer of paper. More money is spent on hard-rock mining in the Temagami area than in the rest of Canada or in Australia, Peru, the United States, and Chile. Our values as Canadians have remained nearly the same since Confederation. More than anything, we remain dedicated to land.

Are the values of the forest, mining, and trapping communities different from those of the rest of our communities? Do we value the environment any less? Do we value clean air and water any less? Do we value aesthetics any less? Do we value recreation in the forest any less? Absolutely not. No group in Canada can claim to hold the value of our environment more highly than we do in the Temagami region or anywhere in northern Ontario.

The creation of a single-use forest in Temagami would present a serious threat to Ontario as a whole. A huge no-development area with restrictions on roads would severely disrupt settlement patterns and the entire region's economy. Already, old transportation routes are being destroyed by the restrictions imposed on the Temagami forest. The impact is being felt by North Bay, Sudbury, and Timmins.

NORTHCARE is committed to local decision-making based on the wise and multiple-use of crown land and water, which constitute over 90 per cent of northern Ontario. Multiple-use is a tradition in the north, and we want to maintain that tradition. As a province and as a country, we have to continue using our resources in a common-sense, cooperative way. And we have to work together; the north's values and concerns can't be ignored any longer.

We in NORTHCARE favour multiple-use over single-use, employment over recreation, the needs of residents over the needs of visitors. It is our view that the values of the residents of Canadian resource communities must be a priority even though these residents are a minority in the province as a whole. If we examine their values carefully we will see that they include the environment and recreation. We will also see that they encompass the complexity of the land and the realities of Canada at large.

APPENDIX: IMPORTANT FACTS ABOUT THE TEMAGAMI FOREST*

FACT: "The 1901 Temagami Forest Reserve was created as an area in which pine forest could be set aside and from which all uses *except lumbering and mining* would be excluded." (Dr John Daniel, Temagami Area Working Group Report, March 1988.)

FACT: 95 per cent of the townships in the Temagami forest have been selectively logged and have regenerated either artificially or naturally. Some townships have experienced logging up to three times. (Ministry of Natural Resources, 1988.)

FACT: Roads have been constructed in the area since 1890. (Dr Bruce Hodgins, *Paradis of Temagami*, 1976.)

FACT: 150 kilometres of two-wheel-drive roads criss-cross the Temagami forest. (Ministry of Natural Resources, Temagami, 1988.)

FACT: 30 per cent of the canoe routes in the Temagami forest are on artificial waterways, controlled by hydro-power structures. (Based on *Canoe Routes of Temagami* by Hap Wilson.)

FACT: Since 1980, 33 million tree seedlings have been planted in the Temagami forest. (Ministry of Natural Resources, Temagami, 1988.)

FACT: "Park's [Canada] research studies have not identified this area [Temagami] as being a representative natural area of Canadian significance." (Bruce Amos, acting director general, National Parks, Parks Canada, 1988).

FACT: "[Job losses] would signal the end of Elk Lake, River Valley and Field and cause serious disruption in the Town of Temagami itself." (Dr John Daniel, Temagami Area Working Group Report, March 1988.)

FACT: The old-age pine forests of Temagami are dying and will not regenerate themselves within the next century. Only through modern forest-management practices that work in tandem with the natural world can we ensure a healthy forest and a healthy working environment for the people of Ontario. (Residents of the Temagami forest region.)

* Prepared by the Women's Action Group of Temagami, April 1988.

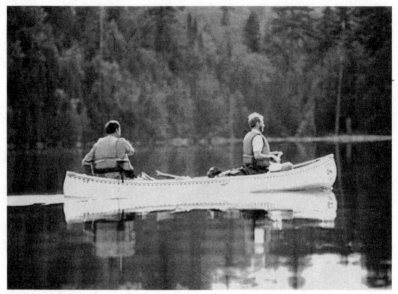

Recreational canoeing on Lake Temagami. *Courtesy: Hap Wilson*

Five

The Importance of Tourism in the Temagami Area

Roman Brozowski

The Temagami area has a varied topography of rugged hills and large and interconnected waterways, and is blessed with mixed flora and fauna. This glaciated area of the Shield has four watersheds flowing in two directions, including to the south via the Sturgeon River towards Georgian Bay, and to the northeast into Lake Temiskaming and into the Ottawa River. The vegetation is largely Boreal forest mixed with Great Lakes–St Lawrence forest. The northern portion of the region is mainly Boreal while the southern sector is dominated by white pine, white birch, poplar, white spruce, and balsam fir, along with some other hardwoods. These physical and vegetative structures have created a habitat for a variety of fish and wildlife. The water areas contain such fish as lake trout, small mouth bass, northern pike, and walleye, while the terrestrial and floral structure of the area is ideal for moose, black bear, and other fur-bearing animals. As well, a variety of Avian fauna, including blue heron, ruffled grouse, osprey, red-tailed hawk, owl, and raven, are present throughout the area.

The combination of these factors has made the Temagami region particularly suited for the tourism and recreation industry which has developed over the last 100 years. As early as 1880, recreational canoeists visited Temagami for the wilderness experience it offered (Temagami District Landuse Guidelines 1983) and began establishing canoe camps on Lake Temagami. By the 1880s accounts of canoe trips into the area began to appear in some magazines (Hodgins and Benidickson 1989). With the construction of the Temiskaming and Northern Ontario Railway, which reached Temagami in 1904, tourists flocked to the region (Temagami: Lake Temagami Plan for Landuse and Recreation 1973) and resort hotels appeared on Lake Temagami (Temagami Area Working Group Report 1988).

The growth of the tourism industry resulted in increased pressure for vacation property on Lake Temagami (MNR Brief to Temagami Area Working Group 1988). Fear of forest fires started by cottagers had caused the government to discourage such development, but public demand finally forced it to allow the leasing of island lots on Lake Temagami in 1905. These island locations reduced the threat of fire to mainland timber stands that were being protected for the forest industry. Similar pressure by tourist groups in the 1920s resulted in the preservation of a skyline reserve on Lake Temagami (Temagami: Lake Temagami Plan for Landuse and Recreation 1973).

The growth of tourism since these early developments has continued to the present day. The construction of the Ferguson highway in the 1920s and 1930s improved the accessibility of the Temagami district for recreational purposes (Brief to Temagami Area Working Group 1988). Over time, this highway No. 11, surpassed the railway in importance and became the primary method for tourists to travel into the area.

THE MAJOR SECTORS OF RECREATION AND TOURISM

The recreation and tourist industry in the Temagami region includes fishing, hunting, canoeing, camping, and cottaging, all supported by an infrastructure of lodges and outpost camps, outfitters and marinas, youth camps and fly-in services (Coopers and Lybrand Consulting Group 1987). For the most part, these recreational land uses, owing to their different requirements, are separated territorially. This allows them to co-exist relatively well.

Access is important to each group. For instance, cottages, because of their permanent nature, tend to be accessible by car or motor boat. Although many cottages are located to take advantage of remote, wilderness conditions and the lack of modern accoutrements, reasonably good access, even if by water, is still usually an important requirement (Coopers and Lybrand Consulting Group 1987). Similarly, expanded access is a main objective of organizations such as the Ontario Federation of Anglers and Hunters, whose members heavily utilize the Temagami area. For fishermen, a good supply of different fish species in lakes that can be accessed is especially important, while, for hunters, road access to wildlife-habitat areas is the key. In particular, these three groups often use the same road and water routes in order to arrive at their various destinations. On the other hand, canoeists, because many desire remote back-country travel, tend to separate themselves geographically from the other user-groups.

Cottaging

Throughout the Temagami area there are 1,800 privately owned cottages with 750 located on Lake Temagami, 214 on the Highway 11 corridor, 180 on Twin Lakes, and the remainder scattered on various lakes (Brief to the Temagami Working Group 1988). Cottages play an important role in the economic structure of the region. The DelCan Survey of 1986 determined that cottagers spend an average of $150 to $200 per week per household during their stay in Temagami. Caretaking, maintenance, boat servicing, and storage expenses generate further monies. Coopers and Lybrand Consulting Group (1987) have estimated that the average cottager on Lake Temagami spends $1,000 annually on groceries, supplies, maintenance, and boat service. Using the total number of 1,325 cottages in the Temagami District (Table 2), they have estimated that $1.33 million (1985 dollars) is contributed annually to the region.

An increase in the number of cottages would benefit the region both during the construction stage and afterwards. The increasing demand for more cottages was considered by the Ministry of Natural Resources (MNR) during the 1970s and 1980s, and the government finally decided in favor of dispersed island development on Lake Temagami and a variety of cottage experiences in other parts of the district. The Temagami District Landuse Guidelines (1983) targeted 300 additional cottages by the year 2000. Most of these would be located on crown land along Lake Temagami. If this number were built, an estimated $1.63 million (1985 dollars) would be spent annually within the district.

Hunting and Fishing

Hunting and fishing are major tourist activities in Temagami, each utilizing different aspects of the environment. The region's water attracted 39,000 fishermen in 1980. In terms of angler days, the estimated numbers were 106,000 in 1983 and 144,500 in 1985. Activity is most intense during the spring, summer, and autumn, but continues during the winter when ice-fishing attracts people to the area. Of the various fish species, such as pickerel, small-mouth bass, and northern pike, found in lakes throughout the area, anglers favour lake trout and walleye. The hunting season, starting in early October and ending in mid-November, involves primarily moose as well as some black bear, which are hunted in the spring. The district attracts 2,000 to 3,000 moose hunters annually and about 400 bear hunters (MNR An Environmental Assessment 1988). An over-harvesting of moose in the past has resulted in a selective harvest system which will allow the population to grow in size so that an increased harvest can be achieved by the year 2000 (Temagami District Landuse Guidelines 1983). This should increase the number of hunters who, in turn, would contribute economically to the area.

Both fishing and hunting contribute substantially to the economy of the region. The 1985 estimate for expenditures by anglers in Temagami was $3.5 million and, for moose and bear hunters, slightly over $1.0 million (Coopers and Lybrand Consulting Group 1987). The total for the two activities amounts to over $4.5 million per year in the Temagami district. It is estimated that by the year 2000 both activities, if properly managed, could be improved so that the increased number of angler and hunter days would bring in $3.8 million and over $1.7 million respectively, or a total of 5.5 million in terms of 1985 dollars (Coopers and Lybrand Consulting Group 1987).

Canoeing and Motorized Camping

Its wilderness setting, well-defined canoe loop route, clear portages, and clean campsites make Temagami an increasingly popular location for canoeists. This recreational activity has been growing rapidly in the 1980s because of good access from major metropolitan centres in both Canada and the United States, improved advertising, and the creation of Lady Evelyn-Smoothwater Park as an alternative to other overcrowded parks (Northern Concepts 1986). Canoe activity in the park and in adjacent areas grew by 15 per cent between 1979 and 1982 (MNR An Environmental Assessment 1988). MNR estimated that, in 1982, there were 8,000 to 10,000 trippers, with 4,000 to 6,000 of these using Lady Evelyn-Smoothwater Park. Assuming this growth rate, the projection was conservatively estimated in 1987 at 9,000 to 11,000 canoe trippers. An estimate by the Northern Concepts organization suggests that the number of canoe campers for 1986 was 23,080.

Undoubtedly, the canoe numbers have increased in the area and further growth can be expected. Better advertising in the southern markets, where the membership in canoeing organizations is expanding, along with the perception by some groups that areas such as Algonquin Park are overcrowded and lack true wilderness environments on corridor lakes (Larenthol and Horwath 1986), will contribute to the growth of canoeing in the Temagami area. Calculating an expenditure by canoeists of $10 to $20 per day, Coopers and Lybrand (1987) have estimated that 90,000 canoe user-days annually contribute $2,250,000 to the local economy. With the industry's continued growth, an additional $440,000 will be added by the year 2000, for a total of $2,690,000.

Non-wilderness motorized camping is the smallest economic contributor to the Temagami district. Estimates suggest that $290,000 is realized annually, primarily from Finlayson Point Park. As use of Finlayson increases, and as Makobe-Grays and W.B. Greenwood are added to the motorized recreational camping facilities for day-use and car camping (Temagami District Landuse Guidelines 1983), this tourist sector is expected to grow dramatically, with expenditures estimated at $1,710,000 annually by the year 2000.

THE INFRASTRUCTURE OF THE TOURIST/RECREATION INDUSTRY

The tourist and recreation industry supports sixty-six tourist establishments and services located within the Temagami district. The camps and lodges, serving mainly anglers and hunters, are located along Highway 11, Lake Temagami, Lady Evelyn, Anima-Nipissing, and Obabika lakes. Seven outpost camps are scattered within the region while eleven youth camps, serving canoeists and other wilderness aficionados, are found primarily on Lake Temagami. Catering to the needs of the wilderness back-country vacationers are several outfitters (Table 1).

This infrastructure of camps, lodges, and outfitters serves 20,000 annual visitors and supports 450 jobs (Coopers and Lybrand Consulting Group 1987). If the boundaries surrounding the Temagami district are drawn to include the area bounded by the Montreal River, Highway 560 to Elk Lake/Gowganda, the headwaters of the Sturgeon River, and Highway 64, the number of camps, lodges, and services increases substantially from 66 to about 100 (Table 1) (Brief to Temagami Area Working Group 1988).

ECONOMIC IMPORTANCE OF TOURISM AND RECREATION

Estimated tourist and recreational expenditures in the Temagami district (Table 2) suggest that angling is the most important activity, followed by the wilderness travel, cottaging, hunting, and non-wilderness travel. If the expenditures for each are added up, $8,435,000 was spent within the district in 1985. The gross annual revenues earned by operators was $8,000,000, a figure which is based on 20,000 visitors to Temagami in 1986 (Table 2) (Coopers and Lybrand Consulting Group July 1986: Field Survey by DelCan 1986). This translated into 450 jobs, or 175 person-years, with wages of $1,500,000. Of these jobs, 55 were full-time and 395 were seasonal. These figures do not include the 60 to 70 owners who operate the tourist lodges, camps, and outfitting establishments.

If projections prove to be relatively accurate, the recreational/tourist activities could result in expenditures of $11.57 million (1985 dollars) by the year 2000. This translates into an increase of 37 per cent over the 1985 expenditures, with an average of 2.5 per cent growth per year during the fifteen-year period. In terms of the contribution of each activity to the total expenditure in the year 2000, angling would be the most important, followed in descending order by wilderness travel, hunting, non-wilderness camping, and cottaging (Table 2). The greatest percentage growth in these sectors would be in non-wilderness camping and hunting, and the smallest in cottaging and angling.

If we assume a similar proportionate growth in employment, such a level of expenditure would translate into a total of 615 jobs. This breaks down, if we use the 1985 full-time/part-time job proportions, into 75 full-time and 540 part-time jobs. Even allowing for some fluctuations, growth in tourist/recreational expenditures and projected jobs during the next decade will be slow and thus will have only a small economic impact upon the area. A Ministry of Tourism and Recreation

Study (1989) on Lake Temagami and along the Highway 11 corridor in the area has indicated that, in 1989, the occupancy level of lodges and motels was only 40 per cent over a 24-week season (May-October). Obviously, a new and better strategy will have to be sought to maintain and to strengthen the tourism and recreation sectors in the Temagami region. Such a strategy should include several approaches:

The maintenance and improvement of existing tourist/recreational activities: A careful maintenance program will be required for hunting and angling (Temagami District Fisheries Management Presentation 1988), both of which activities will be at the maximum limits of sustained yield. Similarly, the cottage-building program will soon be completed, and unless new limits are prescribed, little development potential will remain. Improvement and growth-potential will, however, continue for canoeing and non-wilderness motorized camping. A strategy to attract greater numbers for each activity will be required.

Extending the tourism/recreation season so that the winter will bring more financial benefits to the region throughout the year: The seasonal nature of these activities results in economic slowdowns during the winter months, so that only ice-fishing operates when lakes are frozen. Canoeing and cottaging are spring-to-fall activities which tend to be most intensive during the summer months. Canoeing does attract early May and June "white water tripping" enthusiasts and autumn transient paddlers who enjoy the more serene atmosphere of that season (Northern Concepts 1986). As noted, moose hunting follows the other activities, starting in October and lasting until mid-November, while bear hunting occurs in spring and fall. The need exists for an increased emphasis on outdoor winter sports such as cross-country skiing, snowmobiling, and ice-fishing in order to attract more visitors. This will assist in balancing the financial structure over the whole year.

Developing the potential of hiking and nature-interpretation activities: During the late spring, summer, and fall, more hiking and nature-interpretive trails, such as those being developed on Temagami Island, could be used to entice more visitors to the area. Hiking and nature-interpretation is a rapidly growing activity in Ontario (Larenthol and

Horwath Management Consultants 1986) and, therefore, must receive attention in such a tourism strategy. Work by the Temagami branch office of MNR to identify and select Areas of Natural and Scientific Interest (ANSI) could, in some instances, be used to advertise unique geological and biological areas. Some of these ANSI locations might be integrated into the tourism strategy for the district.

The establishment of some type of tourist/recreation resort complex should also be considered as an important part of the strategy for economic development: The marketing feasibility of such a project will require careful study. In the early 1970s a year-round resort-village complex was proposed for Maple Mountain. A labour force of 450, during construction, and an estimated 800 full-time/part-time jobs, after completion, was expected. However, the venture was aborted by the land-caution obtained by the Teme-Augama Anishnabai, which is still in effect. Recently a proposal to build a $60-million all-season vacation centre at Caribou Mountain has been unveiled (*North Bay Daily Nugget,* Wednesday, 11 October 1989). This resort, with a multitude of recreational opportunities, would also employ approximately 800 people.

Other smaller-scale developments, such as a community welcome centre in Temagami, would assist in the dissemination of tourist information as well as educational and historical material. Cultural and administrative functions would also play an important role at the centre (Temagami Community Welcome Centre Progress Report 1987). Consideration could also be given to acquiring an outdoor education facility similar to those in the Toronto area. This centre would operate on a year-round basis, accepting designated students from all parts of the province. The study of the environment and wilderness would be the focus for such a school. An adjunct could be an institute which would concentrate on research, not only on topics about environmental and economic concerns within the region, but also in the fields of the humanities and fine arts.

A more comprehensive strategy for advertising the variety of tourist/recreation possibilities: This will require the identification of target groups in southern Ontario and the northern United States and the setting up of long-term strategies to attract these people to the region.

The gathering and acquisition of a proper data base for tourism and recreation: Such a constantly updated information base would provide better data on tourism and recreation and would allow for more complete study, analysis, and recommendations about this very important sector of the Temagami economy. It might be possible for the proposed education centre and research institute to coordinate data-gathering and storage.

FIGURE 1 Source: Ontario Ministry of Natural Resources

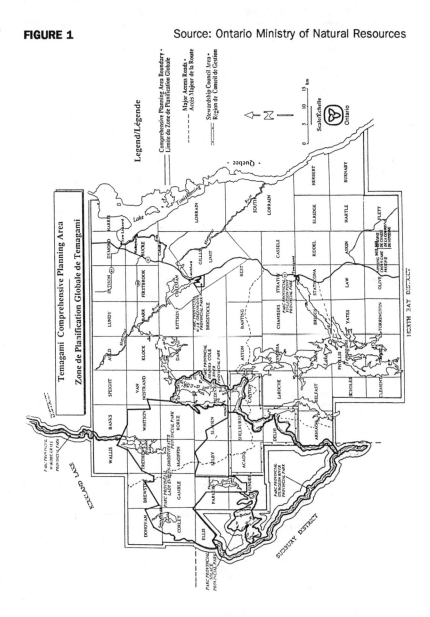

TABLE 1

Temagami District Tourist Establishments and Services, 1987	
Youth Camps on Lake Temagami	11
Commercial Camps off Highway 11	23
Commercial Camps on Lake Temagami	8
Commercial Camps on Anima Nipissing Lake	3
Commercial Camps on Lady Evelyn Lake	7
Commercial Camps on Obabika Lake	2
Outpost Camps	11
Outfitters/Services	4
TOTAL	69

Source: Coopers and Lybrand Consulting 1987, Appendix 1

Temagami Area Tourist Establishments and Services, 1988	
Commercial Camps or Lodges	61
Commercial Youth Camps	12
Commercial Tent and Trailer Parks	3
Commercial Outpost Camps	16
Outfitting Business	3
Marinas	4
TOTAL	99

Source: Ministry of Natural Resources 1988

TABLE 2 — Economic Importance of the Forestry and Tourism/Recreation Industries to the Temagami Area

Economic Contribution of Tourism and Recreation	
Gross Annual Revenues earned by operators	$8,000,000
Annual number of visitors	20,000
Value of Capital Assets	$10,000,000
Annual Wages	$1,500,000
Annual Total Employment	450 jobs
Seasonal Employment	395 jobs
Full-time Employment	55 jobs

Activity	Estimated Tourism and Recreation Activity Expenditures in Temagami District 1985	Economic Contribution of Tourism and Recreation in year 2000 estimated
Wilderness Travel	$2,250,000	$2,690,000
Angling	$3,500,000	$3,800,000
Hunting	$1,070,000	$1,820,000
Cottagers	$1,325,000	$1,550,000
Non Wilderness Camping	$290,000	$1,710,000
Total	$8,435,000	$11,570,000

Source: Coopers and Lybrand Consulting Group. July 1987: 1986 Field Survey by DelCan.

References

An Environmental Assessment for Primary Access Roads in the Latchford Crown Forest Management Unit, MNR, January 1988.

Brief to The Temagami Area Working Group, MNR, January 1988.

Coopers and Lybrand Consulting Group, Economic Importance of the Forestry and Tourism/Recreation Industries to the Temagami Area, July 1987.

Hodgins, Bruce and Jamie Benidickson, *The Temagami Experience: Recreation, Resources, and Aboriginal Rights in the Northern Ontario Wilderness*, Toronto, University of Toronto Press, 1989.

Larenthol and Horwath Management Consultants, Algonquin Park Marketing and Tourism Development Study: Technical Report, prepared for MNR, October 1986.

Northern Concepts Recreation Areas, Consultants and Developers, Economic Overview of the Temagami Canoeing Industry, Temagami, 1986.

Temagami Area Tourism Development Strategy, Ministry of Tourism and Recreation, Northeastern Region, February 1989.

Temagami Area Working Group, Report, 1988.

Temagami Community Welcome Centre, Progress Report, September 1987.

Temagami District Fisheries Management Presentation, MNR, 1988.

Temagami District Landuse Guideline, MNR, 1983.

Temagami, Lake Temagami, Plan for Landuse and Recreation Development, MNR, 1973.

Environmental Perspectives

Wildlife of all sizes abound in the Temagami area. *Courtesy: Hap Wilson*

Six

The Development of a Wilderness Park System in Ontario, 1967–1990: Temagami in Context

Gerald Killan

The controversy surrounding Temagami is profoundly complex and tangled, involving separate but interrelated questions of wilderness preservation and recreation, sustainable forest management, and Native land rights. For politicians, Temagami has become a nightmare that defies easy solution. Former Premier David Peterson described it as "the most difficult issue" he had encountered as a politician.[1] Certainly the controversy has enough dimensions to attract the attention of academics from a score of disciplines. Historians Bruce Hodgins and Jamie Benidickson are in the forefront of this growing number of researchers. Their recent book, *The Temagami Experience: Recreation, Resources, and Aboriginal Rights in the Northern Ontario Wilderness* (1989), a *tour de force* of regional land-use history, painstakingly unravels and interprets the main themes in the Temagami story.

This paper supplements the work of Hodgins and Benidickson by examining Temagami through the lens of provincial-park policy since 1967. The course of events in the region has been frequently shaped by a series of significant park-policy developments. These have included: the 1967 government commitment to create a system of Wilderness parks in Ontario; the conceptualization of a provincial-parks system plan by 1978; the dovetailing of parks-system planning and Strategic Land Use Planning (SLUP) from 1980 to 1983; the creation of Ontario's Wilderness-park system in June 1983 (including the 72,400-hectare Lady Evelyn-Smoothwater Wilderness Park in the heart of Temagami); the 1983 policy imposed by Minister of Natural Resources Alan Pope permitting "non conforming uses" within Wilderness parks; and the revocation of the non-conforming-uses policy in 1988 by linking it with Temagami's Red Squirrel road issue.

I

Ontario first embraced the idea of Wilderness parks in 1967, the year the Conservative government of John Robarts approved a classification policy which included a "Primitive" class of parks.[2] The Department of Lands and Forests, bedevilled by an almost overwhelming set of management problems within the provincial parks, had introduced the classification framework out of desperation. Since 1954 the number of parks had expanded rapidly — from eight to ninety-four — largely in response to the post-war explosion of outdoor recreation. This growth, driven as it was by the recreation imperative, had resulted in a parks system which suffered from a lack of harmony among its users and of balance between its component parts. The primacy of recreation in the parks-planning and development equation had given rise to a recreation/preservation imbalance, problems of overcrowded campgrounds, rowdyism, degraded natural environments, and heightened tensions between user-groups such as hunters and naturalists, motor-boat fishermen and canoeists, commercial loggers, and wilderness preservationists. It had become obvious that no single park could satisfy all these interests, and be all things to all people. Different classes of parks, managed to achieve specific objectives, seemed to offer the best hope of introducing harmony and balance in the system.

The 1967 decision to introduce the classification policy with a Primitive- (today Wilderness) parks component had various sources. The studies and recommendations of the American Outdoor Recreation Resources Review Commission (1958–62) and the International Commission on National Parks had stimulated the Canadian Federal-Provincial Parks Conference to develop a standard classification scheme by

1965.[3] Various Ontario conservation and environmental groups, beginning with the Federation of Ontario Naturalists (FON) in 1958,[4] had also urged the province to introduce a parks-classification and zoning policy. In 1965 Douglas Pimlott, a zoologist at the University of Toronto, renowned for his wolf studies in Algonquin Park and the central figure in the organization of a wilderness-preservation movement in Ontario during the mid-sixties, placed parks-classification at the top of his protectionist agenda. Like most environmentalists of the time, Pimlott took his cue from the United States, where preservationists had succeeded in having Congress pass the Wilderness Act in 1964.[5]

Implementing the new Ontario parks-classification policy proved to be difficult. Northern resource industries and their supporters within the Department of Lands and Forests (the Ministry of Natural Resources, or MNR, after April 1972), generally opposed proposals to create Primitive parks which would result in the removal of large blocks of crown land from timber and mineral extraction. The first Primitive park, announced in April 1968, was Polar Bear, a 1.8 million-hectare goliath around Cape Henrietta-Maria bordering both James and Hudson bays. It evoked little reaction from the resource industries only because it was located in an area deemed to possess low mineral and timber potential. Beyond this initiative, the Robarts government was reluctant to move, especially when the timber industry resisted preservationist demands that the large established Natural-Environment parks — Algonquin and Quetico, Killarney and Lake Superior — be reclassified as Primitive parks where logging would be prohibited.

With the formation of the Algonquin Wildlands League (AWL) in 1968, the stage was set for a major confrontation between wilderness preservationists and loggers over the question of reclassifying the large Natural-Environment parks. During its first years of activity, the league managed to generate, for the first time, widespread public support for the protection of natural areas. Indeed, the league was so successful that it made the management of the large provincial parks a litmus test of the Robarts/Davis governments' sensitivity toward environmental matters.

Ontarians who had experienced and enjoyed their parks and natural environments during the post-war outdoor-recreation boom responded to the environmental clarion call of the AWL. Many of these people were already alarmed by the extent of water and air pollution in their midst. "In the evolution of the rhetoric of ecology," explained Canadian environmental historian Robert Page, "wilderness and pollution were the two key pillars, the two sides of the coin."[6] People now valued parks and natural areas as a necessary element of their rising standard of living and a contributing factor to the quality of their lives. Part of this new way of thinking in the 1960s involved the changing public conception of the crown forests. Unlike traditional so-called "wise-use" conservationists who viewed the forests as a tree farm, environmentally sensitive people were wont to see timbered lands and wilderness as an amenity that was to be enjoyed and that enhanced the quality of their lives.

The AWL and its allies carried on their first crusade for wilderness in Ontario from 1968 to 1974. When the smoke of battle cleared, the successes registered by the preservationists left many government and industry officials shaking their heads in disbelief. Logging had been removed from Killarney and Quetico and both parks had been reclassified as Primitive, in 1971 and 1973 respectively. The Davis government had signed an agreement with Ottawa to create Pukaskwa National Park, and three new Wild-River provincial parks were announced in 1971, including Lady Evelyn-Smoothwater in Temagami. Public consultation had been entrenched as part of the master-planning process for provincial parks, and the Provincial Park Advisory Council was appointed to serve as a watchdog over the system and to seek public input on significant policy matters.[7]

The success enjoyed by the preservationists had a great deal to do with timing and not a little luck. When the AWL appeared in 1968, the Robarts government was suffering the consequences of introducing un-popular programs for tax reform, regional government, and mandatory reorganization of school boards on a county basis. Rather than risk cre-ating another public uproar, the government was inclined to accommo-date the environmentalists by setting up advisory committees for Algonquin and Quetico and opening for public discussion the whole question of wilderness and its importance to society. Later, in April 1971, the window of political opportunity opened wider with the resig-nation of John Robarts and the accession to power of William Davis. In the months prior to the election of October 1971, as the new premier underwent a metamorphosis in image from "bland Bill" to "decisive Davis," preservationists enjoyed some of their most dramatic gains with the political decisions to ban logging in Quetico, to reclassify Killarney as Primitive, and to sign the agreement on Pukaskwa.[8]

During these years, however, the preservationists also discovered the limits of their influence. When economic-impact studies revealed that the regional economies and local communities dependent on timber operations in Algonquin and Lake Superior parks would suffer considerably in the event of a logging ban (alternative sources of timber could not be found outside either park), the government drew the line on preservation and refused to reclassify them as Primitive. Thus, both Algonquin and Lake Superior remained the domain of the timbermen.

After the reclassification battles of 1968–74, preservationists turned their attention to the task of creating a wilderness system. They needed to clarify their thoughts on the questions of how many Wilderness parks should be created, and where they should be located. Accordingly, in 1973, at the annual meeting of the Federation of Ontario Naturalists, representatives of FON, the AWL, the Canadian Nature Federation, the National and Provincial Parks Association of Canada, and the Sierra Club of Ontario formed the Coalition for Wilderness. As its first task, the group drafted a comprehensive position paper for a provincial-wilderness system. The coalition submitted its report, written largely by Bill Addison and Dave Bates of Thunder Bay, to the government in January 1974. The preservationists envisaged a system of 15 Wilderness parks embracing a total area of 23,000 square miles and located to represent all the province's physiographic regions and forest zones. Under this grand scheme, no park was to be smaller than 750 square miles (194,250 hectares).[9]

By this time, MNR's Division of Parks, headed by executive director, James Keenan, was already marching in the same direction as the preservationists. It embarrassed Keenan, the author of the 1967 parks-classification document, that progress in establishing Primitive parks since 1967 had been "more the result of being shoved (Quetico, Killarney), than of leadership," and he advised his minister, Leo Bernier, that "a wilderness policy is one of the most important issues that concerns this Ministry at this time."[10] Under Keenan's direction, the Parks Division launched a comprehensive system-planning effort which culminated in 1978 with the release of two landmark documents: a Cabinet-approved Provincial Parks Policy, and the *Ontario Provincial Parks Planning and Management Policies* manual, the so-called "blue book."[11] These documents constituted nothing short of a planning triumph for the Division of Parks. Across North America, only the United States Parks Service and the state of California possessed similar planning and policy frameworks designed to answer questions which still plagued most park agencies: How many parks of each class were required and why? What natural and cultural features should be preserved in parks and why? How much should be protected and why? What activities should be prohibited or permitted in different park classes and zones?

The "blue book" and policy document now defined Wilderness parks as "substantial areas where the forces of nature are permitted to function freely and where visitors travel by non-mechanized means and experience expansive solitude, challenge, and personal integration with nature." They were to be an average of 100,000 hectares in size, and no smaller than 50,000 hectares, and located to represent each of the province's 13 forest-site regions. Although this proposed Wilderness-park system fell short of the more ambitious scheme desired by the Coalition for Wilderness in 1974, most preservationist organizations were well pleased with the plan and the "blue book," which they soon referred to as "the gospel relating to parks."[12]

Opposition to the plan within MNR had been considerable. During the internal ministry review, some timber, mining, and fish and wildlife managers viewed the plan as a little more than a parks "land grab." To allay this opposition, the Parks Division deleted the program and park-class targets from the policy document submitted to Cabinet in 1978, and included them instead in the "blue book," which received only senior-management approval and thus was more susceptible to amendment.[13]

The release of the Provincial Parks Policy document and the "blue book" marked the end of one phase of the system-planning process and the beginning of another. Ontario now possessed a firm idea of what the ideal parks network should look like. The conceptual and philosophical questions — what? why? where? — had been for the most part resolved. Now it was the turn of regional-parks personnel to undertake the inventories and field research for the system plans which would identify the actual sites required to meet the targets in the "blue book." During this planning process, parks coordinators endeavoured to minimize resource conflicts by rejecting as candidate parks those areas with a high potential for timber, mining, and water power. By early 1981 the regional plans were largely completed. Park planners identified a total of 245 candidate parks necessary to achieve the system-plan objectives.

II

At this juncture, the parks-system plan faced its most difficult test as it was integrated into Strategic Land Use Planning. The 245 candidate park proposals had to be assessed against the land and water requirements of other ministry programs and the needs of other users of crown-land resources. In a perfect planning scenario, the provincial-park and SLUP efforts would have been synchronized so that the regional-parks plans were completed first, and then incorporated into the regional-strategic-planning documents. As it turned out, the proposed strategic plans for northeastern and northwestern Ontario were released in March and June 1980 respectively, before the regional-parks system plans had even been drafted.[14] The response of the advocacy groups was predictable. They charged that MNR had stacked the SLUP process in favour of the resource industries by proceeding with strategic planning before the regional-parks system plans had been completed.[15]

The preservationists were especially alarmed by what the northern SLUP documents contained on the subject of Wilderness parks. None of the six Candidate Wilderness parks identified in the strategic-planning documents had been described in sufficient detail to explain their significance or the reasons for their selection. And why only six, the preservationists asked? What about alternative sites in each region?[16] Ironically, on the other side of the issue, the resource industries as well as many sportsmen, commercial-tourism operators, and Native groups attacked the SLUP regional plans for precisely the opposite reason, that wilderness had been given too much, rather than too little, consideration in the documents.

Fueling this round of the wilderness controversy was the realization by both preservationists and timbermen that they were rapidly running out of time and resources. With so little wild land remaining in Ontario, preservationists saw the SLUP process as their last chance to create a Wilderness-parks system. The timber companies viewed matters from an altogether different perspective. Facing as they were an impending shortage of marketable timber, they bristled at the thought of large areas of productive forest being locked up in Wilderness parks where logging was prohibited. That two of the candidate parks — Ogoki-Albany, to the northwest of Lake Nipigon, and Lady Evelyn-Smoothwater in Temagami — were located in areas where timber commitments had already been made caused them no little anxiety.

Three different companies held timber licences in over one-half the Lady Evelyn-Smoothwater Candidate Wilderness Park. When MNR released the SLUP-Northeast plan, one of the companies, William Milne and Sons Ltd. of Temagami, was in the middle of a $4,000,000-expansion program based in part on obtaining the timber from the volume agreement it held in the proposed wilderness area. The company had already received over $800,000 in federal and provincial subsidies for a modern sawmill suitable for processing all tree species. If the Lady Evelyn-Smoothwater park went forward, argued J.F. McNutt, president of William Milne and Sons, it would reduce the company's allowable cut by an estimated 20 per cent and place "our project in serious jeopardy" together with 200 full-time jobs.[17]

If the trees are not cut in the six Candidate Wilderness parks, announced Ken Greaves, president of the Ontario Forest Industries Association, in a fit of hyperbole, it "can only spell economic disaster for every citizen" in the province.[18] "The facts speak differently," countered the preservationists. The proposed Wilderness parks "involve less than 2% of the productive forest base in Ontario, only a few years cutting at present rates." The future of the forest industry, they argued, lay in the implementation of serious reforestation programs, not in defeating the proposals for wilderness areas. "If the government ... accepts the argument that the road to industry salvation runs through parklands, then the 21st century will bring with it an industry without wood and a province without wild country."[19] The Provincial Parks Advisory Council concurred, and unanimously endorsed the Candidate Wilderness parks.

"The S.L.U.P. process has now eliminated all but the minimal number of Candidate areas required to fulfill the Park Policy mandate and targets," wrote the chairman, George Priddle, in January 1981. If the Ogoki-Albany and Lady Evelyn sites were abandoned because of forest-industry pressure, it would "result in a nearly total commitment of the [Crown owned] Boreal Forest ... to extraction rather than preservation and recreation."[20]

Given the negative reaction of the forest industry to the Candidate Wilderness parks, regional planners had serious doubts that either Lady Evelyn-Smoothwater or Ogoki-Albany would survive the SLUP gauntlet. They believed that they had to demonstrate a willingness to accommodate the timber interests. In the case of Lady Evelyn-Smoothwater, the planners would eventually reject as politically unpalatable options for a park larger than 74,500 hectares. Furthermore, they sought to locate as much of the park as possible (consistent with protectionist objectives) in areas which had already been cut over by the timber companies. They were even prepared to accept, as an anomaly, the continuation of the Liskeard Lumber road which bisected the candidate park, thus maintaining the company's access to its limits to the south of the park. None of this met policy ideals; all the same, parks personnel believed that the proposed candidate park met "blue-book" size requirements, adequately represented the forest-site region, and contained representation of some of the finest Temagami wilderness.[21]

Although most discussion generated in 1980 by the SLUP regional plans centred on the logging versus wilderness issue, other questions complicated the controversy. Mining industry spokesmen objected to the proposed parks as vehemently as did the foresters.[22] So too did many traditional users of the areas contained in the Candidate Wilderness parks — sport hunters, trappers, commercial fishermen, and fly-in tourist operators — all of whom would be denied access if the parks were established. For its part, the Ontario Federation of Anglers and Hunters (OFAH) evoked the "multiple-use" concept and opposed any candidate park in which hunting would be prohibited.[23]

Tourist operators who owned fly-in outpost cabins or commercial lodges in the Candidate Wilderness parks also joined the anti-park forces since "blue-book" policy would require the removal of their businesses. They were supported by some local politicians interested in promoting major resort projects. As a case in point, the representatives of twenty-seven towns and townships, organized as the Temiskaming Municipal Association, opposed the Lady Evelyn-Smoothwater park proposal because they believed it would hinder the kind of tourism investment they envisioned for their region.[24] Local businessmen-politicians realized that a park would end all hope for a four-season resort complex at Maple Mountain. The subject of a comprehensive study by the Ministry of Industry and Tourism in the early 1970s, the Maple Mountain project had been placed in limbo because of a land-caution placed on a 9,000-square-kilometre area of the region in 1973 by the Teme-Augama Anishnabai. Interestingly, Ministry of Industry and Tourism officials objected to the Wilderness-park proposal, arguing that they still considered Maple Mountain as a prime resort-development site. "In our opinion," wrote the director of the Tourism Development Branch, "the classification of the entire area as a wilderness park would represent the least attractive alternative use of the area in terms of the region's economic and employment future."[25]

Not all northern tourist operators opposed the Candidate Wilderness parks; in fact, businessmen could be found on both sides of the controversy. Many recreational canoeing operators who specialized in offering wilderness experiences applauded the SLUP designations and welcomed the creation of provincial parks as a way of preserving the natural areas upon which their enterprises depended. In Temiskaming one of the activists in the Alliance for the Lady Evelyn Wilderness was Trent University historian Bruce W. Hodgins also the director of the Wanapitei Wilderness Centre and a past president of the Ontario Recreational Canoeing Association.

As the SLUP wilderness drama unfolded during 1980–81, most of the actors in the piece were veteran players engaging in well-defined, almost ritualistic, political combat. What distinguished and also complicated this phase of the controversy, however, was the addition of a major new participant in the discussions — the Native peoples of northern Ontario. During the preservation upsurge of the late 1960s and early 1970s, the Native peoples had remained largely in the background as the preservationists struggled to have Algonquin, Killarney, Lake Superior, and Quetico reclassified as Primitive parks. Since the areas in question had already been designated parkland, Native groups were little affected. On the few occasions when new park decisions did impinge upon specific Native communities, the government endeavoured to modify policy to suit the Indians. In creating Polar Bear Provincial Park in 1968, for example, Lands and Forests Minister René Brunelle had insisted that the "traditional hunting and trapping rights of the indigenous Indian population be ... guaranteed."[26]

By the time that the proposed SLUP regional plans appeared in 1980, the Indian bands were not as acquiescent about the establishment of new Wilderness parks as they had been when Polar Bear was created. During the 1970s, the Native peoples across Canada had become more militant and more determined than ever to work for self-determination, to rebuild their self-respect, and to break their dependency on white society. Their concept of "nationhood" rejected "white authority to allocate land ... or to restrict Native use of wildlife."[27] Moreover, the concept of a park was alien to their cultural tradition and their philosophy of being "one with the land."[28]

In Temagami, the Teme-Augama Anishnabai placed a question mark on the future of the Lady Evelyn Candidate Wilderness Park. As early as 1973, to thwart the Maple Mountain project, the Bear Island band had placed a legal caution on over 9,000 square kilometres of crown land (including the park area) and began to press for a resolution of a land claim which had been pending for over a century. Band members argued that, since neither they nor their ancestors had signed a formal agreement surrendering their ancestral homeland to the crown, the area in question remained in the constitutional category of "lands reserved for Indians" and fell under the band's ownership. The 1973 land-caution placed a freeze on most new development — the Maple Mountain project, cottages, mining — although MNR permitted forest operations to continue while the case moved through the courts with glacier-like speed.[29]

Such, then, was the general setting, and the attitudes of the major participants as the SLUP and parks-planning processes approached the critical point of integration. Everyone had expected the Wilderness-parks issue to be a significant element of the strategic land-use planning discussions, but no one seems to have anticipated how dominant that issue would become.

III

At the height of the SLUP wilderness controversy, in the spring of 1981, MNR began to integrate parks-system and strategic planning across Ontario. To bring the two planning programs into phase, the ministry struck a special task force headed by Richard M. Monzon, the deputy regional director of northwestern Ontario. The year between the appointment of the Monzon task force and the release of its report in March 1982 proved to be one of the most stormy periods on record in the relationship between park-advocacy groups and the Ministry of Natural Resources. For a variety of reasons, leading environmentalists concluded that MNR "senior management" had become "increasingly anti-park and pro-resource extraction."[30] Bitter confrontation ensued with some groups calling for the removal of the provincial-parks system from MNR. This occurred coincidentally with the appointment in April 1981 of a new minister of natural resources, Alan Pope, the thirty-five-year-old lawyer and MPP for Timmins. Pope had little opportunity to familiarize himself with strategic and parks planning before he found himself rapidly slip-sliding into the SLUP quagmire.

No sooner had MNR announced the appointment of the Monzon task force than some preservationists smelled a rat. The Algonquin Wildlands League, and even the chairman of the Provincial Parks Advisory Council, George Priddle, charged that the task force had been established to slow down the SLUP process long enough to allow MNR and the large timber companies to negotiate Forest Management Agreements (FMAs)[31]. Once these agreements were in place, argued the environmentalists, the forest industry would enjoy an enormous advantage in the upcoming crown-land allocations. No such plot actually existed. Indeed, the great irony here was that the Monzon task force had been appointed to speed up the synchronization of strategic and parks-system planning, something the preservationists themselves had been insisting upon since the release of the SLUP regional plans.

All the same, by May 1981 many park advocates had begun to have serious doubts whether senior ministry officials wanted to implement the 1978 parks policy. The environmentalists had just learned of the so-called "Sault Ste. Marie massacre," a term coined to describe the contents of a leaked memorandum signed by the Sault-based assistant deputy minister of northern Ontario, G.A. McCormack, "giving mines, forestry, and hydraulic generation priority over potential parks" in land-use planning.[32]

Then, in May, at the "Ontario Provincial Parks: Issues in the Eighties" conference at the University of Waterloo, George Priddle disclosed the details of an acrimonious meeting between the Provincial Parks Advisory Council and William Foster, appointed deputy minister of natural resources in January 1981: "We have a Deputy Minister ... who does not agree with the government's park policy and states that the one overriding commitment of the Ministry is to supply fibre to the mills. This same Deputy Minister has made it perfectly clear that he does not believe in the need to protect representative landscapes" in a system of Wilderness parks and Nature Reserves.[33] Foster made no secret of the fact that he had little enthusiasm for the complex park-policy frameworks fashioned by "the bright, young and zealous" park planners. Their approach to park-system development and management, he believed, smacked of "urban academic elitism." He preferred that MNR pursue a more "populist" approach, one which demanded fewer restrictions on permitted uses, especially in Wilderness and Nature-Reserve parks, and which would not "sterilize large tracts of land."[34]

As environmentalists lost confidence in MNR's capacity to deal objectively with parks issues, they began to demand the removal of the provincial-parks program to another ministry. When Davis restructured his Cabinet and named Reuben Baetz to head a new Ministry of Tourism and Recreation in February 1982, the preservationists urged the premier to transfer the Parks and Recreation Areas Branch to the new ministry.[35] In response, the government appointed Robert Carman, secretary of the Management Board of Cabinet, to chair a senior-level committee to study the matter. The committee eventually decided that the environmentalists' demand was ill advised. By late February 1982 the Monzon task force report had been reviewed internally within MNR and Alan Pope was poised to announce how he intended to bring park planning and SLUP into phase, and place them both on a fast track to completion. It was decided that the removal of the parks program from MNR, the ministry which controlled the crown-land base required for the new parks, might well impede these efforts.[36]

On 12 March 1982 Alan Pope revealed plans to deal with SLUP and provincial parks.[37] The Strategic Land Use Planning program, he explained, would be accelerated and brought to a conclusion by the end of the year. In each administrative district of MNR, staff were rushing to prepare draft district-land-use plans which would be available for public review during a series of open-house meetings scheduled for each district during a two-week span in June. Pope also released the Monzon task force report, which identified and analyzed the 245 candidate provincial parks to be included in the draft district-land-use plans.[38] The minister emphasized that the decisions for or against retaining a candidate provincial park in the final district plans would depend to a considerable extent on the amount of public support, or opposition, registered during the open-house reviews. Unfortunately, Pope also had some bad news for park advocates. He intended to give the whole subject of permitted uses in provincial parks another examination, and to that end announced that the "blue-book" policy manual would be open for public review during the district-planning process.

Park advocates left Pope's 12 March press conference uncertain as to whether they were winning or losing the campaign for implementation of the 1978 policy. They were encouraged by the minister's promise of new parks, but they were unsettled both by his decision to revise the "blue book" and by the extremely tight schedule for the open-house reviews. How, they asked, could individuals and provincial groups obtain a fair hearing when they were expected to register their views on district-land-use options at various open-house meetings in forty-six districts scattered across the length and breadth of Ontario during the same two-week period in June? "This is meaningful public input? Obviously it is not," they grumbled.[39]

Whatever their doubts, the environmentalists had no illusions about one thing. They had now entered what promised to be the most telling period in the history of Ontario's provincial parks. Representatives of eight park-advocacy groups convened in late March in Toronto at the offices of World Wildlife Fund Canada to fashion a strategy for the district-review process. The delegates decided that their best chance for success lay in organizing a committee of activists in each of MNR's administrative districts.[40] The Wildlands League (the word Algonquin had just been dropped to reflect more accurately the organization's broad focus) offered to coordinate the efforts of the scattered groups in the loose parks coalition.

The coalition faced a tough, uphill battle. Its combined membership amounted to only 20,000 people, and its financial resources were limited. Only FON and the Wildlands league could afford full-time staff, and, even then, Arlin Hackman's position at the league was never secure since the organization operated on a meagre annual budget of under $50,000. Still, the parks coalition had strengths no amount of money could buy, particularly the "fire in the belly" enthusiasm of its leaders, and the extraordinary unity of purpose among its members. The 1978 parks policy, the "blue book," the regional-parks system plans, and the Monzon report had galvanized the coalition by providing the member groups with a common agenda and a vision of the ideal parks system.

The organizational effort subsequently put forth by the coalition of park and environmentalist groups paid dividends once the public-review process began; indeed, the turnout of park supporters at the 141 district open houses exceeded expectations. Altogether, some 10,000 people attended the meetings, the majority of whom expressed strong support for the proposed candidate parks and for maintaining the protectionist elements of the "blue book." MNR also received over 10,000 comment sheets, letters, and briefs on land-use issues.[41]

Opponents of the candidate provincial parks also made a strong showing at the meetings. Across northern Ontario, people connected with the timber companies argued vociferously that the proposed parks would seriously reduce the available timber supply and prevent the industry from meeting its future needs, especially for conifer wood. To get its message across to the public, Great Lakes Forest Products purchased television air time in Thunder Bay and distributed a film entitled "Evergreen." Regrettably, forest-industry propaganda to the effect that new parks would destroy the northern economy frightened many people into thinking that the parks issue boiled down to "a clear-cut choice between food on the table and a playground for rich southerners."[42] Such fears were unfounded, insisted the park-advocacy groups, who used the preliminary results of MNR's economic-impact studies for Ogoki-Albany and Lady Evelyn to bolster their case.[43]

In September 1982 the combatants in the land-use struggle got the first measure of their success in influencing district decisions when MNR released for public comment a series of district-land-use planning proposals. Environmentalists were dismayed. "District officials have axed or deferred indefinitely approximately 20% of the candidates, 35% of these in northern Ontario," reported the Wildlands League. "Many that remain are mere shadows of the original proposals, having had their areas reduced drastically."[44] One of the six Candidate Wilderness parks — Aulneau Peninsula on Lake of the Woods — had not survived the review because of strong pressure by organized hunters. The other wilderness areas had been substantially reduced; for instance, MNR had carved 2,100 hectares from the Lady Evelyn-Smoothwater Candidate Wilderness park. Alarm turned to anger when the pro-park groups completed their own *Progress Report on Parks System Planning in Northern Ontario* (September 1982), which provided an overview of all the northern draft district-land-use plans. The report concluded that not only did the proposed park system in the north fall short of "blue-book" targets, but the "draft District Plans consistently demonstrate an anti-parks bias and a willingness to neglect parks policies in favour of other extractive resource policies."[45]

In response to demands exerted by all sides, Alan Pope decided to expand the public-consultation process, and personally chaired a series of seven open forums during November and December 1982. Each meeting was heavily attended with park supporters again in the majority. "Especially surprising," reported FON, "was the support for parks creation in the north, where park advocates outnumbered opponents by a wide margin."[46]

Evidently worried by the show of support for parks manifested at the forums, the Ontario Federation of Anglers and Hunters counterattacked by striking an alliance with the Ontario Trappers Association, the Prospectors and Developers Association, and the Ontario Forest Industries Association to press the minister to impose a two-year moratorium on the establishment of any new park. "It's a major issue with us," asserted Rick Morgan of OFAH. "We feel we need two years to give the government a chance to let people know what happens when you create a park."[47] Firmly committed to wrapping up land-use planning as soon as possible, Alan Pope was not about to cave in to this eleventh-hour demand. Pope was doing everything humanly possible to appear fair to all sides and to familiarize himself with the issues in every part of the province. During personal meetings with each district manager, MNR staff were amazed to discover that the minister's grasp of individual plans often exceeded that of the district managers themselves. He was eager to find compromise positions between the pro- and anti-park coalitions. Accordingly, he called together representatives of twenty-seven different interest groups to meet with him personally in closed sessions on 26 and 27 January 1983 at the Guild Inn, Toronto, in a last-ditch attempt to solve the remaining contentious issues. One entire day was set aside for discussions on the Wilderness parks.

During the Guild Inn discussions, the leaders of the parks coalition attempted to break the deadlock by offering to be flexible on the question of non-conforming activities in the new Wilderness parks. They would never condone forestry and mining in these areas, explained their spokesperson, Monte Hummel, but they were willing to consider limited sport hunting on a park-by-park basis, the continuation of some existing commercial-tourism facilities, controlled mineral exploration, and Native hunting and trapping.

Decisions as to whether or not to allow some or all of these activities in a given park, the environmentalists emphasized, would have to be made during the master-planning process for each park, and, if approved, each permitted activity would have to be conducted in a way compatible with the classification of a Wilderness park. This meant, for example, that sport hunters must be restricted to travelling by non-mechanized means. Should tourism operations be permitted to continue, the operators must be prevented from expanding their existing facilities. The environmentalists opposed the transformation of "present outpost camps in parks into lodges which in turn would service an even broader network of outposts." Hummel also insisted that the tourist operators must not be given unrestricted access to all areas by motor boats or all-terrain vehicles. Any mineral exploration permitted in the new Wilderness parks must be undertaken by aerial geomagnetic surveys or other methods which would have minimal impact on the environment. In the event that a commercially exploitable mineral discovery was found, the affected zone would have to be removed from the park and a comparable area added elsewhere.[48] The sportsmen and industry representatives at the Guild Inn failed to rise to the challenge and continued to argue that Wilderness parks were "unaffordable, undemocratic and unnecessary."[49]

Finally, on 2 June 1983, Strategic Land Use Planning reached its finale when Alan Pope rose in the legislature to outline the contents of his ministry's district-land-use guidelines.[50] "In the guidelines," the minister announced, "we recommend 155 future provincial parks. These will include six Wilderness parks [actually five new parks and an addition to Killarney], 35 natural environment parks, 25 waterway parks, 74 nature reserves, 12 recreational parks and three historical parks. Cabinet has already passed regulations to create the ... Wilderness parks immediately. Therefore, these parks already exist."[51]

It was an extraordinary announcement: the government had created a Wilderness system representative of most of the northern forest-site regions and had committed itself to more than doubling the number of provincial parks. The new Wilderness-park additions included: a major extension to Killarney Provincial Park south of Sudbury; the establishment of Woodland Caribou and Opasquia parks abutting the Manitoba border to the west and north respectively of Red Lake; Wabakimi (a much reduced version of Ogoki-Albany); Lady Evelyn-Smoothwater in Temagami; and Kesagami at the southern tip of James Bay. Combined, these areas added some 1,200,000 hectares to the parks system. Although there would be no Wilderness park for southern Ontario, Pope informed the legislature that, as an alternative, negotiations were underway between the province and Ottawa for "the eventual establishment of a Bruce Peninsula National Park," which would encompass Cyprus Lake and Fathom Five provincial parks near Tobermory.

There was one more item of good news for environmentalists. As a general policy, logging would be excluded from all but two of the new parks. Studies had revealed that the expanded parks system posed no threat to the future of the forest-products industry. "In total, annual available wood supply will be reduced by only one per cent by the year 2000," explained an MNR press release.[52] This loss would be offset by increased timber utilization and through improved forest-protection methods. Pope acknowledged that, throughout the public consultation process, one message had been loud and clear — most Ontarians viewed logging as an inappropriate activity in their provincial parks.

As the minister continued his statement, park advocates learned that a heavy price had been exacted for the historic gains made that day. Ninety of the 245 candidate parks included in the Monzon task force report had been discarded, most being casualties of trade-offs with other resource-users. When the published district-land-use-guidelines documents became available later in the month, it was also evident that drastic cutbacks had been made in the size of many parks. Ogoki-Albany Candidate Wilderness Park, for instance, had been reduced by two-thirds, hence the name change to Wabakimi. "Overall the total area of the 155 new parks," reported the Wildlands League, "will be only about 40 per cent of that contained in the original 245 candidate areas."[53] Nature Reserves had been especially hard hit — their numbers dropped from 150 to 74.[54] Environmentalists took consolation in the fact that MNR intended to protect many outstanding natural features outside the parks system through the new Areas of Natural and Scientific Interest (ANSI) and private-stewardship programs.

Since the elimination of as many as 100 candidate parks had been anticipated by most parks and environmental groups, this feature of Pope's announcement did not create much of a stir. What caused real consternation and burst the bubble of euphoria was the unwelcome news that the government had decided to set aside many of the protectionist features of the "blue book" in managing the new parks. Henceforth, declared Pope, mineral exploration, hunting, trapping, and commercial tourism would be recognized as permitted uses in classes of parks where they had been previously prohibited, including all the new Wilderness parks.

For Monte Hummel, the minister's decision on non-conforming uses smacked of betrayal. As already noted, at the Guild Inn meetings in January, park advocates had been willing to consider compromises on some non-conforming activities in Wilderness parks. "The spirit of our position," Hummel explained, "was that hunting, tourism and mining exploration only be *considered* on a park by park basis, and only *permitted* if they were proposed to take place in such a way that is respectful of the status of a wilderness park." Pope stepped well beyond these parameters by including non-conforming uses "in the regulations for every wilderness park, creating the impression ... that such activities *would* be permitted on the same terms as they had been practiced in the past." Most exasperating of all for Hummel, the MNR information kit issued on 2 June implied that the minister's decision on non-conforming uses enjoyed the support of the environmentalists since it was ostensibly based on compromises they had proposed in January. "In my view," concluded Hummel, "this was *not* a politically honest response to the spirit of the compromises offered at the Guild Inn."[55]

Understandably, most park supporters experienced profoundly mixed emotions as they came to terms with the significance of the minister's decisions on parks. After three years of hanging on tenterhooks over the outcome of SLUP, park activists had fallen short of their goal — the implementation of the 1978 provincial-park policy. Pope had made history by providing the bulk of the land base for an outstanding park system — and by the end of 1985 over 100 of the 155 promised parks had been placed into regulations — but in their eyes he had prevented the proper management of these new parks by discarding the protectionist essence of the "blue book."

Environmentalists now faced the unpleasant prospect of a prolonged and bitter park-by-park struggle against non-conforming uses during the management-planning phase required for each new park. But as fate would have it, the winds of political change freshened in Ontario and gave rise to the hope that this scenario might well be avoided. On 26 June 1985 David Peterson's minority Liberal government assumed power under the terms of a special two-year accord negotiated with the NDP, thereby bringing to an end Ontario's forty-two year Tory dynasty. Environmental groups expected the new administration to reverse Pope's 1983 policy on non-conforming uses. Much to their disappointment, Liberal Natural Resources Minister Vincent Kerrio did not agree with them. As investigative reporter Rosemary Speirs observed, the amiable Kerrio — a former businessman in Niagara Falls, an angler and sport hunter, boating enthusiast and occasional canoeist, and a cottage owner in Temiskaming — saw the "non-conforming uses" question from every side. To him, Alan Pope's 1983 parks policy seemed quite reasonable.[56]

In April 1986, however, Kerrio was surprised to learn that some of his colleagues in the Cabinet Committee on Regulations were of a different mind. When he approached the committee to entrench the "non-conforming uses" in regulations, the chairman, Gregory Sorbara, insisted that the question be reviewed. This action triggered an internal debate within the Peterson Cabinet which lasted two years. Jim Bradley, minister of the environment, and some officials in the premier's office, sided with Sorbara and argued for the adoption of a more "Liberal approach" to provincial-park management. To complicate matters for the government, the public learned of the Cabinet division in early May when confidential documents were leaked to FON.[57]

From that point on, park-advocacy groups gave the government no rest on the "non-conforming-uses" issue. The FON, for example, launched a publicity campaign against hunting in parks. The highlight of the effort involved distributing a so-called "park-user survival device" — a fluorescent-orange triangular safety sticker which read "DO NOT SHOOT. I am not a game species."[58] The demand for the sticker was larger than expected and required the printing of a second run.

Meanwhile, the release of MNR's *Concept Plan Alternatives* (May 1986) for Woodland Caribou Provincial Wilderness Park, a preliminary step in the development of a management plan, also set off a storm of protest. The document proposed to accommodate a wide range of activities in the park — mechanized travel, hunting, trapping, fly-in tourist operations, outfitters located in the interior, 170 boat caches, and 27 private cottages. All of these uses were in keeping with the 1983 district land-use guidelines but inconsistent with the 1978 "blue book." None of these activities should be allowed in a Wilderness park, insisted the preservationists. Since Woodland Caribou was the first of the five new Wilderness parks to receive a management plan, the decisions made here would set precedents for the others.[59] Evidently, all the publicity generated by the environmentalists had the desired effect. In late summer, MNR announced the suspension of the Woodland Caribou management planning process pending the cabinet's decision on whether or not to continue the "permitted non-confirming uses."

Shortly after the ministry had dampened the passions over Woodland Caribou, the embers of another controversy burst into flame. In November 1986 the world's largest alliance of conservation groups, the Swiss-based International Union for Conservation of Nature (IUCN), hearkened to the entreaties of FON and placed Lady Evelyn-Smoothwater Provincial Park on a list of twenty-three protected areas in the world currently being threatened with environmental disaster.[60] The IUCN registry included a site in the Soviet Union threatened by the 1986 Chernobyl nuclear accident, and a park in the Central African Republic where rhinoceros and elephant herds were being decimated by poachers. According to the IUCN, Lady Evelyn-Smoothwater fell into the same category because it was endangered by impending logging activities which would result from the construction of the proposed Red Squirrel road extension and the Pinetorch corridor. Given experience elsewhere in the world, the IUCN believed that the expansion of clearcut logging activities subsequent to the development of these roads would have a disastrous impact upon the wildlife habitat and the prime scenic and recreational values of the Lady Evelyn-Smoothwater Wilderness Park. Apart from the deleterious ecological effects of clearcut logging, forest-access roads would inevitably lead to an influx of hunters, motor boats, and all-terrain vehicles. The environmentalists insisted that the way to protect Lady Evelyn was to designate the disputed area to the south of the park as a wilderness reserve or buffer zone in which logging and mining would be prohibited.[61]

The IUCN's intervention changed what had been a localized logging versus wilderness skirmish into a political *cause célèbre*. Prominent Canadians, alerted to the danger facing the legendary Temagami country, jumped into the fray with all the attendant media coverage they commanded. Authors Margaret Atwood, Pierre Berton, and Timothy Findley, wildlife artist Robert Bateman, and biologist David Suzuki among others formed the Save Temagami Committee, became patrons of the new Temagami Wilderness Society, and squared off against MNR. The issue had developed into the Liberals' first major test for resolving a complex land-use issue, and one which promised to reveal much about the style of government Ontarians could expect in the years ahead.

In July 1987, following the termination of the two-year Liberal-NDP accord, and with the government riding high in the opinion polls, Premier Peterson called an election for 10 September. This meant a further postponement of the decision on parks-management policy since the government did not intend to ignite a series of political explosions across the province during the election campaign. The environmentalists, on the other hand, were eager to keep the issue before the voters.[62] On 21 August they got an opportunity to do so when Natural Resources Minister Kerrio authorized William Milne and Sons Ltd. of Temagami to begin logging a 637-hectare area south of Lady Evelyn-Smoothwater Provincial Park. Unless the company quickly obtained new supplies of timber, explained Kerrio, it would be forced to close down. To minimize the environmental effects, however, MNR rejected the company's application for an access road. The loggers would have to move their equipment by barge and take out the timber in booms via Lake Temagami. In addition, the company would also be required to leave 400-foot (122-metre) shoreline reserves along all waterways and suspend cutting during the summer tourist season.

"Now we are really in a stage where there is a war," declared Timothy Findley. "It's a war between [Kerrio's] department ... and the environment." Gary Potts, chief of the Teme-Augama Anishnabai, considered the logging decision "extremely contemptible" in view of the fact that his band was still in the process of challenging the province's jurisdiction over Temagami in the Ontario Supreme Court. Kerrio was taken aback by the anger over his announcement. In an effort to calm the aggrieved parties, he promised that the government would appoint a citizen's advisory committee to recommend long-term solutions for the disputed area.[63]

After the Liberals won their majority in the September 10th election, the Cabinet could not for long postpone its decision on either provincial-park management policy or the Temagami controversy. But before taking action on the latter question, Natural Resources Minister Kerrio appointed the Temagami Area Working Group, a special advisory committee, to investigate how the government might resolve the conflict over the future of the area around Lady Evelyn-Smoothwater Park. The fifteen-person committee, made up of representatives of all the parties in the dispute, and chaired by John Daniel, president of Laurentian University, was appointed in December and given three months to submit its recommendations. Unfortunately, the group was unable to reach a consensus and broke up in disarray on 5 March 1988.[64] All the same, Daniel submitted a set of recommendations which he hoped would protect the unique landscape, ecology, and wilderness-recreational values of the Temagami wilderness without sacrificing forestry jobs. Among other things, he recommended that the Liskeard Lumber road, which ran through the middle of Lady Evelyn-Smoothwater, be phased out by reallocating existing timber licences in the area surrounding the park. Logging, added Daniel, should be continued in the disputed buffer zone for the sake of the estimated 500 jobs generated by the forest industry in the region. This would necessitate the construction of the Red Squirrel road extension.[65]

Later that same month, the Environmental Assessment Branch of the Ministry of the Environment released its review of MNR's Red Squirrel road environmental-assessment document. The review concluded that despite the narrow focus of the study — it assessed only the potential effects of building the 20-metre wide right-of-way and ignored the impact of the logging activities which would ensue following the completion of the road — it still met the requirements of the Environmental Assessment Act.[66] Preservationists were furious and flooded the minister of the environment, Jim Bradley, with a record 170 applications for a formal environmental hearing on the road extension. Their case was strengthened by the decision of the Toronto consulting firm Deleuw Cather Canada (Del Can) Ltd., which had conducted most of MNR's Red Squirrel road environmental-assessment study, to remove its name from the final report because it considered the scope of the study too narrow to comply with the law.[67]

All of these developments complicated an already intricate situation for the Peterson government. As late as mid-April the Cabinet had yet to reach a consensus on either of the two outstanding wilderness and parks issues. Journalists reported that Environment Minister Jim Bradley favoured both holding an environmental hearing on the Red Squirrel road extension and revoking Alan Pope's 1983 non-conforming-uses policy. Meanwhile, Vince Kerrio and David Ramsay, the minister of correctional services and MPP for Timiskaming, took a more politically pragmatic position on both issues, preferring instead to balance wilderness preservation with the need to foster the economic development of small northern resource communities.[68]

In a noteworthy last-minute effort to provide a fresh perspective on the Temagami controversy, the Canadian Parks and Wilderness Society (CPAWS) issued in early May a brief entitled "The Temagami Crisis: A Critical Evaluation and Proposal for a Sustainable Future." The document was informed by the ideas of the much-heralded book *Our Common Future*, published in 1987 by the World Commission on Environment and Development headed by the prime minister of Norway, Gro Harlem Brundtland. CPAWS challenged the province to embrace the "sustainable-development" concept at the heart of the Brundtland report.[69] It urged the establishment of the Temagami area as a sustainable-development demonstration project, with the goal of promoting "small-scale forestry, wilderness tourism, local processing of timber and other activities meant to diversify the local economy." It also recommended the settlement of the Teme-Augama Anishnabai land claim before any major road construction was undertaken or land-use decisions were made. This far-sighted brief came too late to influence the impending government-policy statement on the Temagami question.

At long last, on 17 May 1988, Vincent Kerrio, with Environment Minister Jim Bradley in tow, convened a press conference to unveil the Liberal approach to managing Ontario's provincial-parks system. The first item of news was stunning. The Liberals had acceded to the demands of park and environmental advocates and were prepared to scrap Alan Pope's 1983 policy allowing "non-conforming" uses in the 155 post-1983 provincial parks. Henceforth, there would be no commercial logging, hunting and trapping (by non-Natives), mining, or hydroelectrical development permitted in any of Ontario's Wilderness and Nature Reserve parks.[70] Only one of the so-called "non-conforming uses" would remain — commercial-tourism operations. In this respect, Kerrio had made a substantial alteration to the "blue book" by deciding that existing tourism operations would be permitted to remain in Wilderness parks, and that some fly-in operations and the use of motor boats outside access areas would be accommodated within individual management plans. Furthermore, status Indians located within treaty areas who owned and operated hunt-camps in Wilderness parks would not be affected by the new policy, and their guests would be permitted to hunt under permit within park boundaries.

As for the other classes of parks, there would be no trapping, mining, or hydro development permitted in them either, and logging would be allowed only in Algonquin and Lake Superior parks under stringent operating rules. All in all, this was one of the most significant park-policy statements ever made. It meant that the "blue book" had been resurrected, and, for the first time, pre- and post-1983 parks would be managed as a unified system according to the same set of policy prescriptions. To cap off his announcement, Kerrio also promised that 53 new parks, all but two being the last of the 155 parks promised in 1983, would be placed into regulations within a year.

After unveiling the new parks policy, Kerrio and Bradley turned their attention to the Temagami question. Kerrio led off with a surprise announcement. Three new waterway parks — Obabika River, Solace Lakes, and Sturgeon River — would be established in the disputed buffer zone, adding some 26,670 hectares of parkland to the 72,400 hectares in Lady Evelyn-Smoothwater. The waterway parks created a circular canoe corridor, offering 225 kilometres of prime canoeing, which linked up with established routes within the Wilderness park. In addition, Kerrio announced that the Cabinet had decided to implement the key recommendations of the Temagami Area Working Group. The government intended to close, in 1994, the section of the Liskeard Lumber road which bisected Lady Evelyn-Smoothwater park. By that time the timber licences issued to the Liskeard Lumber Company would be reallocated in the area north of the park, thereby removing the need for the road. Kerrio also promised to appoint a citizens' advisory council, as recommended by the working group, to assist the transformation of the Temagami district into a "model management area for recreational, forest, tourism and environmental resources."[71]

Once Kerrio had finished, Jim Bradley revealed what the government had decided on the question of the controversial Red Squirrel road extension. "I have accepted the Ministry of Natural Resources' Environmental Assessment for the ... Extension," he announced, and "I have decided not to hold a hearing into this matter," since it would last more than a year, cause undue delay in road construction, and thereby jeopardize the local forest industry. To minimize the environmental impact of the extension, however, Bradley released a list of twenty-nine conditions his ministry had placed on road construction. "I believe this results in a fair and balanced policy serving the needs of Temagami," he concluded.[72]

Was the bundle of policy announcements fair and balanced? As with most political questions, the answer depended upon one's point of view. From the provincial perspective, the government had steered a middle course through the issues, seeking to arrive at a compromise acceptable to all parties. Although some economic interests in northern Ontario might be unhappy over the policy reversal on non-conforming uses in parks, the government hoped that most would be pleased with the removal of the obstacles to logging in Temagami, and with the decision to allow commercial-tourism operations to remain in the new Wilderness parks, including Lady Evelyn-Smoothwater. Similarly, the government evidently hoped that, while some preservationists would be angered over being denied an environmental hearing on the Red Squirrel road extension, the resulting protest would be offset by the euphoria over the decision to remove the non-conforming uses from the wilderness and Nature-Reserve parks.

From the perspective of the Temagami Wilderness Society and the Teme-Augama Anishnabai, the Liberal compromise was neither fair nor balanced. Both the environmentalists and the Indians believed that their primary concerns had been sacrificed for the sake of the preservation of natural areas elsewhere. Not to be denied, both groups took swift action to delay the construction of the Red Squirrel road extension, the Temagami Wilderness Society by filing a lawsuit in June 1988 challenging the minister of the environment's approval of the project, and the Indians by blockading the road right-of-way. When these actions resulted in construction delays, some 300 loggers, mill workers and their families, fearing the imminent closure of William Milne and Sons Ltd., chose the Labour Day weekend to blockade the busy Temagami Lake access road and prevent cottagers and lodge guests from reaching their destinations. This protest received heavy media coverage, especially when a phalanx of Ontario Provincial Police officers, many in riot gear, marched into the demonstrators and arrested fifty-one people. By year's end, the Liberal policy on Temagami had unravelled in the wake of the blockades, court actions, and the collapse of William Milne and Sons in early December.[73]

IV

The battle over wilderness in Temagami continued to capture widespread public attention throughout 1989. Initially, things went badly for the coalition of environmentalists and Indians. In March the Teme-Augama Anishnabai suffered a legal setback when the Ontario Court of Appeal upheld a 1984 decision by the Ontario Supreme Court that the band had, through the Robinson-Huron treaty of 1850, relinquished its claim to its ancestral homeland. Subsequently, the band proceeded with its lawsuit against the province and appealed this decision to the

Supreme Court of Canada.[74] In April the Temagami Wilderness Society also failed in its bid to stop the construction of the Red Squirrel road extension when the Ontario Supreme Court upheld the government's decision to build the road.[75]

Having lost in the courts the TWS intensified its campaign to win the public's support. Taking a cue from the international movement to save the Amazon rain forests which saw rock stars such as Sting and Bruce Cockburn rally to the environmental cause, the society, in cooperation with Beaver Canoe Ltd., organized a benefit concert entitled "Temagami: The Last Wild Stand II" on 27 April at the University of Toronto's Convocation Hall. The concert featured Gordon Lightfoot, Murray McLaughan, and Mary Margaret O'Hara. A month later, on 28 May, 600 environmentalists marched through downtown Toronto to Queen's Park, chanting "Save the trees. Cut down the industries" and "Save Temagami. Dump Peterson."[76] The environmentalists were buoyed by opinion polls indicating that 64 per cent of Canadians considered it more important to preserve forests than to guarantee jobs, and that only 37 per cent of those surveyed viewed forests as a resource primarily to be used for economic benefit.[77]

None of these developments seemed to faze the Peterson government, which steadfastly held to its decision to complete the Red Squirrel road. Accordingly, the TWS turned up the pressure in June by resolving to blockade the road right-of-way and use passive-resistance tactics. As media events, the blockades were enormously successful, particularly when NDP Opposition leader Bob Rae joined the environmentalists in September and was arrested for his trouble. In late November, the Teme-Augama Anishnabai also resumed their blockade. Tiring of these tactics, on 17 November the government obtained a permanent Ontario Supreme Court injunction prohibiting further blockades. Although more arrests followed, construction of the Red Squirrel road proceeded rapidly to completion on 10 December 1989.[78]

Notwithstanding the failure to stop the road, all was not lost for those who opposed logging in the Temagami wilderness. As it happened, the Peterson government had not been unaffected by the considerable negative publicity it received over this issue. Furthermore, the Ministry of Natural Resources could not ignore the scientific findings of the TWS's Tall Pines Project, a forest-research program launched in

1988 under the supervision of Dr Peter Quinby. Drawing on Quinby's fieldwork, the society had increasingly played up in its public-relations efforts the importance of Temagami as the last significant old-growth pine ecosystem in North America. Old-growth forests, the society emphasized, were essential for soil stabilization, water purity, nutrient retention, wildlife habitat, and as a gene pool; but even more importantly, they possessed incalculable benefits for forest research and could well hold the key to both forest regeneration and the long-term future of the forest industry.[79] The sudden concern about "old-growth" values caught MNR by surprise. During the early 1980s when the ministry selected the area for Lady Evelyn-Smoothwater Wilderness Park, the concept of old-growth forest had not even been part of the planners' vocabulary. Park planners had been mainly concerned about protecting recreation values and cold-water fishing, not old-growth forests.[80] It was not until Quinby and the TWS initiated the Tall Pines Project in 1988 that anyone had attempted to identify the specific qualities of an old-growth forest in northeastern North America!

Evidently, the findings of the Tall Pines Project and the TWS's strategy of focusing on the need to preserve "old-growth" values paid dividends. On 20 November, 1989, two weeks before the completion of the Red Squirrel road, the new minister of natural resources, Lyn McLeod, announced that the government intended to place a freeze on an environmentally sensitive 585-hectare area of Temagami's Wakimika Triangle pending further studies.[81] Two months later, in January 1990, at a conference presented by the Faculty of Forestry at the University of Toronto, the minister revealed that her officials were currently preparing a new policy designed to identify and protect tracts of old-growth forest.[82]

In April 1990, the Teme-Augama Anishnabai also made gains both for Native self-government and the protection of the Temagami forests by signing an historic agreement with the Ontario government for joint stewardship of some 40,000 hectares (four townships) in the region opened to logging by the completion of the Red Squirrel road. Henceforth, the area covered by the agreement is to be administered by a stewardship council comprised of equal numbers of band representatives and government officials. The membership of the council effectively gave the band a veto over logging in the stewardship zone. As part of the agreement, the beleaguered William Milne and Sons mill in Temagami was to be closed and its assets purchased by the Ontario Development Corporation.[83]

It remains to be seen whether these initiatives by the former Peterson government will achieve a *modus vivendi* between the disputants in Temagami. Initial responses are not encouraging. The environmentalists continue to claim that too little is being protected; the timber interests challenge this assertion, while the Teme-Augama Anishnabai insist that the stewardship agreement is merely "the first step toward a treaty of co-existence."[84] With such conflicting values and so little middle ground, especially between loggers and environmentalists, it appears that the battle over wilderness in Temagami is not yet close to playing itself out.

---

[1] Quoted in "Temagami Madness," Toronto *Star,* 4 Dec. 1988.

[2] *Classification of Provincial Parks in Ontario 1967* (Parks Branch, Dept. of Lands and Forests). See also Legislative Assembly of Ontario, *Hansard,* 16 March 1967, 1447. The park classes established in 1967 were: Natural Environment, Nature Reserve, Primitive, Recreation, and Wild River. The classification scheme was revised during the system-planning program of the 1970s. Today, provincial parks are classified as Historical, Natural Environment, Nature Reserve, Recreation, Waterway, and Wilderness parks.

[3] Archives of Ontario (AO), RG–1, IA–7, box 5, file 2–3–5–1, *passim,* and "Proposed Basis for a Park Classification System, July 17, 1963."

[4] Federation of Ontario Naturalists (FON), "Outline of a Basis for a Parks Policy for Ontario," Dec. 1958.

[5] For Pimlott, see George Michael Warecki, "Protecting Ontario's Wilderness: A History of Wilderness Conservation In Ontario, 1927–1973," (unpublished Ph.D. dissertation, McMaster University, 1989), 195–208. See also Douglas H. Pimlott, "The Preservation of Natural Areas in Ontario," *Ontario Naturalist,* vol. 3, no. 2 (1965), 8–24.

[6] Robert Page, *Northern Development: The Canadian Dilemma* (Toronto: McClelland and Stewart, 1986), 35.

[7] I have examined all these themes in a manuscript commissioned by the Parks and Recreational Areas Branch, MNR, tentatively entitled *Ontario's Provincial Parks: Towards System and Balance,* chapters 4,5, publication forthcoming.

[8] A.K. McDougall, *John P. Robarts: His Life and Government* (Toronto: University of Toronto Press, 1986), chapters 15–16; Claire Hoy, *Bill Davis* (Toronto: Methuen, 1985), 89; and Jonathon Manthorpe, *The Power and the Tories: Ontario Politics 1943 to the Present* (Toronto: Macmillan, 1974), chapters 10–11.

[9] "Wilderness in Ontario: A Submission to the Government of Ontario from Coalition for Wilderness," January 1974.

[10] AO, RG–1, IB. acc. #14300, sched. #1096, temp. box 1, file 11–1–1, Keenan to Bernier, 9 April 1974.

[11] *Ontario Provincial Parks Policy* (MNR, 1978). *Ontario Provincial Parks Planning and Management Policies* (MNR, 1978).

[12] Parks and Recreational Areas Branch, file MO–3–P (Parks Policy), J.K. Reynolds, deputy minister, to Mike Singleton, FON, 8 Jan. 1979.

[13] Interview with Ronald J. Vrancart, director of the Parks Division (1976–81), 9 Feb. 1989. For the internal MNR opposition to the system plan see Parks and Recreational Areas Branch (PRAB), file MO–3–P (Parks Policy), *passim.*

[14] *Strategic Land Use Plan: Northwestern Ontario* (Toronto: MNR, 1980); *Proposed Strategic Land Use Plan: Northeastern Ontario* (Toronto: MNR, 1980).

[15] Arlin Hackman, "A Response to the Strategic Land Use Plan For Northwestern Ontario," *Park News,* vol. 17, no. 1 (Spring 1981), 26.

[16] Arlin Hackman, "Strategic Land Use Planning and the Future of Wilderness in Ontario," *Park News,* vol. 16, no. 4 (Winter 1980), 36.

[17] PRAB, file NE–3, J.F. McNutt to W.G. Cleaveley, regional director, northern region, 1 May 1980.

[18] Quoted in *Globe and Mail,* 4 March 1981. See also *Wildland News,* vol. 14, no. 5 (Nov. 1982), 7, in which Greaves is quoted as saying that the potential loss to the economy of establishing provincial parks in northwestern Ontario would amount to $24 billion. An environmental economist for the Wildlands League demonstrated this estimate to be grossly exaggerated.

[19] Arlin Hackman, "Shaping a Future for Ontario Parks: The Protagonists," *Seasons,* vol. 22, no. 2 (Summer 1982), 28.

[20] PRAB, file NC–3, George Priddle to James H.C. Auld, 22 Jan. 1981.

[21] Interview with Cameron Clarke, 3 Oct. 1989.

[22] J.W. Griffith, general manager, Prospectors and Developers Association, "Forum: Mining Industry," *Seasons*, vol. 22, no. 2 (Summer 1982), 38–9.

[23] R.G. Morgan, executive vice-president, Ontario Federation of Anglers and Hunters (OFAH), "Forum: Hunting and Fishing," *ibid.*, 39–40.

[24] The *North Bay Nugget*, 30 Jan. 1981.

[25] PRAB, file NE–3, R.L. Brock to R.B. McGee, district manager, Temagami, 3 Sept. 1981. For the background of the Maple Mountain project, see Bruce W. Hodgins and Jamie Benidickson, *The Temagami Experience: Recreation, Resources, and Aboriginal Rights in the Northern Ontario Wilderness,* (Toronto: University of Toronto Press, 1989), chapter 12.

[26] OA, RG–1, IA–5, box 1, file 13–2–3, Brunelle to J.K. Reynolds, 19 Oct. 1967.

[27] Ron Reid, "The Native Question," *Seasons*, vol. 22, no. 4 (Winter 1982), 46.

[28] Wally McKay, "Forum: Native People," *Seasons*, vol. 22, no. 2 (Summer 1982), 40–1.

[29] "The Temagami Land Caution," *Wildland News*, vol. 14, no. 5 (Nov. 1982), 8. See also Hodgins and Benidickson, *Temagami Experience*, chapter 12.

[30] *Wildland News*, vol. 13, no. 1 (June 1981), 7.

[31] Robert Matas, "Ontario Stalls Public Participation in Forest Planning, Naturalist Says," Toronto *Globe and Mail*, 7 May 1981. Forest-management agreements were introduced by the Davis government to address the reforestation problem in Ontario. It greatly embarrassed MNR officials that twice as much forest was being logged as was being regenerated across the province, a state of affairs which made a mockery of Premier Davis's promise in 1977 to plant two trees for every one cut. The new agreements established long-term contractual arrangements between the crown and the large forest companies whereby the latter undertook, with government subsidies, forest-management practices, including the construction of access roads, harvesting, and reforestation. Theoretically, the agreements would provide the companies with a continuous supply of timber while ensuring forests were harvested and rejuvenated on a sustained-yield basis. During the eighteen months prior to Pope's appointment as minister, five agreements had been signed with four companies covering some 4.9 million hectares of crown land. MNR intended to sign agreements for another 15.5 million hectares over the next four years.

[32] PRAB, file MO-3L, Lorne Almack, president, FON to Alan Pope, 26 May 1981.

[33] George B. Priddle, "Parks and Land Use Planning in Northern Ontario," *Environments*, vol. 14, no. 1 (1982), 49.

[34] Interview with William Foster, 11 April 1989.

[35] Ron Reid, "Ontario Parks: Last Chance for Survival?" Toronto *Globe and Mail,* 26 Feb. 1982.

[36] Interview with Norm Richards, 15 March 1989.

[37] Copy of "Statement to the Legislature by the Honorable Alan W. Pope, Minister of Natural Resources, Friday, March 12, 1982," appended to MNR *Newsrelease,* 12 March 1982. See also "Background Information on Land Use Planning and Park System Planning in Ontario," March 1982, 4.

[38] MNR, *Report of the Task Force on Parks System Planning,* vol. 1 (Sept. 1981), vol. II, appendices.

[39] Ron Reid, "Wilderness Waltz," *Seasons,* vol. 22, no. 2 (Summer 1982), 24.

[40] Jeff Port, "Gambling with Our Resources," *Park News,* vol. 18, no. 3 (Fall 1982), 24. See also Arlin Hackman, "Ontario's Park System Comes of Age," in Monte Hummel (ed.), *Endangered Spaces: The Future for Canada's Wilderness* (Toronto: Key Porter Books, 1989), 173.

[41] "Annual Meeting: President's Report 1983," *Wildland News,* vol. 15, no. 3 (June 1983), 10.

[42] *Wildland News,* vol. 14, 1 (April 1982), 11, and "Hot Spots," 8–11 for the forest-industry campaign against parks. See also *ibid.,* vol. 14, 2 (June 1982), 10.

[43] *Ibid.,* vol. 14, nos. 3–4 (Sept. 1982), 15.

[44] *Ibid.,* 20.

[45] *Ibid.,* 21–2.

[46] "Minister's Forums Draw Crowds," *Seasons,* vol. 23, no. 1 (Spring 1983), 8. For the heavily attended London meeting, see London *Free Press,* 7 Dec. 1982.

[47] Burt Dowsett, "Sportsmen Buck Parks," London *Free Press,* 15 Dec. 1982.

[48] Canadian Parks and Wilderness Society (CPAWS) office, Toronto, vertical file, SLUP (Ont.) folder, Monte Hummel to Hon. Vince Kerrio, 17 Sept. 1985. In this letter Hummel provides a detailed account of the park advocates' position at the Guild Inn meetings.

[49] "Pope's Roundtable Talks Lead in Circles," *Wildland News,* vol. 15, no. 2 (March 1983), 5. See also *Park News,* vol. 19, no. 1 (Spring 1983), 27.

[50] Hackman, "Ontario's Park System Comes of Age," 178, explains how Leo Bernier, minister of northern affairs, persuaded Pope that it would create a better "public image in the north" if the district plans were called guidelines.

[51] Information Kit: Land Use Guidelines, "Statement to the Legislature by the Hon. Alan Pope, Minister of Natural Resources, Thursday, June 2, 1983."

[52] *Ibid.,* MNR *Newsrelease,* 2 June 1983, "Natural Resources Minister Announces Resource Land Use Guidelines."

53 *Wildland News,* vol. 15, no. 3 (June 1983), 4.

54 "The Canadian Assembly: Part II," *Park News,* vol. 21, 4 (Winter 1985/86), 20.

55 CPAWS Office, Toronto, vertical file, SLUP (Ont.) folder, Hummel to Kerrio, 17 Sept. 1985. See also MNR, *Backgrounder: Land Use Guidelines* (June 1983), 9.

56 Rosemary Speirs, "Parks Issue Catches Peterson in a Crossfire," Toronto *Star,* 16 Jan. 1988.

57 Don Huff, "Earthwatch," *Seasons,* vol. 26, no. 3 (Autumn 1986), 4, and David Israelson, "Minister Wants Mining, Hunting in New Parks," Toronto *Star,* 12 May 1986.

58 The sticker was distributed in *Seasons,* vol. 26, no. 2 (Summer 1986). See also Barry Kent MacKay, "Should Mining, Hunting Be Allowed in Our Parks?" Toronto *Star,* 13 July 1986.

59 Jennifer Young, "A New Wilderness Policy for Ontario? Woodland Caribou: Update," *Wildland News,* vol. 18, no. 2 (Spring 1986), 10–12, and Daniel Brunton, "Woodland Caribou," *Seasons,* vol. 26, no. 23 (Autumn 1986), 36.

60 David Israelson, "Wilderness Area Put on World List as Threatened Site," Toronto *Star,* 27 Nov 1986.

61 Don Huff, "Earthwatch," *Seasons,* vol. 27, no. 1 (Spring 1987), 4–5. See also Julian A. Dunster, "Roads to Nowhere: Incremental Access and the Shrinking Wilderness," *Alternatives,* vol. 15, no. 3 (Sept./Oct. 1988), 22–9.

62 David Israelson, "'War' Waged over Future of Ontario's Wilderness," Toronto *Star,* 10 July 1987.

63 John Temple, "Logging Approved in Virgin Forest," Toronto *Star,* 22 Aug. 1987.

64 John Temple, "Wilderness Committee Breaks up in Disarray," Toronto *Star,* 6 March 1988. See also Hodgins and Benidickson, *Temagami Experience,* 284–5.

65 Temagami Area Working Group, *Final Report* (Toronto: MNR, March 1988).

66 Review of the Environmental Assessment for Primary Access Roads in the Latchford Crown Forest Management Unit [Red Squirrel Road Extension/ Pinetorch Corridor] (Toronto: Ontario Ministry of the Environment, 1980). Environmental Assessment Branch, EA file no. NR–NE–02.

67 Christie McLaren, "Temagami Logging Roads Given Go-ahead," Toronto *Globe and Mail,* 13 April 1989.

68 Christie McLaren, "Wilderness Use to Test Cabinet," Toronto *Globe and Mail,* 7 April 1988.

[69] World Commission on Environment and Development, *Our Common Future* (Oxford, New York: Oxford University Press, 1987).

[70] MNR, *Newsrelease*, "Ontario Announces New Parks and More Protection for Wilderness and Nature Reserves," 17 May 1988.

[71] MNR, *Newsrelease*, "Natural Resources Ministry Announces Decision on *Temagami Land Use*," 17 May 1988; MNR, "Speaking Notes for the Hon. Vincent Kerrio ... Regarding the Temagami Area Land Use Decision 17 May 1988, 12:30 p.m." Both these documents were contained in an information kit distributed on 17 May.

[72] "Statement by Jim Bradley, Minister of the Environment Regarding Ministry of Natural Resources' Environmental Assessment for Primary Access Roads," 17 May 1988.

[73] "Loggers Charged in Road Protest," London *Free Press*, 3 Sept. 1988; "Protestors Threaten 'Worse' Action," Toronto *Sunday Star*, 4 Sept. 1988; Christie McLaren, "Ontario Set for Another Conflict on Logging Roads in Wilderness," Toronto *Globe and Mail*, 22 Nov. 1988; Christie McLaren, "Ontario Going to Court in Indian Dispute," *ibid.*, 30 Nov. 1988; Thomas Walkom, "Trouble in the Northern Bush," *ibid.*; Mary Gooderham, "Loss of Sawmill Loan is the Latest Wrinkle in Temagami Battle," *ibid.*, 5 Nov. 1988; Christie McLaren, "No Aid for Sawmill, Peterson Says," *ibid.*, 10 Nov. 1988; Christie McLaren, "Stymied Ontario Sawmill Goes Under," *ibid.*, 3 Dec. 1988.

[74] "Choices in Temagami," Toronto *Globe and Mail*, 1 March 1989.

[75] Christie McLaren, "Temagami Logging Roads Given Go-ahead," *ibid.*, 13 April 1989.

[76] Lisa Shimko, "Save Temagami, Liberals Urged," *ibid.*, 29 May 1989.

[77] Christie McLaren, "Canadians Want Logging Changed, Poll Finds," *ibid.*, 19 May 1989.

[78] Darcy Henton, "Fight on to Save Temagami's Pine Giants," Toronto *Star*, 11 June 1989; "Temagami: 'Camp-in' Planned over Road Extension," London *Free Press*, 26 Aug. 1989; *Insider's Dispatch: News of the Temagami Wilderness Society*, vol. 4, no. 1 (Sept. 1989); Rachel Leaney, "Road Foes Gearing for 'Passive' Protest in Temagami Forest," Toronto *Globe and Mail*, 18 Sept. 1989; Timothy Appleby, "Rae Arrested at Temagami Demonstration," *ibid.*, 19 Sept. 1989; Donald Grant, "Natives to Resume Logging Road Blockades," *ibid.*, 3 Nov. 1989; "OPP Arrests 46 in Logging Road Protest," *ibid.*; "Chief Arrested in Road Protest," *ibid.*, 16 Nov. 1989; Thomas Claridge, "Temagami Injunction Permanent, Court Rules," *ibid.*, 18 Nov. 1989.

[79] "Save Temagami Trees, Scientist Says," *ibid.*, 15 Feb. 1989; "Old Growth as a Weapon," *Insider's Dispatch: News of the Temagami Wilderness Society*, vol.

4, no. 1 (Sept. 1989); Brad Cundiff, "New Ideas about Old Growth," *Seasons,* vol. 29, no. 4 (Winter, 1989), 31–35; Peter A. Quinby, "Old Growth Forest and Temagami: A Literature Review," Tall Pines Project, *Reserach Report No. 1;* Peter A. Quinby, "Old Growth Forest Survey in Temagami's Wakimika Triangle," Tall Pines Project, *Research Report no. 2* (January 1989); Peter A. Quinby, "Self-Replacement in Old Growth White Pine Forests," Tall Pines Project, *Research Report No. 3* (January 1990).The Tall Pines Project reserach reports were published by the Temagami Wilderness Society.

[80] Interview with Cameron Clarke, 3 Oct. 1989.

[81] Gene Allen, "Ministry Wants Freeze on Temagami Logging," Toronto *Globe and Mail,* 21 Nov. 1989.

[82] David Israelson, "Ontario Moves to Protect Oldest Forests from Logging," Toronto *Star,* 21 Jan. 1990.

[83] MNR, *Newsrelease,* "Province and Teme-Augama Anishnabai Sign Historic Stewardship Agreement," 23 April 1990.

[84] Gene Allen, "Ontario Gives Natives Veto over Logging in Temagami to Save Ancient Pine Tracts," Toronto *Globe and Mail,* 24 April 1990; Craig McInnes, "Not Quite Out of the Woods Yet," *ibid.,* 28 April 1990.

Chief Gary Potts and then Minister of Natural Resources Lynn McLeod at the signing of the historic joint-stewardship-council agreement on 23 April 1990. *Courtesy: Ontario Ministry of Natural Resources*

Seven

Contexts of the Temagami Predicament

Bruce W. Hodgins

Chief Gary Potts, in defending the land claim of the Teme-Augama Anishnabai and outlining his view of stewardship, has made the Native position clear: "The government claimed that we are trying to shut down the North. Far from it: we are trying to save the North for the future .... The environmental impact of the removal of a forest is longterm: the economic gain is not. We made it clear to the government that the wish of our people for the future is to have our traditional area governed by an area residents' land-use council that cannot be overruled by short-sighted politicians who do not appreciate fully the principles of sustained life and development."[1] Besides affirming the wise, temperate environmentalism of Gro Harlem Brundtland,[2] the Temagami Indians echo the great thoughts of Aldo Leopold, written in 1949: "Despite nearly a century of propaganda, conservation still proceeds at a snail's pace."[3]

In the popular press, some reviews of the *Temagami Experience*,[4] written by myself and Jamie Benidickson, have mildly criticized us for being "too academic," too lacking in passion, too intent on giving the pro-development side a fair shake; indeed the reviewer for *Canadian Geographic* noted that our writing was "tedious,"[5] although she praised the book's content and explained it correctly. In our defence, we started research for that book in 1973, before the current crises. We meant it to be a detailed, many-sided "bio-regional study," a phrase not even invented then. It was about the history of recreation, resource management, and aboriginal rights in the northern Ontario wilderness. Perhaps our scholarly efforts camouflaged some of our passion. Good historical studies need a viewpoint. This paper should certainly leave no doubts about the position of its author.

Most readers of this volume probably know the basic Temagami story — at least back to that great Temagami non-event, the Robinson-Huron Treaty of 1850, and on past the establishment of the Temagami Forest Reserve in 1901, a reserve intended for perpetual-yield scientific forestry and for non-intrusive recreation in a rapidly urbanizing province and continent. If I am wrong about the extent of the readers' knowledge, information can be found in the *Temagami Experience*. In it, however, the Temagami Wilderness Society (TWS) only secures first mention fourteen pages before the end, and Laurentian's President John Daniel one page later. Brian Back, the TWS director, is in the footnotes, but he is not in the text. Our last additions and changes, alas, were made in the mid-summer of 1988, before the most recent clashes.

Two basic problems with regard to the Temagami crises emerge out of the recent history of our province. The first relates to the failure of the Davis-Peterson governments to give provincial and national leadership on the aboriginal-rights question, leadership that could have reversed the semi-racist and assimilationist features of Ontario's and Canada's earlier historical record.[6] Instead they hid behind platitudes and legal niceties. They perpetuated nineteenth-century attitudes of condescension and terminal paternalism with regard to that question: they showed considerable charity but little regard for Native self-respect or self-determination. They championed so-called "legal fact," which was often historical error. This has been especially true with respect to the Peterson government's approach to the Teme-Augama Anishnabai. In that government, Ian Scott, who as minister responsible for Native affairs was pledged to advance Indian causes, fought as attorney general against the Temagami Indians with every means at his disposal.

Yet the federal and provincial authorities, and, indeed, even Mr Justice Steele of the Ontario Supreme Court and the Ontario Appeal Court judges, all agreed that the Temagami Indians had not signed the Robinson Treaty. No dispute exists on that vital matter. That historical fact will survive even if the Supreme Court of Canada, aided and abetted by the Ontario attorney general, "finds" that the Temagami Indians have no legal interest in their own lands. As late as two years ago the crisis with the Indians could have been avoided. But it was not avoided, largely because of the Peterson government's lack of vision and its subservience to hinterland politics. Such politics are the historical legacy of mainstream leadership in this imperial province.

The second problem arises from the failure of the Forestry Group (with its two branches) of the Ministry of Natural Resources (and its predecessors) and through it the Ontario government to fulfill its broadest mandate, that of protecting the crown domain[7] and its renewable resources. The ministry (MNR) argues, despite Indian claims, that Temagami lands are indeed a part of crown domain. Yet, over the years, MNR has failed to enforce and stimulate pine-lands conservation, whether inside or outside specific parks. MNR has failed to advance its own thinking and action beyond the era of winter logging, short-haul bush roads, and water transport; it has failed to see the northern Ontario bush as more than a tool for the forestry industry which in return would act as a limited employment agency. The Forestry Group failed outright to challenge the lumber interests' outdated definition of "multiple-use" and those interests' promotion of the divisive north-south dichotomy. MNR was trapped in hinterland politics, unable to grasp the fact that the pine resource was dwindling and that policies of "sustainable development" (or preferably "sustainable life") should have been taking over from the destructive idea of unlimited "economic progress."

Through most of the twentieth-century history of Temagami, a complex history which we described in our book, we saw a sort of balance of diverse and rival forces competing over land use. The Temagami Indians were unfortunately clearly marginalized. Yet, courageously, they somehow survived, needling away at the dominant credo, never collectively giving up (though some individuals despaired and were demoralized). Their determination provided hope for a more enlightened future. In the *Temagami Experience*, we were critical of the Viv Nelles thesis on northern Ontario, one that saw all problems as coming from the external economic forces which the provincial government refused, or lacked the courage, to control for the democratic good of the people of Ontario.[8] Instead, we argued that the varied and often conflicting objectives of the several constituencies interested in the landscape and resources of Temagami had maintained or had been forced to maintain a sort of balance. Amid dialogue, compromise, and on occasion neglect, no group had been able to sustain a position of exclusive dominance over the pattern of development. Despite intermittent conflict and tension among divergent groups, and despite very different values, severe clashes were generally minimized or avoided. Then, in the late 1970s, as the new-style, year-round logging industry, both local and national, pushed harder for its lopsided, unecological view of the future, the fundamental failure of MNR and the Ontario government became ever clearer. Ironically, the Nelles thesis gradually took on more meaning. This, then, is the basis for the present paper's emphasis on hinterland politics.

Yet Bob Rae's action, as leader of the Opposition, of standing on the Red Squirrel road right-of-way on 20 September 1989, and thereby being arrested,[9] was neither an expression of hinterland politics nor something unique in the social-democratic tradition. Donald Mac-Donald had complained bitterly in the legislature of Ontario in the mid-1960s about the original Johns-Manville road that was built along Red Squirrel Lake,[10] and Stephen Lewis in 1973 criticized as misguided the proposed Maple Mountain project in the heart of the Temagami wilderness.[11] Furthermore, it was Sudbury's Local 6500 of the United Steelworkers, and not the government of Ontario, that during the 1970s led the early battle against acid rain in northeastern Ontario.[12]

Three objectives, each with deep historic roots, call for serious consideration with regard to the Temagami country: the self-determination, economic viability, and socio-cultural integrity of the courageous aboriginal community now centred (involuntarily) on Bear Island; secondly, the protection of the area's priceless and long-appreciated wilderness heritage; and lastly the implementation, finally, of forest stewardship involving both sustainable harvesting and some preservation. The short-term sacrifice of the last old-growth pine on the ancestral lands of the Teme-Augama Anishnabai furthers none of these three objectives.

In 1901 and 1903 the Ontario government designated the Temagami country as a forest reserve with the stated intention that sustainable-yield forest management might be implemented there under the direction of professional foresters. Despite reaffirming this goal periodically, provincial governments never succeeded in managing the once-rich pine forests for perpetual yield or sustainability. Before 1970 the presence of competing users, notably canoeists and cottagers, hardly interfered seriously with forest management. If anything, the presence of both the recreational interests and the Indians served to moderate somewhat the manner and pace of forest-cutting. Thus the current generation has been given the chance to return to the issue of sustainability. It now has the benefit of greater knowledge of the scientific principles involved and a greater ecological understanding of the risks of continued failure. From the beginning of this century, canoe-oriented youth camps were in the forefront of that protective impulse. Camp Keewaydin and Camp Temagami, American and Canadian respectively, both arrived on Lake Temagami in 1903. Organized canoe camping has ever since then been a vital activity in the area.

As the twentieth century progressed, Ontario gradually and brilliantly curtailed the extent of forest fires in the Temagami pinery (despite the setback with the great 1977 fire). Thus, in a sense, the purest form of wilderness was eliminated, but the concept of wilderness is a relative one. Intervention to control fire was never accompanied by sufficient intervention in planting and harvesting techniques to ensure sustainable-yield pine forestry. The replacement of red and white pine did not keep pace with cutting, especially in the mixed stands of forests which became the common focus for timber operations. In the late 1970s, attention shifted more and more to jack pine and spruce and to their regeneration and even to poplar and other hardwoods. Based on presumed market requirements and alleged oversupply of "over-mature" stands of various species, MNR's 1983 Land Use Guidelines called for a dramatic increase of almost 200 per cent in the local cutting of conifers and a 500-per cent increase in the cutting of local hardwoods. This faulty vision — using skyline and shoreline reserves to help inflate the supply side — helped contribute to the determination of resource planners and lumber companies, who had just shifted to year-round work and trunk-road delivery, to enter the most remote sections of the Temagami forest. The accompanying road-construction projects were paid for mainly by the urban taxpayers of Ontario, projects that are now the subject of prolonged protest and outrage on the part of environmentalists and Indians.

Throughout the 1970s MNR was failing in its stewardship role and was too close to the lumber industry's lobby. It also lacked the funds to regulate and replant; it could rather easily designate, for example, pine stands as mixed stands and thus relegate them to "natural regeneration" — in reality, to a deteriorating forest with hardwood domination. Though planting drastically increased in the 1980s, MNR failed to establish sustainable-yield forestry, and allowed granite ridges to be cut and clearcutting techniques to continue. It also allowed the lumbermen's ridiculous interpretation of the term "multiple-use" to become a bad joke for Indians, vacationers, and environmentalists. So environmentalists had to abandon the term, though they continued to believe in multiple economic activities in northern Ontario, all based on a mix of strict overall conservation practices and specific preservationist sites.[13] In recent years resource-use decisions began severely to undermine the enjoyment of the Temagami country by others. Appreciative users, who had been encouraged by government to enjoy Temagami since the turn of the century, sought some indication that their long-term interests in the quality of the landscape would be respected.

Meanwhile, the best of our Canadian forestry schools taught some good conservation but gave little attention to the concepts and imperatives of preservation.[14] MNR continued to direct what recreational concerns it had outside provincial parks to sports hunting and fishing. Today the Ontario government still promotes and encourages such hunting, unrelated to clearly defensible aboriginal hunting for country food.

Can one imagine the "sport" of hunting surviving into the mid-twenty-first century?

On Lake Temagami, for some time, none of these MNR deficiencies seemed to affect traditional cottagers. The shoreline and skyline reserves protected and insulated them from the environmental reality. Then two things, which apparently escaped the notice of MNR, happened to the cottagers. First, in 1971, the Temagami Lakes Association (TLA) was taken over, in a quasi *coup d'état*, by year-round, youngish Canadian and American environmental activists, acid-rain opponents, back-country-oriented youth camps, and so on. The TLA ceased primarily to be a ratepayers organization; it became sophisticated, and it was well connected to all three political parties.

Secondly, the shift by the logging industry to year-round activity, which focused on trunk-road access, alarmed the cottagers. Their "Islands Only Development" hinged for its protection on the sanctity of the mainland. The Johns-Manville road by Red Squirrel Lake went within a few hundred metres of Camp Wanapitei on Sandy Inlet of the lake's north arm. The TLA soon objected. The provincial NDP also objected. Both were ridiculed. MNR, both regionally in Sudbury and provincially in Toronto, seemed oblivious to the change. More remote roads began to be built. All this combined to awaken the TLA to the long-standing pleas from the canoe camps, which had formed their own association, that it be concerned about the back-country. The youth camps saw themselves as educational institutions, with ideological commitments first and business interests second. This struggle then merged with the campaign to prevent the construction of a resort on Maple Mountain. Yet, in 1973, it was the Temagami Indians who stopped that very silly project when they secured in the courts the land-caution on their homeland.

Especially unnoticed by MNR was the change on Bear Island. Since 1877 the Indians had "wanted in," having been "left out" of the Robinson-Huron Treaty. The federal government gave lukewarm, spasmodic support; Ontario always stonewalled. The resource potential was too great, and so phoney arguments about recent "post bands" were created. All in all, a semi-racist perspective was maintained, one which certainly looked like a policy of gentle cultural genocide. But, in 1973, with vigorous new leadership, the Teme-Augama Anishnabai fought back. Having stopped the Maple Mountain venture, they demanded a major role in management of the resources of the Temagami area. They wanted an economically adequate land base, dedicated to sustainable forest stewardship, and a share of the economic benefits. The Association of Youth Camps fully backed the Indian land claim.

The nucleus of the three-fold local entente against trunk-road development and forest depletion was thus in place. Again MNR did not take meaningful notice.

Locally, MNR was slow to see the implications of the changing forest technology. Insufficient money was spent on forest reclamation, as logic implied it would have to be under the 1962 Crown Timber Act, which gave the government, not industry, full responsibility for replanting. MNR was also slow to integrate into any local policy the full implications of fire curtailment and the new scientific knowledge concerning the possible natural permanence of pine forests (in contrast to the old idea of pine as a relatively temporary "climax forest").[15] Short-term goals repeatedly took precedence. Roads were largely paid for by the government; mills were kept going by massive subsidies and grants. Today it is estimated that almost two-thirds of the direct and indirect costs of harvesting pine in the Temagami country, including paying for and policing the road-building, may be paid for by the taxpayers and not by the entrepreneurs of the Milne, Field, Goulard, Liskeard, and other lumber concerns.

Recently, some northern news media and local authorities have attributed the problem of timber supplies to the pressure of the environmental lobby and the recalcitrance of the Temagami Indians. But with or without the environmentalists, the Indians, and the new roads, a serious interruption in Temagami pine-cutting now seems to be no more than a few years away. If a serious effort to place the local forest industries on a more modest, realistic, and sustainable footing on suitable lands is not soon made by choice, it will have to be made on the basis of absolute necessity. By that time, however, the old-growth pine forest will be gone and with it the only opportunity to understand a unique forest ecology. Compromised too would be the chance to nurture a sustainable activity around a treasured wilderness and the opportunity to demonstrate Ontario's respect for the aboriginal people of the area by honouring their claims to an unsurrendered homeland which they are willing to share. In any event, for a long time to come, the limited future for logging around Temagami will primarily be in hardwoods rather than in pine. Professor Crandall Benson, both in 1984 and in 1989,[16] reporting to the Teme-Augama Anishnabai, has warned us all about this. Dr Peter Quinby has also done so in his studies for the Temagami Wilderness Society.[17]

The imminent decline in Temagami's pine harvesting is the fault of the provincial government. It is Ontario's historic style of hinterland politics, a style of politics that conflicts with the Ontario public's apparent environmental commitments. Futhermore, despite what the government and its friends assert, the Indians and the preservationists have all suggested socio-economic alternatives for Temagami, even if they have proved inadequate in selling their ideas to the local Euro-Canadian public or to government. With great condescension, MNR has always dismissed these alternatives, citing statistics of dubious value and insisting on financial quantification. The Temagami Advisory Council will do no better than MNR has if it continues to rely on MNR as its secretariat and refuses to listen both to the Indians and to provincial environmental groups whose head offices happen to be south of North Bay.

How valuable is a wilderness sunset? Quantify the quality of a semi-wilderness experience. What are the financial losses for the dominant society of restoring and guaranteeing a proper land base for the Temagami Indians?

And what about Temagami village? Part of the problem there has again been the provincial government. In the 1960s that government created Temagami North as a resource town, mainly for the Sherman iron mine, outside the Georgian Bay watershed, in a field by Net Lake (in the Ottawa Valley!). Temagami North was cut off from Lake Temagami and its back-country. The aim was to starve out the old townsite, which had iron ore beneath it but had been a recreation-oriented community since its 1905 inception with the arrival of the railway. This misguided policy continued until the early 1980s, though it was a failure from the beginning. It left the incorporated Temagami Township with two rival urban centres in two diverse major watersheds. But, with a few exceptions, the merchants of even the old town failed to respond adequately to two events — the opening of the Temagami Mine road south of the village in 1958, a road which encouraged cottagers and suppliers to "turn off" before Temagami village, and then the provincial shutting down in 1965 of the service of the Ontario Northland Boat Lines, further severing the villagers' vital links with the vacationers on the lake. The youth camps and lodges henceforth bought much of their supplies, certainly food, elsewhere — mainly from North Bay and Sturgeon Falls. No wholesale operations emerged in the village to supply the growing lake business. With this break between village and lake came a severe decline in vital village-Bear Island links, so significant and obvious in the past, to which the Metis population is a happy testament.

There developed a scorn in the village for the non-exploitive vacationers who were clearly the wave of the future: the cottagers and canoeists who did not hunt and rarely fished. Meanwhile the canoe camps and canoeing outfitters increased their travel in the remote backcountry, which otherwise only the most enthusiastic snowmobiling villagers knew anything about. The poorly run International Canoe Festival, held in 1985, received little cooperation from the village. By 1988 conditions had reached a low point, with villagers throwing personal abuse at Smoothwater Outfitters, Temagami Canoe, and some of the lake membership of the first joint planning board.

But there is more than one village in the Temagami country. To the northwest in Elk Lake, during the summer of 1989, the refusal of the Petro Canada station, the only petroleum outlet, to sell gasoline to vehicles carrying canoes pointed to behaviour even more bitter and potentially more dangerous and self-defeating.

Logging roads in 1989 seemed central to the Temagami crises, but they were only symbolic.[18] Of far greater importance, beside the just claims of the Temagami First Nation, is the integrity of the forest, or what is left of that forest behind the precarious shoreline reserves and in the once partly cut over and much too small Lady Evelyn-Smoothwater Wilderness Park. At least the main area of the tall old-growth ecosystem must be preserved. Parts of the rest of the forest, back of the waterways, could be carefully conserved through strict sustainable-yield cutting without trunk roads. All this definitely means reducing employment in white-pine harvesting, but it could also mean much more labour-intensive tree planting and more hardwood cutting. Furthermore, Stone Consolidated (formerly Consolidated Bathurst) should probably lose its hold on lands east of Highway 11. There should be careful examination of the Geraldton plantation experiment. We need further study of the serious current proposals to make the village of Temagami into a tourist destination and cultural attraction. We must move to strict environmental sanity. Some people who migrated to the area in the late 1960s to work in the iron mine and in the pine mills may have to move on, with public help, if they are unwilling to adjust. A large percentage of the forest workers, however, in the past came to work from outside the area, many from Quebec.

Hinterland politics are at the centre of the problem. The concept was explained years ago by Harold Innis, and more recently interpreted by Mel Watkins[19] and other political economists. Hinterland politics are linked to the so-called demographic imperative (a great conundrum for democracy) and to the influence of the metropolitan economic-power base. Traditional provincial political elites do not depend heavily on the north for their electoral success, though northern seats here and there might marginally help. The north is seen primarily as a source of wealth for the provincial economy or as an embarrassingly depressed area of mass unemployment. These elites help prop up local entrepreneurs and the government relies mainly on them to keep the economy going and unemployment under some control. They promote the extraction of resources for the short-term wealth of the province, public and private, and the government pays something back in welfare and subsidies. This style of economic and political management peaked in the 1930s under the Mitch Hepburn Liberals, with their support of the gold-mining magnates and their opposition to the organizational efforts of the industrial unions. And the magnates were all backed by the new *Globe and Mail*. In part, history does repeat itself.

But we are now in a new situation. In virtually all surveys of opinion, Ontarians, most of whom now live in the south and in Sudbury and Thunder Bay, rate "Environmental Concerns" at the top of their political agenda. A majority also supports aboriginal self-government, even though many may be unclear about its significance.[20] All the Ontario and many of the national environmental organizations support the thrust of the Temagami Wilderness Society; most also support the Teme-Augama Anishnabai. All oppose MNR on the issue of Temagami logging, and most are linked through "Forests for Tomorrow" in their overall critique of MNR in the Environmental Class Assessment of its forests stewardship and planning. The intellectual and literary leadership of the province also condemns MNR. Most of the private citizens serving on the Premier's Environmental Round Table are extremely critical. So far all this has not yet persuaded a provincial government to change its policies. Ultimately this enlightened pressure may succeed. I firmly believe that it should.

In the near future, from a committed academic's perspective, the Temagami Indians must have a large area totally under their self-governing control, with provisions for possible venture enterprises based on the models suggested by Chief Gary Potts[21] and the Gro Harlem Brundtland commission.[22] Beyond this area, but still within the old N'Daki Menan or homeland, the Teme-Augama Anishnabai's influence must be felt in all planning and monitoring bodies. All this requires Ontario to engage in serious negotiations with the Teme-Augama Anishnabai without expecting them to deny their history or abandon their aboriginal rights. It certainly means taking to heart their second Benson report and the principles of the federal Coolican report.[23] It means looking clearly at the models being worked out in the far north with the Inuit, the Dene, and the Yukon Indians.

The Temagami country should also have self-governing, recreational-based municipalities, such as the proposed Lake Temagami Archipelago, legally separate from the current Temagami Township. It is vitally important that the Temagami country, to use the unofficial name,

be identified distinctively by the Ontario government, especially by ad-
justing significantly the present boundaries of MNR's Administrative
District of Temagami. That district's present inappropriate boundaries
include the Tri-towns, an urban complex never socio-culturally a part
of the Temagami country. To include New Liskeard, Haileybury, and
Cobalt in the district skewers all the statistical analysis of social and economic activity and sustains an impossible political conundrum. The
1903 boundary of the Forest Reserve south of the Arctic watershed, a
boundary which is roughly the same as the Indians' N'Daki Menan,
would be most appropriate.

Incorporated traditional townships like Temagami must become
oriented totally to environmentally sensitive activities such as recycling
and ecological study, and to recreation in all its non-exploitive aspects:
wilderness-venture travel, winter recreation, cottager supplying, up-
scale destination and conference facilities, and aboriginal art and cultural displays. This means eventually the end of both sports hunting,
except with cameras and easels, and trophy fishing. It also means the
electoral overthrow of the type of local administrations that now exist
in Temagami, Elk Lake, and Latchford. Temagami Village should and
can become the jewel of northern Ontario. It could be a more attractive
place than either Lake Placid, New York, or Eli, Minnesota — with the
canoe finally becoming Temagami's genuine rather than phoney icon.

An obsession with old and unsound economic-development
modes of thinking, combined with the habits of hinterland politics, can
lead to the view that the land claims of the Teme-Augama Anishnabai
or the preservationist proposals of even the more moderate advocates
in the TWS verge on the outlandish. But that is the old way of thinking,
one which has brought us to our present world ecological crisis. The
demands are not absurd as we move toward ecological sanity. They are
not absurd as we think of the aboriginal or fourth world peoples' long-
term, historic commitment to sustainable life. The projection of forest
stewardship by the Temagami Indians, with their own core land base
and a significant role in a shared resource-management council for their
entire old homeland, is the correct projection. The just claims and goals
of the Teme-Augama Anishnabai, like those of many other aboriginal

groups in Canada and like those of the Kaypo in the Brazilian forest, are intrinsically ecological in nature.[24] The dominant Ontario society needs to recognize this imperative for its own and all humankind's survival.

ADDENDUM

After the above paper was presented and then revised for publication, the Teme-Augama Anishnabai and the Ontario government, on 23 April 1990, signed a "Memorandum of Understanding" which provided for the establishment of a stewardship council, with Temagami Indian representation to be 50 per cent. The council would control resource development in the four crucial townships of the Wakimika Triangle on the basis of strict "stewardship" or sustainable life. In the meantime, no timber harvesting would take place, nor would the Red Squirrel road in this area be significantly upgraded or used for truck-hauling. This council was announced to be a step toward the establishment of a "treaty of co-existence" between Ontario and the Temagami Indians, regardless of the outcome of the appeal to the Supreme Court of Canada (to be heard on 25 November 1990). The Ontario government also bought the Milne Lumber mill and closed it down, giving Roger Fryer increased and controversial cutting rights just south of Lake Temagami. These developments, followed by the September 1990 electoral victory of Bob Rae's New Democratic Party in Ontario, suggest that perhaps a significant if tentative new beginning is now underway in Temagami.

---

[1] Chief Gary Potts, "Teme–Augama Anishnabai: Last–Ditch Defence of a Priceless Homeland," in *Drum Beat: Anger and Renewal in Indian Country*, Boyce Richardson, ed. (Toronto, 1989), 201–28; quotation from 209–10.

[2] World Commission on Environment and Development, Chair: Gro Harlem Brundtland, *Our Common Future* (Oxford, 1987).

[3] Aldo Leopold, *A Sand County Almanac* (New York, 1949), quoted by Monte Hummel in his edited *Endangered Spaces: the Future for Canadian Wilderness* (Toronto, 1989), 267.

[4] Bruce W. Hodgins and Jamie Benidickson, *The Temagami Experience: Recreation, Resources, and Aboriginal Rights in the Northern Ontario Wilderness* (Toronto, 1989). Where not otherwise documented, most of the historical analysis in this paper is extrapolated from that book. But note also our "Temagami: the Road to Ruin," *Globe and Mail*, 11 December 1989, 8. Both authors camped on Lake Wakimika with the Temagami Wilderness Society demonstrators on 16–17 September 1989 when the blockade of the Red Squirrel road extension began. Both were later arrested again when supporting the road blockade of the Teme–Augama Anishnabai (which began on 11 November 1989) in opposition to the injunction secured by the attorney general.

[5] Margaret Mironowitz, review in the October/November 1989 issue, 92–93. Note also the reviews in the *Whig–Standard Magazine* (Kingston), 12 August 1989, and *Quill and Quire*, August 1989.

[6] Note, for example, J. Miller, *Skyscrapers Hide the Heavens: A History of Indian-White Relations in Canada* (Toronto, 1989), note 16. Also see both Boyce Richardson, "Concealed Contempt," *Canadian Forum*, December 1989, 15–20, and Gary Potts, in Richardson, ed., *Drum Beat*, 201–28.

[7] See, for example, the Ontario sections of Peter R. Gillis and Thomas R. Roach, *Lost Initiatives: Canada's Forest Industries, Forest Policy and Forest Conservation* (New York, 1986).

[8] H.V. Nelles, *The Politics of Development: Forests, Mines and Hydro–Electric Power in Ontario, 1849–1941* (Toronto, 1974).

[9] Wayne Roberts, "Temagami Forest Standoff," *Now* (Toronto), 28 September–4 October 1989. (Roberts, himself, was arrested at the Temagami Wilderness Society (TWS) blockade along Wakimika Lake, on 18 September, two days before Bob Rae's arrest.) See also the *Temiskaming Speaker* (New Liskeard), 20 September 1989 and the *Star* (Toronto), 25 September 1989.

[10] Ontario Legislature, *Hansard*, 9 June 1966, 4474. The author of this paper has extensive correspondence between himself and Donald C. MacDonald, and with various Lands and Forest officials concerning the extension of the Johns–Manville road (now the Red Squirrel road) during June, July, and August of 1966.

[11] *Temagami Times*, autumn, 1973 and spring 1974.

[12] The Temagami Lakes Association was also aroused in the early 1970s by the "SO_2 problem." See the *Temagami Experience*, 256–7 and notes 21 to 25 on 344. Note also various *Temagami Times*, for 1972 and 1973 and especially the spring of 1980, as well as Carol (Cochrane) Bangay, "The Dragon's Breath," *Alternatives* vol. 2, no. 2 (Winter, 1973), 36–47.

[13] Note George M. Warecki, Protecting Ontario's Wilderness: A History of Wilderness Conservation in Ontario, 1927–1973 (unpublished doctoral dissertation, McMaster University, 1989). Note also Arlin Hackman, "Ontario's Park System Comes of Age," in Hummel, ed., *Endangered Spaces*, 165–82.

[14] Yet the American–based Forest History Society, with heavy industrial backing, gives a prominent place in its *Journal of Forest History* to conservation– and preservation–oriented articles. Jamie Benidickson, Peter Gillis, and this author won the Weyerhauser Award in 1983 with an article on the failure of Ontario and Quebec forest reserves: "The Ontario and Quebec Experiments in Forest Reserves, 1883–1930," *JFH*, vol. 26, no. 1 (January 1982), 20–33; The society's Vancouver conference in 1985 had all of us and other preservationists give various talks and papers. The society also helped publish the critically important *Lost Initiatives* . But back in Canada, at the turn of the century, *Rod and Gun in Canada* served as a magazine for both the wilderness buffs and the Canadian Forestry Association.

[15] Note the following: Henry A. Wright and Arthur W. Bailey, *Fire Ecology: United States and Southern Canada* (New York, 1982); William C. Clark and R.E. Munn, eds., *Sustainable Development of the Biosphere* (Cambridge, 1987); Harold K. Steen, ed., *History of Sustained Yield Forestry: A Symposium* (Santa Cruz, 1984); and David Kelly and Gary Braasch, *Secrets of the Old Growth Forest* (Salt Lake City, 1988).

[16] C.A. Benson, *et al.*, *Forest Management in N'Daki Menan of the Teme– Augama Anishnabai* (May 1982) and his *The Need for a Land Stewardship, Holistic Resource Management Plan for N'Daki Menan* (July 1989).

[17] See, for example, his reports in various recent issues of the TWS's *Wilderness Report* and Brad Cundiff, "New Ideas about Old Growth," *Seasons*, vol. 29, no. 4 (Winter 1989), 31–5. Note also Ben Moise, "Temagami Wilderness under Seige: Indians, Environmentalists, Loggers and Hunters Square off in Northern Ontario," *Canadian Geographic*, Feb./March 1989, 28–39, and Jeff Outhit, "Wood, Wilderness and Justice," *Whig–Standard Magazine*, 11 November 1989, 4–10.

[18] Roger Fryer alleged at the Laurentian conference, in response to this draft paper, that the trunk roads through the Wakimika Triangle (in Shelburne and Delhi townships) were never the economic issue, that he had a "promise" from MNR concerning long-term forest harvesting off the yet unconstructed westbound Pinetorch Corridor road. This caused quite a sensation, because

such a "promise" seems not to have been made public, if indeed it even exists. He would retrieve logs from the corridor, he claimed, via the Red Squirrel road to Temagami, not southward to Field, and Liskeard Lumber would not haul logs northward from the corridor through the park (where the road is to be closed in mid-decade). Certainly all this needs clarification. The corridor area may be less sensitive. But road construction should await new environmental assessment, a settlement with the Indians, and agreement on the route for hauling, if hauling is to take place.

[19] See Mel Watkins, "The Staple Theory Revisited," in Bruce W. Hodgins and Robert Page, eds., *Canadian History Since Confederation: Essays and Interpretations* (2nd ed., Georgetown, 1979), 573–89; Nelles, *Politics of Development*; and Wayne Roberts, "Temagami Forest Standoff," *Now*, 28 Sept.– 4 Oct. 1989.

[20] J. Rich Ponting, "Public Opinion on Aboriginal Peoples' Issues in Canada," *Canadian Social Trends* (Statistics Canada), no. 11, (Winter 1988), 9–17; also note *Globe and Mail*, 19 April 1984.

[21] Chief Potts's sophisticated proposals have been endorsed by the Teme–Augama Anishnabai Tribal Assembly and are found in various of its reports. He eloquently outlines his position in his recent article in *Drum Beat*, 201–28, and in his unfortunately relatively brief appearance on 22 November 1989 before the Ontario legislature's Resource Development Committee. See the draft transcript of those hearings.

[22] *Our Common Future*. The Brundtland report supports aboriginal self-government and links that support to environmental protection.

[23] Department of Indian and Northern Affairs, *Living Treaties: Lasting Agreements: Report of the Task Force to Review Comprehensible Claims Policy* (Murray Coolican, Chairman, Ottawa 1985). Note Bruce W. Hodgins, John S. Milloy, and Kenneth J. Maddock, "'Aboriginal Self-Government': Another Level or Order in Canadian and Australian Federalism?" in Hodgins, John Eddy, Shelagh D. Grant, and James Struthers, eds., *Federalism in Canada and Australia: Historical Perspectives, 1920–88* (Peterborough, 1989), 452–87. Also see Rudy Platiel, "Wider self-rule for Natives foreseen in 90s," *Globe and Mail*, 3 January 1990.

[24] The author would like to thank his Trent University colleague Jonathan Bordo, who was arrested during the TWS blockade, for help in articulating this vital ecological link between the claims of the Temagami Indians and the demands of the environmental groups. Note also Harold Eidsvik, "Canada in a Global Context," in Hummel, ed., *Endangered Spaces* 300–45.

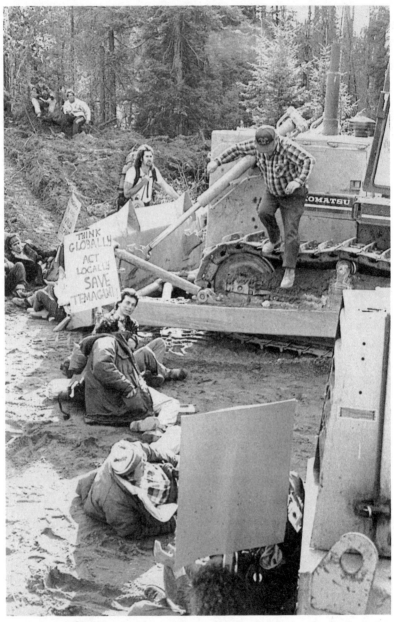

The Temagami Wilderness Society's blockade of the Red Squirrel road extension in the fall of 1989. *Courtesy: Temagami Wilderness Society*

Eight

Temagami: An Environmentalist's Perspective

Brian Back

Temagami is probably the most contested piece of land in North America. We are now into the 112th year of the Teme-Augama Anishnabai struggle to regain their homeland. In the past five years alone Temagami has been the subject of seven court decisions, three road blockades, and at least 124 arrests on the Temagami Wilderness Society's blockade of the Red Squirrel road. About one-third of the blockaders have been from northern Ontario; the remainder have come from as far away as France and Wales. Native people from the area, the Teme-Augama Anishnabai, and even from Malaysia, have been involved. The oldest person arrested was seventy-seven years of age. He insisted on being arrested, in spite of a heart condition, because he felt so strongly about making a personal statement.

The Temagami Wilderness Society (TWS) has proposed a wilderness reserve for the area. This reserve would not be a park, but a land trust to be held for the Teme-Augama Anishnabai. There is no provision in either the Provincial Parks Act or the National Parks Act for a wilderness reserve. The proposal is entirely designed for the unique situation in Temagami.

The Teme-Augama have lived in Temagami for 6,000 years and have never surrendered their rights. This is the TWS's position and it does not hinge on a court decision. The land belongs to the Teme-Augama.

Readers may be familiar with the TWS's Tall Pines Project. It is the largest field study of old-growth forest in Canada. The Tall Pines team discovered that Temagami contains the largest known stand of old-growth red and white pine in Ontario. We did not know this until April 1989. The Ministry of Natural Resources (MNR) did not know it either. Only since then has MNR recognized old growth as a distinct and sensitive feature of the Temagami environment. But even now it has no protection policy, only a logging policy:cut the trees as quickly as possible.

There are some myths about old growth that should be dispelled. Old growth does not consist just of emperors of the forest — the big, old trees. Old-growth red- and white-pine ecosystems *do* contain trees at least 140 years of age, but that is not sufficient. The *entire* ecosystem is old. In it there are snags (standing dead trees) and deadfalls, and a thick floor of organic material — the emperors of past generations. In Temagami these pine ecosystems have been evolving for 500 to 700 years. Interestingly, the oldest trees found in Temagami are 375-year-old white pine. They are outside the parks and are unprotected.

When a tree dies it is not the end of life, but the beginning. It becomes home to a different set of flora and fauna. Eventually it recycles back into the soil to support new tree growth. We are trying to preserve not the big trees, but the processes of the ecosystems that preserve the forest. Old-growth forests are ancient fortresses of life that have preserved the processes and the species, the blueprints for restoring our lost forests.

Unfortunately, Temagami has been undergoing successive destruction at the hands of the Ontario government. The "production policy," as it is called by MNR, is an Ontario-wide effort that is the sum of logging targets set in each district, including Temagami. This policy, which has resulted in doubling Temagami's logging volume since 1980, is based on a fifty-year rotation. It assumes that the forests of Ontario will be logged over fifty years and all of them will grow back in the same length of time.

But Ontario's forests cannot grow back in fifty years. Nature cannot do it. Even the MNR's Temagami policy states that white and red pine take 120 years to regenerate while jack pine needs eighty years. The fastest growing species in northern Ontario is poplar and it still takes sixty years to grow back. MNR has built into its planning process the ultimate demise of the forest industry.

Half of the ministry's grand theory involves logging and the other half regeneration. It assumes that everything logged is regenerated. In the case of conifers, the theory requires replanting or reseeding. But only 50 per cent of Ontario's logged areas are replanted. In the district of Temagami for 1980-87, only 26.5 per cent was replanted. In fifty years little of our heritage will be left because MNR is not keeping its promise to our forests, to our industry, to our First Nations, or to the public.

The only independent field audit of replanted areas in Ontario that we have found was conducted by the provincial auditor in 1985. The study found that two-thirds of the audited areas had no commercially viable forest returning. The forests of Temagami will not return because the Ontario government does not know how to bring them back. There is not going to be a forest, an industry, or a future.

But there is hope for the future of the people of Temagami. Members of the local community are standing up and saying that they intend to create a sustainable future. Look at the Temcor proposal for a destination resort which, local entrepreneurs hope, will create up to 400 permanent jobs. But, of course, it will succeed only if the forests remain.

Recently, in the *Globe and Mail's Report on Business* magazine, I read an interesting comment by Lieutenant Governor David Lam of British Columbia. I want to cite it because BC is similar in so many ways to northern Ontario: "The unfortunate part of a natural-resource based economy is that it limits one's imagination and flexibility and adaptability. It creates a complacent, fatalistic attitude that says, 'Destiny governs, what can I do?' Such an attitude is not conducive to creating a mind geared to the competitive world of the 21st century." I think the people of Temcor and the town of Temagami already know where the future is, and it is not in logging anymore. It is in sustaining our resources.

The people of Temagami are trying to bring together many groups to work on their project for sustainable development, including the Teme-Augama Anishnabai. Until we can come to terms with the people living on the land, we will never come to terms with the other life forms on the land, and we will never protect our environment.

The Native Dimension

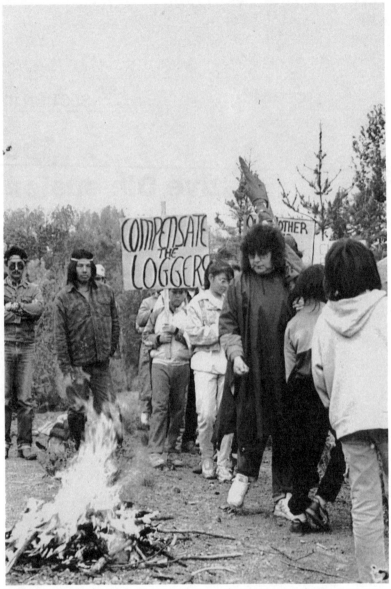

The Teme-Augama Anishnabai blockade of the Goulard lumber road, 1989. *Courtesy: Temagami Wilderness Society*

Nine

The Native Dimension: Key Dates

This list was compiled by the Teme-Augama Anishnabai

The Teme-Augama Anishnabai have documented 6,000 years of occupation of their homeland, N'Daki Menan, which surrounds the Lake Temagami area in what is now called northeastern Ontario. At the time of the Royal Proclamation in 1763, through to and beyond the signing of the Robinson-Huron Treaty in 1850, the People of the Deep Water were a self-governing nation possessing over 9,000 square kilometres of geographically defined lands. Possession of lands and civil affairs were regulated by a communal system of law. Each family maintained its own tract of 500 to 800 square kilometres. Wendaban and Misabi are the names of two such traditional family grounds.

1877   Chief Tonene asks to be taken into treaty to gain protection of his people from encroaching lumbermen and settlers.

1883   The federal government recognizes the omission of the Teme-Augama Anishnabai from the 1850 Robinson-Huron Treaty, arranges for annuity payments, and promises to survey a reserve.

1884   A 260-square-kilometre reserve is surveyed at the southern outlet of Lake Temagami.

1894   The federal government states the Teme-Augama Anishnabai case before a board of arbitrators: "The Dominion on behalf of the said [Temagami] Indians says that the lands are subject to the interest of the said Indians and that the Province ought to allow a reserve to be set apart, or approve of the reserve so surveyed by the Dominion upon such terms as to surrender of the Indian title in the remaining portions of the tract."

Amelius Irving, counsel for Ontario, successfully argues that the case is a matter for treaty, not arbitration, and a decision is deferred.

1901   Ontario establishes the Temagami Forest Reserve.

1901   Aubry White, assistant commissioner of crown lands for Ontario, writes: "[The reserve] taking in a great portion of Lake Temagami and many million of pine timber ... was entirely out of keeping with the Indian population ... no action was taken."

1910   The Department of Indian Affairs (DIA) asks Ontario for a reserve for the Teme-Augama Anishnabai. Ontario again cites the value of timber in its refusal.

1910   Ontario harasses the Teme-Augama Anishnabai. Chief François Whitebear writes to the Indian agent: "We have to get permission from the chief fire ranger to cut even firewood."

1911   Ontario establishes the Temagami Game and Fish Reserve and harassment escalates. The Teme-Augama Anishnabai are prohibited from hunting and fishing in the reserve.

1912   The Whitebear family settlement on Whitebear Lake is flooded by a hydroelectric development in its territory.

1921   Cross Lake is flooded also, causing loss and hardship to the Nebanegwune family.

1929   Ontario charges rent to Teme-Augama Anishnabai living on Bear Island. The DIA asks "special permission to remain without charge until ... a reserve might be obtained ... "

1930   Ontario replies, saying that "as time goes on there seems to be less and less reason why lands should be set aside for the Temagami Indians."

1933   The federal government insists that "the Province has a moral as well as a legal obligation to provide these [Temagami] Indians with a reserve."

1939   Ontario again states that the area surveyed for a reserve is "too valuable from a timber point of view ... [the Temagami Indians] should be allotted a portion of Bear Island."

1939   The Teme-Augama Anishnabai are forbidden to trap without purchasing an Ontario licence and trapping areas are cut down to 93 square kilometres.

1943   The federal government purchases Bear Island from Ontario for $3,000.

1945-7 The Teme-Augama continue attempts to secure the reserve surveyed in 1884.

1948   The Katt (Wendaban) family settlement is flooded at Diamond Lake.

1954   Chief John Twain writes to Ontario, saying that "Bear Island is not a reserve by any means ... We have every right to live wherever we decide to live because the Temagami Band is in the same position as before ... we never surrendered our hunting grounds or any of our original rights to the Crown. We never signed the treaty with no government ... all these troubles we got now will be put before the Supreme Court of Canada to definitely settle the whole matter for once and for all."

1970   Bear Island Indian Reserve Number 1 is created by an Order in Council issued by the governor-general of Canada.

1973   Chief Gary Potts files land-cautions in 110 townships within the Teme-Augama Anishnabai traditional lands and asserts Teme-Augama Anishnabai ownership.

1978   Ontario sues the Teme-Augama Anishnabai in the Supreme Court of Ontario.

1982   In June trial proceedings commence before Justice Donald Steele of the Supreme Court of Ontario. The trial continues for 119 days over the next two years.

1983   Ontario escalates its administrative and legislative actions on the Teme-Augama Anishnabai lands. It creates the Temagami Planning Area and the Lady Evelyn-Smoothwater Provincial Park.

1984   In December Justice Donald Steele finds against the Teme-Augama Anishnabai, saying that a chief to the west signed away any land rights. He also finds that the present Teme-Augama Anishnabai are descendants of the people who occupied the land in 1763.

1984   Four days after the Supreme Court of Ontario decision the Teme-Augama Anishnabai file notice of appeal.

1987   In November the minister of Indian affairs, William McKnight, withdraws funding of the appeal proceedings, stating that $400,000 was a "huge commitment for an appeal" and "those who have a stake in the outcome should raise the balance." The Teme-Augama Anishnabai remind McKnight of his trust responsibility and the fact that they had raised $1.6 million at the trial stage.

1988   In April appeal hearings are scheduled for January 1989.

1988   On 17 May the minister of natural resources, Vince Kerrio, announces that construction of the Red Squirrel extension and the Pinetorch corridor will go ahead.

1988   The Teme-Augama Anishnabai Tribal Council decides at its annual assembly on 22 May to blockade any further road developments on N'Daki Menan.

1988   In December the Ontario Court of Appeal rules on injunctions brought forward by Ontario which sought the order of the court to remove the then six-month-old Teme-Augama Anishnabai blockade of the Red Squirrel road. In a compromise ruling, the Teme-Augama Anishnabai were ordered to remove their blockade and Ontario was ordered to stop all construction until the outstanding title issue had been addressed by the Ontario Court of Appeal.

1989   The Teme-Augama Anishnabai appeal to overturn Justice Donald Steele's 1984 decision proceeds from 9 to 27 January.

1989   On 27 February the Ontario Court of Appeal upholds the lower court decision, denying the Teme-Augama Anishnabai's ownership of their ancestral lands with the argument that the aboriginal title had been surrendered and extinguished by any number of means. The Teme-Augama Anishnabai immediately direct legal counsel to apply for leave to appeal to the Supreme Court of

Canada and reaffirm their intention to take the case to the international courts in their continuing struggle for justice.

1989   On 28 March the Teme-Augama Anishnabai stage a one-day blockade on the Goulard logging road to serve notice to the Ontario government that the *status quo* and the devastation of the land by clearcut logging will not be tolerated.

1990   On 23 April the Teme-Augama Anishnabai and the government of Ontario sign an agreement to create a stewardship council to regulate resource development in four critical townships in the Wakimika Triangle.

Native rock painting in Temagami. *Courtesy: Temagami Wilderness Society*

Ten

Prehistoric Occupations at Lake Temagami

Diana Gordon

In any debate, such as that on Tema-
gami, involving differing and competing views of land and resource utilization, archaeology can play an important role. First, archaeological
sites are themselves "resources" worthy of protection and consideration. They represent the only extant, physical record of human occupations prior to the arrival of Europeans on this continent. Secondly,
through the study of the archaeological record, prehistorians can reconstruct the economy, settlement, and technology of people in the distant
past. Understanding what resources these former inhabitants utilized in
their daily lives and what strategies they developed to survive on this
same landscape offers a greater temporal context to the current debate.

This paper presents an overview of the prehistoric occupations of
Lake Temagami (Figure 1) and environs. The author conducted archaeological field-work on Lake Temagami in 1986 and 1987 for her
doctoral dissertation (Gordon 1986, 1987, 1988a, 1989, n.d.). Drawing
on this and other research, the present paper will describe the nature of
archaeological resources in the Temagami area, the variety of sites encountered, and the different prehistoric occupations. For the purposes
of this paper, the Temagami region is defined as the Sturgeon River

drainage, which includes Lake Temagami and the western portion of the upper Ottawa River drainage. The latter includes Lake Timiskaming (Figure 2).

The Temagami region is an important study area in understanding the archaeology of Ontario for several reasons. The landscape with its deep lakes, rivers, and forests provided fish, waterfowl, game, and fresh water, all of which were basic necessities for prehistoric hunter-gatherers. For this reason, the area is rich in archaeological sites, as demonstrated by preliminary surveys of various lakes and river systems (Ridley 1966; Pollock 1972, 1976; Knight 1972, 1977; Noble 1982; Conway 1986b; Conway and Conway 1989; Gordon 1987, 1989, n.d.). Major travel routes cut through the region, including the Lake Temagami-Sturgeon River route to Lake Nipissing and the Great Lakes and the Montreal River-Lake Timiskaming route to the lower Ottawa River and St Lawrence River (Figure 2). These routes cross several ecological zones and watersheds, making possible contact and communication between prehistoric peoples living to the north and to the south of the Temagami region. Historical accounts from the seventeenth century describe contacts between the Iroquoian-speaking horticulturalists of Huronia and Algonquian-speaking hunters of the Canadian Shield (Heidenreich 1971: 241; Trigger: 1985; 205-7, 276; Hodgins and Benidickson 1989: 14-17).

The third reason that the archaeology of Temagami is important is the dynamic environment. One major question in archaeology is how human beings, through the medium of culture, have adapted to changes in the environment. Since deglaciation about 10,500 years ago (Veillette 1988), the Temagami area has undergone dramatic shifts in palaeohydrology, vegetation, and climate (Veillette 1983, 1988; Liu and Lam 1985; Liu n.d.; Gordon n.d.). Prehistoric hunting groups living in close relationship with the land would have made adjustments to these environmental changes over time. The archaeological record can reveal cultural changes in technology, subsistence, and settlement patterns.

ARCHAEOLOGICAL RESEARCH IN THE TEMAGAMI REGION

As is true for all northern Ontario, archaeological exploration of the

Temagami region is in its infancy. At the turn of the century isolated artifacts and rock-painting sites were reported. Among the lists of accessions to the provincial museum are stone tools, for example, a "weathered knife or spear [from] Smooth Water Lake" (Boyle 1900:6) and a "large argillite gouge or chisel" (Boyle 1900:6) from "Lake Temagaming" (Boyle 1904:63, 1905:27). One interesting item is a "birch bark canoe (two fathom), made by an Indian named Quill [from] White Bear Lake between Lake Temiscaming and Lake Temagami" (Boyle 1902).

Rock-painting sites have been recorded by various researchers. W.H.C. Phillips (1907) published illustrations of rock paintings from Diamond Lake and Lady Evelyn Lake in 1907. Later, Selwyn Dewdney and Kenneth Kidd (1967:92-3) recorded one rock-painting site on Diamond Lake and two on Lake Temagami. Thor Conway has recently recorded rock paintings on Lake Temagami, Obabika Lake, and other locations in northeastern Ontario (Conway 1984, 1986b; Conway and Conway 1989).

Although surveys and actual excavations of archaeological sites have increased in the past twenty years, research is limited and analyses are preliminary. Pioneering work in northeastern Ontario was conducted by Frank Ridley, an amateur archaeologist. Between 1948 and 1962 he identified major site areas in northeastern Ontario, testing and excavating sites on Lake Nipissing (Ridley 1954, 1966), Lake Timiskaming, and Lake Abitibi (Ridley 1956, 1958, 1963, 1966). Ridley's research laid the groundwork for many subsequent archaeological projects, such as Lake Nipissing (Brizinski 1980; Brizinski and Savage 1983) and Lake Abitibi (Lee 1965; Kritsch-Armstrong 1982; Pollock 1984).

In 1969 Dean Knight (1977) extensively excavated Ridley's Montreal River Site (Ridley 1966) on Lake Timiskaming. Knight (1972, 1977) also conducted surveys on the west side of Lake Timiskaming and the lower Montreal River in 1971 and 1972. In the early 1970s John W. Pollock surveyed the Montreal, Blanche, Englehart, Larder, and Misema lake and river systems of the upper Ottawa River drainage (Pollock 1972, 1976), and excavated sites at Smoothwater Lake, Duncan Lake, and Larder Lake (Pollock 1975, 1976). William C. Noble (1982) continued further survey and excavation at Larder Lake in 1977.

In 1978 and 1981 Thor Conway conducted salvage excavation of one multi-component site on Lake Temagami (Conway 1986a) and surveyed northern sections of the lake (Conway 1986, p.c.). Excavation was conducted at a second multi-component site in 1982 and 1983 (Conway 1982; Smith 1983). The northern two-thirds of adjacent Lake Obabika were also surveyed in 1981 and 1984 (Conway 1984; Conway and Conway 1989).

In 1986 and 1987 the author identified eight archaeological sites on the shorelines and islands of the central "Hub" of Lake Temagami during eleven days of survey. Excavation of the stratified, multi-component Three Pines Site (Druid's Cove) CgHa-6 was the main focus of this fieldwork (Gordon 1986, 1987, 1989, n.d.). The site, originally located by Conway (1986, p.c.; Borden Form 1981), was very productive. A total of 15,036 artifacts were recovered from the excavation of 84 one-metre-square units. Excavation was done in three-cm levels, with the spatial distribution of all artifacts and soil features recorded on individual plan maps for each level. Sterile soil was generally reached at a depth of 15 to 20 cm.

From the nearby peatbog a pollen core was extracted and analyzed by geologist John H. McAndrews of the Royal Ontario Museum (Figure 3). Archaeological sediments, off-site soils, lithic tools, and rock samples were identified by geologist Geof Burbidge (1988) of the University of Ottawa. In her doctoral dissertation (Gordon n.d.), the author has incorporated these analyses to reconstruct the palaeoenvironments of Lake Temagami and the Three Pines Site following Butzer's (1982) contextual approach to archaeology. In addition, a stratigraphic analysis of archaeological sediments and artifacts was done following Harris (1979) in order to reconstruct the temporal sequence of natural processes and cultural activities which have interacted to create the Three Pines Site as it exists today.

THE NATURE OF THE ARCHAEOLOGICAL RECORD

In order to develop a better understanding of the way of life of prehistoric inhabitants of the Mixed and Boreal Forest zones of the Canadian

Shield, archaeologists incorporate information from ethnographic and ethnohistorical studies of native Indian groups living in similar environments in Ontario and Quebec (e.g. Speck 1915a, 1915b; Jenkins 1939; Rogers 1962, 1963a, 1963b, 1966, 1969, 1973; Rogers and Black 1976; Tanner 1979; Francis and Morantz 1983). Ethnographic studies indicate that hunting, trapping, and gathering of seasonally available food resources is the major, traditional economic activity. Hunter-gatherers' subsistence and settlement strategies are characterized by an annual, seasonal economic round. From fall to spring, small kin-based groups periodically moved to different camping locations in order to exploit fish, mammal, bird, and plant resources as they became available. In the summer, when life was more relaxed, these groups would amalgamate at one location for a few weeks of socializing, trading, and preparing for the long winter to come.

The archaeological record consists of the preserved material remains left by these hunter-gatherer occupations. Archaeological research is much like detective work. Archaeologists piece together the past from a few clues left behind, reconstructing how people lived, what tools they made, what animals they hunted, and what changes occurred in their settlement patterns, subsistence, and technology over time in response to environmental change and other impetuses. The true challenge in Mixed/Boreal forest archaeology is the fact that artifacts are relatively scarce and limited in variety. Many items prehistoric men and women used for their tools, clothing, and dwellings decomposed over time in the acidic podzolic soils. Organic materials such as hides, fur, sinew, animal bone, wood, and bark are rarely recovered from these archaeological sites. What is preserved are stone tools, fired-clay pottery vessels, calcined or burned animal bone, occasional native copper implements, and red ochre.

In addition to portable artifacts, soil features can also be found. For example, at the Three Pines Site fire-reddened soil with calcined animal bones were found, as were thick deposits of light gray sand with a high ash content. These features are remnants of cooking or disposal hearths. High-temperature, localized fires would reduce wood, animal bone, and other organic materials to ash, while the heat would oxidize iron in the underlying soil. These hearths occasionally contain cobbles brought onto the site from the nearby beach. In a few cases, rocks were laid to the southeast of the hearths, as if for a wind-break. The occasional post mould was also encountered, possibly from a conical tent dwelling or meat/hide smoking structure.

Archaeological sites in the Temagami region are multi-component, which means that they have been repeatedly occupied over many thousands of years. Because of shallow soil development and the seasonal nature of the prehistoric occupations, however, these sites are quite fragile and easily destroyed. One modern camper burying his garbage, or one shovel full of dirt to smother a picnic fire, not to mention larger-scale landscape modifications, can easily destroy 6,000 or more years of prehistory.

VARIETY OF ARCHAEOLOGICAL SITES

A range of archaeological sites of different sizes, locations, and functions have been recorded in the Temagami area. These sites include short- and long-term habitations, summer-gathering areas, quarry sites, lithic-processing sites, rock paintings, and sites with a religious significance. For habitation sites, the amount of level ground suitable for camping can be used as a rough measure of length of occupation and/ or group size. On this basis, the author has identified a number of surveyed sites on Lake Temagami as short-term camps. These are located on narrow points and small islands. Testing of such sites produced a few waste flakes from resharpening a lithic tool and occasionally an arrowhead or piece of pottery. Such sites may have housed one or two families for a few days, or perhaps were travel or stopover camps for two men hunting away from the main base camp (Rogers and Black 1976; Chism 1977, 1978).

Sites with more extensive flat and well-drained terrain could have been occupied by a few families for longer periods, or perhaps housed more people for a short period of time. Such sites are usually well situated for fishing, as fish provided a stable dependable resource for hunting groups (Rogers 1973; Tanner 1979; Gordon 1980). Other factors that determined the settlement patterns of prehistoric people were expanses of well-drained ground, protection from cold winds, sunny exposures, and accessibility to water, firewood, and constructional resources such as tent poles, spruce roots, and saplings (cf. Chism 1977, 1978; Irimoto 1980; Rogers 1967, 1973; Gordon 1985, 1988a). Sites which offered all these features were the most favoured locations, with groups repeatedly returning to them over many years. This accounts for the greater quantity of artifacts and soil features on such sites, compared to that on the small travel camps.

The three major excavated sites on Lake Temagami occur in such favourable locales. One is atop a sand and gravel esker, while the other two are located on sandy terraces (Conway 1982, 1986a; Gordon 1988a). One of the largest areas of flat sand is at Sandy Inlet (Camp Wanapitei), the location of Father Paradis's chapel of the late nineteenth century (Hodgins 1976). According to Bruce Hodgins (1986 p.c.), the inlet was an important summer-gathering area with many families camped across it in the nineteenth century. It was also a prehistoric site. Hunting groups would have been attracted to the well-drained ground, fresh water, and fish at the inlet, and the gently sloping beach which allowed greater safety for children playing along the shallow shoreline (cf. Gordon 1985, 1988b).

In addition to seasonal and multi-functional habitation sites, there are several special-function sites. These include quarry sites, as prehistoric people relied on hard conchoidal fracturing rock from which to make projectile points, scrapers, and knives. Vein quartz was one raw material exploited by some stone-tool makers. This material was quarried from lakeside veins of quartz, such as those found on Lake Temagami (Gordon 1987, n.d.) and Obabika Lake (Conway 1984; Conway and Conway 1989). Material from such veins was often transported and worked further at nearby campsites (Gordon 1987, n.d.).

Certain sites probably had religious meaning, such as the numerous rock-painting sites on Diamond Lake, Lady Evelyn Lake, Lake Temagami, and Obabika Lake (Phillips 1907; Dewdney and Kidd 1967; Conway 1984, 1986b). Conway and Conway (1989) report religious or sacred sites identified by Teme-Augama Anishnabai elders on Obabika Lake. One site contains two large free-standing rocks, probably glacial erratics, called "My Grandfather and Grandmother Rocks," where offerings were left (Conway and conway 1989:55). Another similar site occurs on the northwest arm of Lake Temagami (Conway 1986, p.c.).

CULTURAL CHRONOLOGY

The prehistory of northeastern North America is broadly divided into different time periods, based on major changes in the material cultures and radiocarbon dates from archaeological sites. In Ontario these periods include Palaeo-Indian (12,000–7,000 B.P.), Archaic (7,000–3,000 B.P.), Initial Woodland (3,000–1,000 B.P.), and Terminal Woodland (1,000 B.P. to Contact) (Wright 1972b).

Paleo-Indian Occupations (12,000–7,000 B.P.)

The first human occupations of Ontario occurred between 11,500 and 10,200 B.P., when hunting groups moved into areas made available as the continental ice sheets retreated. Palaeo-Indian occupations are now well recognized in southwestern and south-central Ontario from systematic survey of proglacial Lake Algonquin and Lake Iroquois strandlines (Storck 1978, 1979, 1982, 1984; Deller 1976; Ellis and Deller 1982). Early Palaeo-Indians camped on the shores of these cold lakes, hunting caribou herds with specialized fluted-point spears. In northeastern Ontario, Late Palaeo-Indian components (c. 10,200–7,000 B.P.) have been identified on the north shore of Georgian Bay and Manitoulin Island (Greenman 1943; Lee 1957; Storck 1984) as well as in the Lakehead area of northwestern Ontario (MacNeish 1952; Fox 1980; Dawson 1983; Julig 1988). With the exception of the problematic "Temiscaming complex" in northwestern Quebec (Martijn 1985; Martijn and Rogers 1969), no Palaeo-Indian sites have been confirmed in northeastern Ontario inland from the Great Lakes. Some researchers consider it a strong possibility that such occupations exist but have not been fully recognized (Pollock 1984; Gordon n.d.).

From palaeoenvironmental and geochronological studies, Palaeo-Indian occupation of Temagami-Timiskaming is a distinct possibility. Recent detailed studies of regional deglaciation and proglacial lake formation by geologist Jean Veillette of the Geological Survey of Canada indicate that the Temagami area was ice-free by at least 10,500 B.P. (Veillette 1983, 1988, 1988 p.c., 1989). The northeast arm of Lake Temagami was inundated by proglacial Lakes Post-Algonquin and Barlow-Ojibway at their maximum extent. Veillette's work opens the potential for finding Early Palaeo-Indian sites (*c.* 11,500–10,200 B.P.) on the same proglacial lake strandlines as were occupied in southern Ontario (Storck 1982). If access to water were a key factor in settlement selection, then any early groups would have favoured proglacial lakeshores. Settlement choices, travel routes, and resource use would be in considerable flux in this period. Climatic warming and isostatic rebound would have caused shifts in lake levels and drainage directions (Veillette 1988) while the vegetation changed from tundra (Saarnisto 1974) to an early boreal woodland (10,500–9,000 B.P.) to a closed boreal forest (9,000–7,350 B.P.) (Liu n.d.).

In order to locate these hypothesized Palaeo-Indian sites, a different archaeological survey strategy will be necessary than the methods currently employed. Based on the distribution of glaciolacustrine deposits between Lake Timiskaming and Lake Temagami (GSC 1987; Veillette 1988), the shorelines of the ancient proglacial lakes are many kilometres inland from current lakeshores. The technique of examining present-day shorelines (e.g. Conway 1984; Gordon 1987, 1989) is inadequate to locate potential Palaeo-Indian occupations. The author has begun research on developing alternative archaeological-survey strategies for Lake Temagami and environs. This involves palaeohydrological reconstructions to help predict early Holocene site locations, which will then be tested through archaeological field work. Systematic surveys of proglacial lake strandlines is a technique which has resulted in an explosive growth in Palaeo-Indian research over the past fifteen years in both southern and northwestern Ontario (Storck 1978, 1979, 1982, 1984; Deller 1976; Ellis and Deller 1982; Dawson 1983; Julig 1988).

Archaic Period (7,000–3,000 B.P.)

Many sites have been identified with Archaic components, for example, Smoothwater Lake (Pollock 1975, 1976), Larder Lake (Pollock 1976; Noble 1982), Montreal River (Knight 1977), and three sites on Lake

Temagami (Conway 1982, 1986a; Gordon n.d.). With only a few sites excavated and very few absolute dates, however, occupations of this period are not well known. Hunter-gatherers living on the Canadian Shield manufactured a wide variety of larger stone-spear and other projectile points, knives, and hide scrapers. At the Three Pines Site certain artifacts are representative of the Archaic period. From one hearth (Feature 20) a very fine-grained, olive-green sandstone side-notched projectile point, a bluish-grey quartzite-bipointed biface, and an unfinished biface of very dark gray chert were recovered. In another hearth (Feature 4) a narrow blade, olive-green siltstone projectile point, a large snub-nosed gray chert scraper, a clear quartz biface tip, and a large rectangular greenish-gray mudshale flake knife were found together. Several Archaic stone tools from Three Pines show definite similarities with tools identified from sites on Lake Abitibi (Marois 1973; Kritsch-Armstrong 1982) and Lake Nipissing (Ridley 1954).

The Archaic period tool makers were highly specialized craftspeople, knowledgeable in the properties of different lithic materials and in the locations of lithic sources. While many types of stone used by Three Pines Site knappers were locally obtained, others are exotic to the area (Burbidge 1988). For example, fine-grained siltstones, sandstones, quartzites, and the softer mudrock are all available in local bedrock outcrops (Table 1). Exotics to Lake Temagami include clear quartz and several cherts which prehistoric knappers may have imported directly or obtained through trade with other groups. One type of chert, a light gray fossiliferous one, is found locally as nodules on the beaches of Lake Temagami. Although rather poor in flaking qualities, it was used for the occasional tool at the Three Pines Site. The material resembles Thornloe Formation cherts from the Palaeozoic Temiscaming outlier north of Lake Timiskaming. Its presence in the Temagami basin is due to glacial action. The continental ice sheets crossed the Temagami area in a south-southwest direction, scouring the Palaeozoic outlier and depositing chunks of this chert many kilometres from its source (Veillette 1989; Burbidge 1989 p.c.).

The earliest radiocarbon date obtained from a reliable stratified archaeological context in the Temagami region is 5,030+/-240 B.P. (GaK-

2802) at the Montreal River Site, which dates the early Archaic occupations of this site (Knight 1977). At the Three Pines Site, no charcoal samples were deemed from a sufficiently reliable stratigraphic context to submit for dating. Yet a pollen core was extracted from the adjacent peatbog in order to obtain a minimum date by which the terrace/bog complex could have been established and thus occupied. The basal organics of the four-metre long core gave a date of 6,400 +/- 80 B.P. (WAT-1987). Thus the Three Pines Site could have been available for occupation by at least 6,400 years ago.

Analysis of the Three Pines Bog pollen core (Figure 3) by McAndrews reveals the changing forest composition and climate of the Temagami region over the past six millennia. The zonation of this core correlates with cores (Figure 2) from Nina Lake near Sudbury, Jack Lake near Gogama, and Lake Six near Timmins (Liu and Lam 1985; Liu n.d.). In the Archaic period, represented by Zone 3a, the climate was warmer, possibly with a mean annual temperature of 1 to 2^0 higher than that of today (Liu n.d.). This Hypsithermal period is characterized by an increased and northward-migration spread of white pine (*Pinus strobus*), causing the Mixed Forest/Boreal Forest ecotone to migrate to the edge of the Canadian Shield, 140 km north of its present position (Liu n.d.).

Thus Archaic period hunter-gatherers in the Temagami region had a more favourable climate than today. Increased temperatures would allow range extension of animals normally associated with a mixed forest, such as deer, and fewer boreal-forest adapted animals, such as moose and caribou. A warmer climate would result in longer periods of open water, which would be reflected in seasonal usage of certain sites. For example, warm-weather sites and island locales could be occupied for longer periods between break-up and freeze-up. Slightly drier conditions would mean an increase in the frequency of forest fires, which would also affect settlement location and hunting areas.

Initial Woodland Period (c. 3,000 – 1,000 B.P.)

The Initial Woodland archaeological period is marked by the introduction of ceramic technology. The pottery vessels are coil manufactures, conical shaped with various pseudo-scallop shell, rectangular dentate, and linear stamp impressions. These Laurel ceramics are widespread across northern Ontario, Minnesota, and Michigan (Wright 1967; Hamilton 1981), and are represented on sites in the Temagami region (Conway 1986a; Knight 1977; Noble 1982; Pollock 1975, 1976).

At the Three Pines Site, Laurel pottery makers used either Nipissing quartz diabase or granitoid rocks as pottery temper, which would have required considerable pounding. Initial Woodland (Laurel) lithic tools are generally smaller than those of the preceding period, and are fashioned from different raw materials (Wright 1972a). Three Pines triangular end-scrapers and smaller, side-notched projectile points and bifaces are fashioned on colourful Hudson Bay Lowland (HBL) chert. This material is homogeneous with good conchoidal fracture, making it desirable for flintknappers. It occurs as nodules in glacial drift in northern Ontario, brought southward from the Hudson Bay Lowland Palaeozoic formations by glacial scouring. However, HBL nodules were not found on the beaches of Lake Temagami by either the author or geologist Burbidge, and this type of chert does not occur in the Temiscaming outlier. Karrow and Geddes (1987) suggest that the steep drop in the carbonate content of tills south of the Chapleau moraines marks the southern extent of reworked Palaeozoic sediments from the Hudson Bay Lowland. This suggests that the prehistorically used HBL chert was not deposited as far south as Lake Temagami. It was brought onto Lake Temagami sites by Initial Woodland flintknappers either by travelling farther north to find the material or by trading with other groups (Gordon n.d.).

The Initial Woodland period in the Temagami region corresponds to Zone 3b on the Three Pines Bog pollen core, beginning at 3,540 +/- 70 B.P. (WAT-2088). This zone shows a decrease in white pine with an increase in jack or red pine, birch, and spruce. The change marks the onset of Neoglacial cooling, when the Boreal Forest migrated southwards from the edge of the Shield. The present-day ecotone boundary, which is situated north of Lake Temagami (Figure 1), was stabilized around 2,600 B.P. (Liu n.d.).

Terminal Woodland (1,000 B.P. to Contact)

The Terminal Woodland period is characterized by different types of pottery vessels. Terminal-Woodland occupations at Lake Temagami are represented by cord-wrapped, stick-impressed, and cord-textured vessels (Conway 1986a; Gordon 1987, n.d.). At the Three Pines Site, one vessel is very thin walled, with a complex cord-impressed design and dark-gray diabase temper. None of the Terminal-Woodland vessels at Lake Temagami, nor those described on other sites in the Temagami region (Knight 1977; Pollock 1976), fit comfortably into the category of Blackduck or Selkirk pottery which is well represented on upland Shield sites in northwestern Ontario, Manitoba, and Minnesota (Hamilton 1981; Gordon 1985).

A different type of vessel found on two sites on Lake Temagami has linear-incised or trailed decorations with collars and castellations. This style of vessel resembles those found farther south in the sedentary horticultural villages of the Huron and other Iroquoian-speaking groups (Conway 1982, 1986a). Such vessels are also found in the upper strata of sites from Lake Nipissing and as far north as Lake Abitibi (Ridley 1954, 1966; Brizinski 1980). Cross-dating with Huron Incised pottery shows these vessels to date to the mid-to-late sixteenth century (Noble 1982).

The occurrence of "Iroquoian-like" vessels in northeastern Ontario sites suggests contact either direct or indirect between horticultural groups to the south and the northern hunter-gatherers. As noted earlier, north-south riverine travel corridors cross the Temagami region. In historical records such as the Jesuit Relations, there are accounts of trading relationships, over-wintering of Algonquian-speaking groups with the Huron, Hurons fishing in Lake Nipissing, and Iroquois raids as far north as James Bay (Trigger 1985: 205-7, 276; Heidenreich 1971: 241; Hodgins and Benidickson 1989: 14-17). Native oral histories also include accounts of Iroquois raids in the Temagami region (Speck 1915b; Conway and Conway 1989:36).

Historic (Contact 1900) and Modern (20th Century) Periods

The presence of mass-manufactured items generally signals the historic (period of written documents) or post-contact period. At Three Pines a series of nineteenth-century occupations are represented by various hearth features. In one hearth (Feature 22/23) a complete beaver jaw and deer phalanges were found together with a clay pipe and gunspalls from flintlock muskets. The pipe stem was stamped "Henderson/Montreal" and was manufactured between 1846 and 1876 (Smith 1986). A greater number and variety of nineteenth-century items were recovered from another site on the lake (Conway 1982) which is situated closer to Bear Island. Mass-manufactured items became locally available in 1834 when the Hudson Bay Company opened an outpost on Lake Temagami. This post was subsequently moved to Bear Island in 1877 (Mitchell 1977). Bear Island is centrally located on Lake Temagami and would have been an ideal summer-gathering locale in the prehistoric past, just as it is today as the Indian reserve and village of the Teme-Augama Anishnabai.

On prehistoric archaeological sites, modern or twentieth-century occupations are considered by some archaeologists as intrusive disturbances. But, in fact, these occupations are as much a record of the cultural sequences of a site as the prehistoric occupations are. For example, various twentieth-century artifacts and soil features were noted at the Three Pines Site. These include food containers, construction hardware, coinage, ammunition, fishing and boating items, as well as a New York City transit token (Gordon 1987). Older hunting-camp hearths are indicated by thick organic deposits, cobbles, burned animal bone, ammunition, and coins dated 1939 and 1945. More recent features such as garbage-disposal pits, drainage ditches for tents, a large burnt-sand and cobble-picnic fire, and two outhouses built by the Ministry of Natural Resources attest to the varied recreational activities which occur at the site today. Some of these activities have buried and protected several features, while others have destroyed the underlying prehistoric layers (Gordon n.d.).

SUMMARY

The archaeological record of the Temagami region reveals a long period of occupation by prehistoric hunter-gatherers. Earliest occupations may extend back as far as deglaciation at 10,500 years ago. In the Archaic period, early occupations at one site on Lake Timiskaming are radiocarbon-dated to 5,000 years ago, while the Three Pines Site on Lake Temagami could have been occupied at least 6,400 years ago, based on site geochronology. Archaic-period occupations fall within the Hypsithermal climatic period when temperatures were higher and the Mixed Forest extended much farther north. The ceramic makers of the Initial Woodland period had a cooler climate. Laurel ceramic vessels are well represented in the Temagami region, as are tools of Hudson Bay Lowland chert, a favoured lithic resource. The Terminal Woodland period is signaled by the earlier cord-impressed vessels and later "Iroquoian-like" pottery, indicative of trade and other contacts with horticultural Iroquoian-speakers south of the Canadian Shield.

Although archaeological research in the Temagami region has barely "scratched the surface," many questions and possible avenues of future research have arisen. For example, finding hypothesized Palaeo-Indian occupations will require a different archaeological-survey strategy than that currently employed. It will be necessary to reconstruct regional palaeohydrology and then survey systematically ancient proglacial lakes and other former shorelines. Preliminary work indicates that these strandlines occur far inland from present-day lakes and rivers. Inland locations may also have been used by Archaic and Woodland groups as winter-habitation sites, when the need for protection from cold winds was a dominant factor in settlement selection. It is premature to propose formulae concerning the maximum distances at which archaeological sites should be found from present-day shorelines, without adequate archaeological research in the Mixed/Boreal Forest or without consideration of how drainage systems have altered since deglaciation with the combined effects of isostatic rebound and climatic change.

As stone tools and debitage are the most frequent artifacts recovered from Mixed/Boreal Forest sites, the accurate identification of tool

lithology by specialists in geology is increasingly important to archaeological research. By determining which specific materials were selected
by prehistoric tool makers, and drawing on information about local
bedrock formations and exposures, future archaeological researchers in
the Temagami region should be able to locate quarry sites and nearby
lithic-reduction sites. This technique was successfully used at Lake
Abitibi to locate the Mt. Goldsmith quarry and related sites (Pollock
1984; Kritsch-Armstrong 1982). In addition, by examining what local
lithic raw materials were exploited, and identifying the exotics in lithic
tool assemblages, archaeologists will be able to make more accurate
statements concerning prehistoric group movement and trade.

The archaeological resources of the Temagami region are valuable,
but also fragile. A single archaeological site, although occupied only on
a seasonal basis for a few weeks or months, can reveal a long record of
human activity over centuries, even millenia. Hunters and gatherers lost
or discarded a few items each time they reused a site. After centuries of
seasonal occupations, the most attractive locations will yield high-arti-
fact frequencies. Such sites are often situated on sand and gravel, the
same types of deposits and locales that have been used for logging-
boom access to the lakes, road-construction material, and tourist campsites.

Archaeological sites in the Temagami region, with their long record
of human occupation, can offer information on prehistoric hunting and
gathering technology, economy, and settlement patterns. They can
show how people adjusted and responded to changes in the natural
and cultural environments. The past of this country, of this Canada, is in
the ground — if only we have eyes to see it.

Acknowledgements: The Ontario Heritage Foundation provided major funding for the archaeological fieldwork and analysis through Archaeological Research Grants 333 and
337. Thesis proposal research was funded by the Presidential Committee on Northern
Science Training and Research, McMaster University. I would also like to acknowledge
the support of the Social Sciences and Humanities Research Council through the Doctoral Fellowship Program.

TABLE 1 — Stratigraphic Column for the Temagami Area (after Burbidge 1988) and Local Sources of Three Pines Site Lithics (Gordon n.d.)

PHANEROZOIC

Cenozoic   Glacial Deposits: Unconsolidated Sand and Gravel[1]
                 unconformity

Paleozoic   Temiscaming Outliner: Limestone, Dolostone[6]
                 unconformity

PRECAMBRIAN

Late Proterozoic   Grenville Province: Gneisses, Metagranitoid Rocks[5]
                         Grenville Front

Early Proterozoic   Nipissing Quartz Diabase[2]
                              intrusive contact
                         Huronian Supergroup (Southern Province)
                              Cobalt Group
                                   Bar River Formation [4]
                                   Gordon Lake Formation [4]
                                   Lorrain Formation [3,4]
                                   Gowganda Formation [1]
                                        Firstbrook Member
                                        Coleman Member
                                        unconformity

Late Archean   Metagranitoid, Metavolcanic, Metasedimentary Rocks
                     (Superior Province)

Legend: Local Raw Material Sources for Three Pines Site CgHa-6 Lithic Tools

[1] mudrocks, wackes and low metamorphic grade sandstone

[2] vein quartz; pottery temper

[3] hard granitoid and sandstone cobbles in glacial deposits; pottery temper

[4] metamorphosed olive-gray quartz siltstone

[5] mafic gneiss

[6] fossiliferous 'local' chert nodules in glacial deposits

FIGURE 1

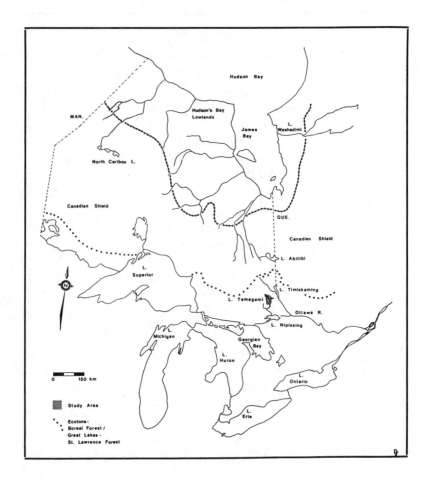

FIGURE 2

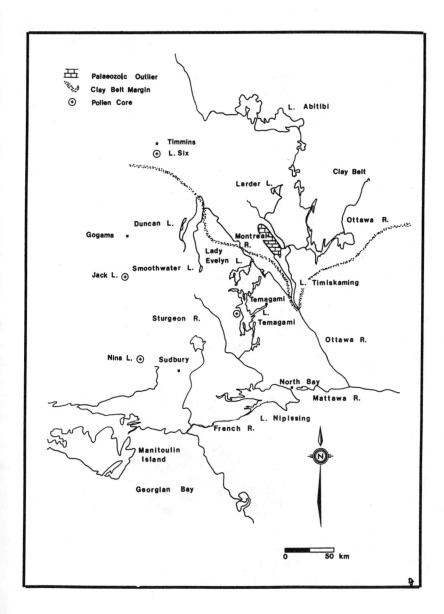

FIGURE 3 — Three Pines Bog

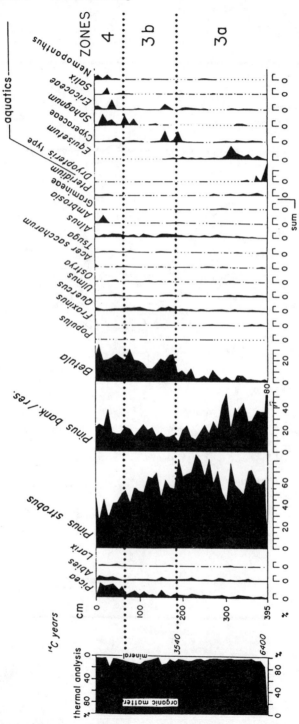

Glossary

Archean: Earliest Precambrian rocks

Argillite: A rock derived from siltstone, claystone, or shale

B.P.: Years before present

Basal: From the base

Biface: A stone tool worked on both faces

Calcinate: The removal of carbonates and hydrates from an organic or inorganic substance by burning or roasting

Cambrian: The earliest period of the Paleozoic era, thought to have covered the span of time between 570 and 500 million years ago

Castellation: One of a number of regular, pointed protuberances rising from the lip of a clay vessel

Cenozoic: The latest era of geologic time, which includes the Tertiary and Quaternary periods and which is characterized by the evolution of mammals, birds, plants, modern continents, and glaciation

CgHa-6: A code derived from the Borden Site Designation Scheme and referring to the Three Pines Site

Chert: A very fine-grained natural silicate with predictable flaking characteristics

Conchoidal: The shell-shaped fracture characteristic of a number of lithic materials used for aboriginal tool manufacture

Debitage: The waste material produced by tool knapping

Dentate: Tooth-like

Ecotone: The transition zone between two biologic communities

Erratics: Rocks transported, by glacial action, to another site

Esker: An often long, winding gravel ridge deposited by a subglacial stream

Flintknapper: A person who makes tools or other objects from flint

GaK-2802: A code referring to a specific radio-carbon test

Glaciolacustrine: Produced by the action of a glacier and water

Gneiss: A foliated (or layered) rock formed by regional metamorphism

Granitoid: Having the granular, crystalline structure of granite

Gunspall: A form of gunflint made by a punch technique which leaves a bulb of percussion

Holocene: Period dating from the end of the Pleistocene Age, 10,300 B.P.

Hypsithermal: That period of the geologically recent past (9,000 to 2,600 B.P.) when relatively warm conditions prevailed in the northern hemisphere

Igneous: Said of a rock or mineral solidified from molten or partially molten material. Igneous rocks constitute one of the three main classes into which rocks are divided, the others being metamorphic and sedimentary

Isostatic rebound: The return of a region of the earth's surface to its previous elevation following the retreat of a glacier

Knapper: The general term for a person who flakes stone to produce tools

Laurel: An initial Woodland culture common to northern Ontario

Lithic: Stone

Mafic: Said of igneous rock composed of one or more ferromagnesian, dark-coloured minerals

Mesozoic: An era of geologic time from the end of the Paleozoic to the beginning of the Cenozoic, or from about 225 to about 65 million years ago

Meta-: A prefix which, when used to describe rock, means changed

Metamorphic rock: Any rock which has been altered by heat or intense pressure, causing new minerals and structures

Moraine: An accumulation of earth and stones carried and ultimately deposited by a glacier

Outlier: A part of a formation left detached through the removal of surrounding parts by denudation

Palaeo: Ancient

Palaeohydrology: A study of ancient water levels

Paleozoic: An era of geologic time from the end of the Precambrian to the beginning of the Mesozoic, or from about 570 to about 250 million years ago.

Palynology: The study of ancient flora

Phalanges: A series of articulating bones of the hand or foot

Phanerozoic: That part of geologic time represented by rocks in which the evidence of life is abundant, that is, Cambrian or later times

Podzolic: A leached, zonal soil found under conifers

Precambrian: Dating from *c.* 2,000 million to 500 million B.P.

Proglacial: Situated just beyond the edge of a glacier

Proterozoic: The geological time and deposits of the Precambrian era, which lies between the Archeozoic era and the Cambrian period of the Paleozoic era

Rebound, Isostatic: See Isostatic rebound

Riverine: Produced by, or associated with, a river or river action

Sedimentary rock: Resulting from the consolidation of loose sediment that has accumulated in layers

Strandline: Line of contact between a lake and the land

Till: An unsorted mixture of clay, sand, gravel, and rocks which has been transported and deposited by a glacier

Wacke: A "dirty" sandstone that consists of a mixed variety of angular and unsorted or poorly sorted mineral and rock fragments in an abundant matrix of clay and fine silt

References

Borden Form
  1981   CgHa-6. Archaeological Site Record Form.
          Heritage Branch, Ontario Ministry of Culture and Recreation.

Boyle, David
  1900   *Archaeological Report 1899. Being Part of Appendix to the Report
          of the Minister of Education Ontario.* Toronto: L.K. Cameron.

  1902   *Archaeological Report 1901. Being Part of Appendix to the Report
          of the Minister of Education Ontario.* Toronto: L.K. Cameron.

  1904   *Archaeological Report 1903. Being Part of Appendix to the Report
          of the Minister of Education Ontario.* Toronto: L.K. Cameron.

  1905   *Archaeological Report 1904. Being Part of Appendix to the Re-
          port of the Minister of Education Ontario.* Toronto: L.K.
          Cameron.

Brizinski, Morris A.
  1980   Where Eagles Fly: An Archaeological Survey of Lake Nipissing.
          M.A. dissertation. Department of Anthropology, McMaster Uni-
          versity.

Brizinski, Morris A. and Howard Savage
  1983   "Dog Sacrifice among the Algonkian Indians: An Example from
          the Frank Bay Site." *Ontario Archaeology* 39:41-56.

Burbidge, Geof H.
  1988   Lake Temagami Archaeology: Geological Report on the Lithic
          Material from the Three Pines Site CgHa-6. Ms.

Butzer, Karl W.
  1982   *Archaeology as Human Ecology.* Cambridge: Cambridge Univer-
          sity Press.

Chism, James V.
  1977   Archaeology at Washadimi: The 1977 Field Summary. Ms. Direc-
          tion d'Archéologie et Ethnologie. Québec: Ministère des Affaires
          culturelles.

1978   Archaeology at Washadimi: the 1978 Chism Field Summary. Ms. Direction d'Archéologie et Ethnologie. Québec: Ministère des Affaires culturelles.

Conway, Thor
1982   A Preliminary Report on the Witch Point Site, Lake Temagami. Ms. Heritage Branch, Ontario Ministry of Citizenship and Culture.

1984   An Archaeological Assessment of Obabika Lake. Ms. Heritage Branch, Northeastern Region, Ministry of Citizenship and Culture.

1986a   The Sand Point Site. Ms. Heritage Branch, Northeastern Region, Ontario Ministry of Citizenship and Culture.

1986b   Algonkian Settlement Patterns in the Upper Great Lakes 1600 to 1900. Paper presented at the 19th annual meeting of the Canadian Archaeological Association. May. Toronto, Ontario.

Conway, Thor and Julie Conway
1989   "An Ethno-Archaeological Study of Algonkian Rock Art in Northeastern Ontario, Canada." *Ontario Archaeology* 49:34-59.

Dawson, K.C.A.
1983   "Cummins Site: A Late Palaeo-Indian (Plano) Site at Thunder Bay, Ontario." *Ontario Archaeology* 39:1-29.

Deller, D. Brian
1976   "Paleo-Indian Locations on Late Pleistocene Shorelines, Middlesex County, Ontario." *Ontario Archaeology* 26:3-19.

Dewdney, Selwyn and Kenneth Kidd
1967   *Indian Rock Paintings of the Great Lakes.* Toronto: University of Toronto Press, Second edition.

Ellis, C.J. and D. Brian Deller
1982   "Hi-Lo Materials from Southwestern Ontario." *Ontario Archaeology* 38:3-22.

Fox, William A.
1980   "The Lakehead Complex: New Insights." *Collected Archaeological Papers.* D.S. Melvin, ed. 127-51. Ontario Ministry of Culture and Recreation Archaeological Research Report 13.

Francis, Daniel and Toby Morantz
1983   *Partners in Furs: A History of the Fur Trade in Eastern James Bay 1600-1870.* Kingston: McGill-Queen's University Press.

Geological Survey of Canada (GSC)
1987   *Surficial Geology Map 1624A-Haileybury.* Ottawa: Surveys and
        Mapping Branch, Geological Survey of Canada.

Gordon, Diana Lynn
1980   "Reflections On Refuse: A Contemporary Example from James
        Bay, Quebec." *Canadian Journal of Archaeology 4:83-97.*

1985   *North Caribou Lake Archaeology.* Conservation Archaeology Re-
        port, Northwestern Region, Report No. 9. Ontario Ministry of Citi-
        zenship and Culture.

1986   Lake Temagami Archaeology, 1986. Preliminary Report on file at
        the Ontario Heritage Foundation, Ministry of Culture and Com-
        munications, Toronto.

1987   Archaeology at Lake Temagami, 1986. Final Field Report on file at
        the Ontario Heritage Foundation, Ministry of Culture and Com-
        munications, Toronto.

1988a   "Lake Temagami and the Northern Experience." *Arch Notes* 88-2:
        25-30, and *Nexus* 6: 3-9.

1988b   "Discovering Patterns of Change at North Caribou Lake in the
        Post-Contact Period: Implications for Finding and Interpreting the
        Archaeological Record." *Boreal Forest and Sub-arctic Archaeol-
        ogy.* C. S. Reid, ed. Occasional Publications of the London Chap-
        ter, Ontario Archaeological Society No. 6.

1989   Lake Temagami Archaeological Research: 1987-1988. Final Re-
        port. Ms. Ontario Heritage Foundation, Ministry of Culture and
        Communications, Toronto.

n.d.   A Contextual Approach to the Archaeology of Lake Temagami.
        Ph.D. dissertation. Dept. of Anthropology, McMaster University.

Greenman, Emerson
1943   "An Early Industry on a Raised Beach near Killarney, Ontario."
        American Antiquity 8: 260-5.

Hamilton, Scott
1981   *The Archaeology of the Wenasaga Rapids.* Archaeology Research
        Report 17. Toronto: Ontario Ministry of Culture and Recreation.

Harris, Edward C.
1979   *Principles of Archaeological Stratigraphy.* New York: Academic
        Press.

Heidenreich, Conrad
   1971   *Huronia: A History and Geography of the Huron Indians 1600-1650.* Toronto: McClelland and Stewart.

Hodgins, Bruce W.
   1976   *Paradis of Temagami.* Cobalt: Highway Book Shop.

Hodgins, Bruce W. and Jamie Benidickson
   1989   *The Temagami Experience: Recreation, Resources, and Aboriginal Rights in the Northern Ontario Wilderness.* Toronto: University of Toronto Press.

Irimoto, Takashi
   1980   *Chipewyan Ecology: Group Structure and Caribou Hunting System.* Senri Ethnological Studies No. 8. Osaka: National Museum of Ethnology.

Jenkins, William H.
   1939   *Notes on the Hunting Economy of the Abitibi Indians.* The Catholic University of America Anthropological Series No. 9.

Julig, Patrick J.
   1988   The Cummins Site Complex and Palaeo-Indian Occupations in the Northwest Lake Superior Region. Ph.D. dissertation. Department of Anthropology, University of Toronto.

Karrow, P.F. and R.S. Geddes
   1987   "Drift Carbonate on the Canadian Shield." *Canadian Journal of Earth Sciences* 24: 365-9.

Kritsch-Armstrong, Ingrid D.
   1982   Queries Near the Quarry: A Technological Analysis of the Jessup Lithic Workshop Site. M.A. dissertation. Department of Anthropology, McMaster University.

Knight, Dean H.
   1972   "Montreal River Salvage Operations – 1972." *Canadian Archaeological Association Bulletin* 4: 107-8.

   1977   The Montreal River and the Shield Archaic. Ph.D dissertation. Department of Anthropology, University of Toronto.

Lee, Thomas
    1957   "The Antiquity of the Sheguiandah Site." *Canadian Field-Naturalist* 71(3):117-37.

    1965   *Archaeological Investigations at Lake Abitibi 1964.* Travaux Divers 10. Centre d'Etudes Nordiques, Université Laval, Québec.

Liu, Kam-Biu
    n.d.   Holocene Paleoecology of the Boreal Forest and Great Lakes–St. Lawrence Forest in Northern Ontario. Ecological Monographs. In press.

Liu, Kam-Biu and Nina Siu-Ngan Lam
    1985   "Paleovegetational Reconstruction Based on Modern and Fossil Pollen Data: An Application of Discriminant Analysis." *Annals of the Association of American Geographers* 75(1) 115-30.

MacNeish, Richard S.
    1952   "A Possible Early Site in the Thunder Bay District, Ontario." *National Museum of Canada Bulletin* 126:23-47.

Marois, Roger J.M.
    1973   "Trois Rivières/Lac Abitibi." *Canadian Archaeological Association Bulletin* 5:146-8.

Martijn, Charles
    1985   "Le Complexe Plano de Temiscamie est-il une Illusion?" *Recherches Amèdiennes au Québec* 15 (1-2):161-4.

Martijn, Charles and Edward S. Rogers
    1969   *Mistassini-Albanel: Contributions to the Prehistory of Quebec.* Centre d'Etudes Nordiques, Travaux Divers 25, Université Laval.

Mitchell, Elaine Allan
    1977   *Fort Timiskaming and the Fur Trade.* Toronto: University of Toronto Press.

Noble, William C.
    1982   "Algonquian Archaeology in Northeastern Ontario." In *Approaches to Algonquian Archaeology.* 35-55. M. Hanna and B. Kooyman, eds. Chacmool: University of Calgary.

Phillips, W.H.C.
    1907   "Rock Paintings at Temagami District." *Archaeological Report*

1906. Being Part of Appendix to the Report of the Minister of Education Ontario, 41-7. Toronto: L.K. Cameron.

Pollock, John W.

1972   Report on an Archaeological Site Survey of Swastika District 1972. Unpublished Report. Ontario Ministry of Natural Resources.

1975   "Algonquian Culture Development and Archaeological Sequences in Northeastern Ontario." *Canadian Archaeological Association Bulletin* 7:1-53.

1976   *The Culture History of Kirkland Lake District, Northeastern Ontario*. Archaeological Survey of Canada. Mercury Series No. 54. Ottawa: National Museum of Man.

1984   A Technological Analysis of Lake Abitibi Bifaces. Ph.D. dissertation. Department of Anthropology, University of Alberta.

Ridley, Frank

1954   "The Frank Bay Site, Lake Nipissing, Ontario." *American Antiquity* 20:40-50.

1956   "An Archaeological Reconnaissance of Lake Abitibi, Ontario." *Ontario History* 43(1):18-23.

1958   "Sites on Ghost River, Lake Abitibi." *Pennsylvania Archaeologist* 28(1):3-20.

1963   "The Red Pine Point Site." *Anthropological Journal of Canada* 2(3):7-10.

1966   "Archaeology of Lake Abitibi Ontario-Quebec." *Anthropological Journal of Canada* 4(2):2-50.

Rogers, Edward S.

1962   *The Round Lake Ojibwa*. Art and Archaeology Occasional Papers 5. Toronto: Royal Ontario Museum.

1963a   "Changing Settlement Patterns of the Cree-Ojibwa of Northern Ontario." *Southwestern Journal of Anthropology* 19(1):64-88.

1963b   *The Hunting Group-Hunting Territory Complex among the Mistassini Indians*. National Museum of Canada Bulletin 195.

1966   "Subsistence Areas of the Cree-Ojibwa of the Eastern Subarctic: A Preliminary Study." In *Contributions to Anthropology* 1963-64, Part II, 87-118. National Museum of Canada Bulletin 204.

1967   *The Material Culture of the Mistassini*. National Museum of Canada Bulletin 218.

1969   "Band Organization among the Indians of Eastern Subarctic Canada." In *Contributions to Anthropology: Band Societies*. D. Damas, ed. 21-50. National Museum of Canada Bulletin 218.

1973   *The Quest for Food and Furs: The Mistassini Cree, 1953-1954*. Publications in Ethnology No. 5. Ottawa: National Museum of Man.

Rogers, Edward S. and Mary Black
1976   "Subsistence Strategy in the Fish and Hare Period, Northern Ontario: The Weagamow Ojibwa 1880-1920." *Journal of Anthropological Research* 32(1):1-43.

Saarnisto, Matti
1974   "The Deglaciation History of the Lake Superior Region and its Climatic Implications." *Quaternary Research* 4:316-39.

Smith, Beverley A.
1983   Faunal Analysis of the Witch Point Site (1982 excavation). Unpublished Ms.

Smith, Robin H.
1986   "Analysis of the Clay Tobacco Pipe Assemblage from the Front Street Site (AjGu-15), Toronto." *Ontario Archaeology* 46:55-61.

Speck, Frank G.
1951a   *Family Hunting Territories and Social Life of Various Algonkian Bands of the Ottawa Valley*. Geological Survey Memoir 70, Anthropological Series No. 8. Ottawa: Canada Department of Mines.

1915b   *Myths and Folk-lore of the Timiskaming Algonquin and Timagami Ojibwa*. Geological Survey Memoir 71, Anthropological Series No. 9. Ottawa: Canada Department of Mines.

Storck, Peter L.
1978   "Some Recent Developments in the Search for Early Man in Ontario." *Ontario Archaeology* 29:3-16.

1979   *A Report on the Banting and Hussey sites: Two Palaeo-Indian Campsites in Simcoe County, Southern Ontario*. Archaeological Survey of Canada. Mercury Series 93. National Museum of Man.

1982   "Palaeo-Indian Settlement Patterns Associated with the Strandline of Glacial Lake Algonquin in Southcentral Ontario." *Canadian Journal of Archaeology* 6:1-31.

1984   "Research into the Paleo-Indian Occupations of Ontario: A Review." *Ontario Archaeology* 41:3-28.

Tanner, Adrian
    1979   *Bringing Home Animals: Religious Ideology and Mode of Production of the Mistassini Cree Hunters.* St. John's: Memorial University of Newfoundland.

Trigger, Bruce G.
    1985   *Natives and Newcomers.* Montreal: McGill-Queen's University Press.

Veillette, Jean
    1983   "Déglaciation de la Vallée Supérieure de l'Outaouais, Le Lac Barlow et le Sud du Lac Ojibway, Québec." *Géographie physique et Quaternaire* 37(1):67-84.

    1988   "Déglaciation et Evolution des Lacs Proglaciaires Post-Algonquin et Barlow au Temiscamingue, Québec et Ontario." *Géographie physique et Quaternaire* 42(1):7-31.

    1989   "Ice Movements, Till Sheets and Glacial Transport in Abitibi-Timiskaming, Quebec and Ontario." In *Drift Prospecting.* R.N.W. Dilabio and W.B. Coker, eds. Geological Survey of Canada Paper, 89-120.

Wright, J.V.
    1967   *The Laurel Tradition and The Middle Woodland Period.* National Museum of Canada Bulletin 217.

    1972a   *The Shield Archaic.* Publications in Archaeology 3. National Museum of Man.

    1972b   *Ontario Prehistory.* Toronto: Van Nostrand and Reinhold.

At dispute in the Teme-Augama Anishnabai land claim are sacred sites such as the Conjuring Rocks on Obabika Lake. *Courtesy: Hap Wilson*

Eleven

The Temagami Indian Land Claim: Loosening the Judicial Strait-jacket*

Kent McNeil

The controversy over ownership, use, and development of the lands around Lake Temagami has many facets, all interconnected. Spiritual, ethical, and cultural values mingle with economic, political, and legal concerns. Given this complexity, no single approach can provide adequate solutions. This is particularly evident when *legal* solutions to the Temagami Indian land claim are sought. The Euro-Canadian legal system is simply not equipped to deal with many of the issues which must be addressed because they lie outside the realm of traditional legal analysis. But the difficulty extends much deeper than this. The aboriginal peoples of Canada have had virtually no input into the creation of the Euro-Canadian legal system, which for most of them is a foreign imposition. It does not reflect their values: indeed in many cases it has shown itself to be incapable of taking those values into account. For this reason, the appropriateness of deciding issues of aboriginal rights in Euro-Canadian courts needs to be questioned very seriously.

* I would like to thank Professor Brian Slattery for his very helpful comments on a draft of this article.

The Temagami Indian land claim has nonetheless come before the courts, and must be dealt with in the context of the Euro-Canadian legal system, however unsatisfactory that may be. So, keeping in mind the very real limitations of legal analysis, I am going to undertake a discussion of the main issues arising out of the Ontario Court of Appeal's decision on this claim, delivered on 27 February 1989, in *Attorney-General for Ontario* v. *Bear Island Foundation* (hereinafter the *Bear Island* case).[1] The Court of Appeal upheld the decision of Mr Justice Steele,[2] the trial judge in the Ontario Supreme Court, denying the Teme-Augama Anishnabai (the "Deep-Water People," referred to as the Temagami Indians in the judgments)[3] any right to the approximately 9,000 square kilometres of land claimed by them around Lake Temagami. On 19 October 1989, the Supreme Court of Canada granted leave to hear an appeal of the Court of Appeal's decision.

The case was the result of applications by the Bear Island Foundation, acting on behalf of the Teme-Augama Anishnabai, to file cautions in the Land Titles offices for Temiskaming, Nipissing, and Sudbury against the province of Ontario's alleged title to the lands. The Teme-Augama Anishnabai claim the area as their traditional homeland, which they call "N'Daki Menan" and which is referred to in the judgments as the "Land Claim Area." In response to those applications, the attorney general for Ontario commenced legal action against the foundation and certain members of the Teme-Augama Anishnabai, asking for, among other things, a declaration of the title of the Crown in Right of Ontario and a denial of any right of the defendants to the lands. The defendants counterclaimed for a declaration of their own title, based on their aboriginal rights and the terms of the Royal Proclamation of 1763, by which George III had reserved certain lands to the Indians for their use until they decided to dispose of those lands, which could be done only by sale to the crown at a public meeting of the Indians called for that purpose.[4]

Steele held that the province of Ontario was entitled to the declarations it sought, and that the defendants had failed to establish that they had aboriginal rights in the Land Claim Area, whether south of the height of land dividing the Hudson and the St Lawrence–Great Lakes watersheds, where the Royal Proclamation applies, or north of the height of land, where he held (erroneously, in my view) that the proclamation does not apply.[5] He decided that this aspect of the defendants' case failed because they did not prove to his satisfaction "that their ancestors were an organized band level of society in 1763; that, as an organized society, they had exclusive occupation of the Land Claim Area in 1763; or that, as an organized society, they continued to exclusively occupy and make aboriginal use of the Land Claim Area from 1763 or the time of coming of settlement to the date the action was commenced."[6] Apart from his questionable requirement, for which no authority was given, that occupation had to be continuous up to the commencement of legal action,[7] the criteria applied by Steele for proof of aboriginal title were enumerated in 1980 by Mr Justice Mahoney in *Baker Lake* v. *Minister of Indian Affairs.*[8]

Although the matter cannot be pursued here, I think that there are serious difficulties with Mahoney's criteria. For example, Mahoney did not explain why an organized society is a prerequisite to aboriginal title. If the explanation for this is that aboriginal title depends on the existence of an aboriginal system of property law which could arise only in an organized society,[9] what if that law did not provide for exclusive occupation by the society, another of Mahoney's requirements?[10] In this respect, Mahoney's criteria appear to be potentially inconsistent with one another, a problem arising from his failure to distinguish aboriginal law and occupation as distinct sources of aboriginal title.[11] One may ask as well why one aboriginal group could not replace another as the holders of aboriginal title to particular land after the crown's acquisition of sovereignty.[12]

In addition to the problems inherent in Mahoney's tests, it is doubtful whether those tests were even relevant to most, if not all, of the Land Claim Area. Even if Steele was correct in concluding that the lands north of the height of land were within Rupert's Land, the lands in the St Lawrence–Great Lakes watershed would have been within the former French colony of New France, which had been ceded to Britain by the Treaty of Paris in 1763 at the end of the Seven Years' War. Mahoney's tests for aboriginal title relate to a territory, such as Rupert's Land, which was deemed by the British crown not to be under the jurisdiction of a recognized sovereign, and which could therefore be acquired by the original mode of colonial acquisition known as settlement. They are inappropriate for a territory acquired derivatively by conquest or cession from another European sovereign, as New France had been, because in that case the law of the former sovereign and its application to the aboriginal peoples would have to be taken into account.[13] One cannot get around this complicating factor, as Steele attempted to do, by using 1763 as the relevant date for applying Mahoney's tests in the portion of Canada acquired by cession from France at that time.[14] To do so is to treat the French regime and French law as irrelevant to aboriginal rights, thereby offending the fundamental principle of British colonial law that in conquered and ceded territories the laws of the former sovereign, and any rights held by virtue of those laws, continue until repealed or abrogated by legislative act.[15]

On appeal from Steele's judgment, the Ontario Court of Appeal did not find it necessary to address the issue of proof of aboriginal title. Without "necessarily approving the views" of Steele in this regard, the Court of Appeal was "prepared to assume, without deciding, that the Temagami Indians in 1850 enjoyed aboriginal rights to at least some part of the Land Claim Area and that these rights extended to the use and occupation of the lands in the traditional ways of a band."[16] It was in 1850 that William Robinson, acting on behalf of Queen Victoria, signed the Robinson-Huron Treaty with named chiefs and "principal men" of the Ojibwa Indians inhabiting and claiming the eastern and northern shores of Lake Huron.[17] By that treaty, the Ojibwa signatories, on behalf of their respective tribes or bands, surrendered to the Queen all their rights to the territory described by the treaty in exchange for a lump-sum payment and perpetual annuities. Excluded from the territory surrendered were reservations, set forth in the schedule to the treaty, which were to be held and occupied in common by the Ojibwa chiefs and their tribes for their own use and benefit. In addition, by the treaty the Queen and the government of the province of Canada promised to allow the said chiefs and tribes "the full and free privilege" to hunt and fish as they had been "in the habit of doing" in the surrendered territory, except in portions sold or leased to individuals or companies.[18]

While avoiding the issue of whether the Temagami Indians had established their claim to aboriginal title, the Court of Appeal agreed with Steele that any aboriginal land rights they may have had prior to 1850 had been extinguished by the Robinson-Huron Treaty. The Court of Appeal based this conclusion on three different grounds, which may be briefly stated. First, the court said that the Temagami Indians were parties to the treaty. Secondly, even if they were not parties originally, they adhered to the treaty by accepting benefits under it, and so became parties. Thirdly, even if they did not surrender their aboriginal title by signing or adhering to the treaty, the crown unilaterally extinguished their title by means of the treaty because their lands were included within the treaty area. I am going to discuss each of these grounds in turn, under headings adopted from the Court of Appeal's judgment.

EXTINGUISHMENT BY SIGNING THE ROBINSON-HURON TREATY

The Court of Appeal decided first of all that one of the Ojibwa chiefs who signed the treaty, Chief Tawgaiwene,[19] represented the Temagami Indians and signed on their behalf. The Teme-Augama Anishnabai deny this. The issue, which is vital, is mainly a question of historical fact, to be decided (in the absence of a jury, as in this case) by the trial judge on the basis of all the evidence. Since, as Steele held at trial, the burden of proving extinguishment of aboriginal title is on the crown,[20] the onus was on counsel for the province of Ontario to establish on a balance of probabilities that the Temagami Indians were represented by Tawgaiwene when he signed the treaty. Steele found that this burden had been met. Although it is not my intention to review the evidence relied on by him in arriving at this conclusion, I would like to draw attention to two matters.

First, Steele prefaced his discussion of this issue with a significant statement of law: "A treaty is not a conveyance of title because title is already in the Crown. A treaty is merely a simple acknowledgement that may be formal or informal in nature."[21] This statement relates back to Steele's earlier treatment of the law respecting aboriginal title.

Whether arising independently or as a result of the Royal Proclamation of 1763, for him aboriginal title does not appear to be proprietary in nature.[22] Relying in part on the words of Lord Watson in 1888 in *St. Catherine's Milling and Lumber Company* v. *The Queen* that "the tenure of the Indians was a personal and usufructuary right, dependent upon the good will of the Sovereign,"[23] Steele concluded that there was no legal obligation on the British crown to acquire Indian lands by a formal surrender of aboriginal title. Since the crown already had title to those lands (the question of how the crown *obtained* title remains unanswered[24]), the negotiation of land-surrender treaties was merely a prudent policy designed primarily to avoid Indian insurrections.[25]

In my view, Steele misinterpreted this aspect of the *St. Catherine's* decision. In that case, Lord Watson held that Indian tenure under the Royal Proclamation was dependent upon the good will of the sovereign because the reservation of lands for Indian use by the proclamation had been "for the present," that is, until the further will of the crown should be known.[26] The significance of this will be discussed further below. The point made here is that, although his Lordship qualified Indian tenure in this way and described it as "a personal and usufructuary right," he did not deny that the Indians had a proprietary interest in the lands reserved for them. On the contrary, he concluded that they did have "an interest other than that of the Province,"[27] within the meaning of section 109 of the *British North America Act, 1867* (now the *Constitution Act, 1982*).[28] Subsequent cases have clarified that the term "personal" simply means that the Indian interest is inalienable, other than by surrender to the crown.[29] In a 1988 unanimous decision in *Canadian Pacific Limited* v. *Paul*, the Supreme Court of Canada did not accept an interpretation of the *St. Catharine's* decision that "Indian title is merely a personal right which cannot be elevated to the status of a proprietary interest so as to compete on an equal footing with other proprietary interests."[30]

In light of the *Canadian Pacific* decision in particular, Steele was clearly mistaken when he denied proprietary status to aboriginal title. That mistake led him to the equally erroneous conclusions that an Indian treaty "is not a conveyance of title" and therefore formalities appropriate to a conveyance of title need not be present. The suggestion made here is that these erroneous conclusions of law may have affected Steele's findings of fact. Because he thought a treaty could be "informal in nature," he may have been more willing to infer that Chief Tawgaiwene had signed the Robinson-Huron Treaty on behalf of the Temagami Indians, even though the evidence that Tawgaiwene represented them appears to have been largely circumstantial.[31] The question which I think needs to be asked in this context is whether Steele would have come to the same conclusion had he regarded aboriginal title as a proprietary interest in land to be protected by law like any other property interest until conveyed by appropriate formalities.[32]

The second matter I would like to draw attention to concerns the way Steele dealt with the evidence relating to this issue of whether Tawgaiwene represented the Temagami Indians. On more than one occasion, he drew inferences from action or inaction on the part of the Indians in relation to the treaty. For example, he found that Nebene-gwune, who, although chief or headman of the Temagami Indians, did not sign the treaty, acknowledged by accepting payment under the treaty that Tawgaiwene's signature bound him and his group.[33] Moreover, Steele concluded that"the other Indians who were present would have objected if Nebenegwune and his people were not entitled to be paid, because every payment could have had the effect of reducing the amount available to those who were entitled."[34] The problem with these inferences is that they rest on the assumption that Ojibwa Indians living around Lake Huron in 1850 would react in much the same way as persons of European origin would react in similar circumstances. This assumption reveals a regrettable lack of appreciation of cultural differences, which can often result in serious misunderstanding. Rupert Ross, a crown attorney in Kenora, Ontario, who is responsible for prosecutions on twenty-two remote Indian reserves, has provided perceptive insights on this problem in a recent article.[35] After twenty years' experience in northern Ontario, Ross writes that he is only beginning to understand the extent to which the culture and ethical norms of Indian communities differ from those of mainstream Canadian society. He gives a poignant illustration, which is best quoted in full:

192 / Kent McNeil

Most Europeans, for example, have an expectation that someone who will not look you straight in the eye is demonstrating
evasiveness. We suspect that we are being either brushed off or
lied to. When we wish to demonstrate our own sincerity and
respect, we make a point of squarely facing the other and establishing the strongest eye contact we can sustain. I have
learned, to my chagrin, that in some northern reserve communities looking another straight in the eye is taken as a deliberate
sign of disrespect, for their rule is that you only look inferiors
straight in the eye. Fortunately, I have not insulted too many
people, though only because they knew I was just an ignorant
white man who did not even know *how* to behave civilly. More
unfortunate was the fact that for many years I had been misin-
terpreting them, especially on the witness stand. I had been
reading evasiveness and insincerity and possible lies when I
should have been reading only respect and sincerity.[36]

To avoid grave errors when interpreting the words and actions of Indian persons, Ross says "we must learn, as best we can, to leave our
white eyes behind to a very significant degree."[37] So without evidence
that Ojibwa Indians would have reacted similarly to whites in the circumstances surrounding the signing of the 1850 treaty, there is no justification for drawing the kind of inferences Steele drew from Ojibwa behaviour.

No attempt can be made here to resolve the difficult question of
whether Steele was right or wrong in concluding that Chief Tawgaiwene signed the treaty on behalf of the Temagami Indians. The point is
simply that, if Steele's decision was influenced by an erroneous view of
the legal nature of aboriginal title and dubious assumptions respecting
the behaviour of Ojibwa Indians at the time the treaty was signed, his
conclusion on this essentially factual issue should not be accepted. The
rule is that an appeal court should not overturn findings of fact unless
the "trial judge made some palpable and overriding error which affected his assessment of the facts."[38] The judges of the Ontario Court of
Appeal decided that Steele's factual findings generally, and regarding

this matter in particular, did not constitute palpable and overriding error; moreover, they agreed with his findings.[39] Although they did not expressly adopt Steele's views on the nature of aboriginal title, the discussion in the following parts of this paper will show that they must have regarded aboriginal title as non-proprietary. As for relying on assumptions based on attitudes of Euro-Canadian society, the Court of Appeal drew the same kind of inferences from Ojibwa behaviour in 1850 as Steele had done.[40] It is therefore suggested that this aspect of the Court of Appeal's decision is no more reliable than Steele's. The matter can and should be re-examined by the Supreme Court of Canada because the erroneous views and questionable assumptions of the lower-court judges with respect to aboriginal title and Ojibwa society were palpable and overriding errors which probably affected their assessments of the facts.

EXTINGUISHMENT BY ADHESION TO THE ROBINSON-HURON TREATY

Even if the Temagami Indians were not made parties to the Robinson-Huron Treaty by the signature of Chief Tawgaiwene, the Court of Appeal agreed with Steele's alternative conclusion that they later adhered to the treaty by accepting benefits under it, specifically annuity payments and a reserve.

From 1850 to about 1856, annuity payments for the Temagami Indians appear to have been made to either Nebenegwune or Tawgaiwene pursuant to the treaty. These payments were then discontinued. In 1883 the Department of Indian Affairs, which had previously concluded that the Temagami Indians were *not* parties to the treaty,[41] decided to add them to the annuity list because they had expressed a willingness to come into the treaty. Annuity payments were made continuously from that year until 1979, when the cheques were returned by the Temagami Indians, who asserted that they had never surrendered their aboriginal rights.[42]

Although Steele concluded that the reserve designated by the treaty for Tawgaiwene and his band must have been for the Temagami Indians,[43] the Teme-Augama Anishnabai do not appear to have resided there. In 1881 their chief, Tonene, requested a reserve and annuity pay-

ments in return for the surrender of their lands.[44] We have seen that annuity payments began in 1883, but, in spite of repeated requests by the
Temagami Indians,[45] reserve lands were not set aside for them until
1943 and were officially made a reserve only in 1971 when the Bear Island Reserve was created.[46]

On the facts just summarized, Steele and the Court of Appeal decided that the Temagami Indians had adhered to the treaty. But although adhesions to Indian treaties are common enough, this is the
only instance I am aware of where an Indian tribe has been held to
have adhered to a treaty merely by accepting the benefits of it. Adhesions generally take the form of officially executed documents, which
are signed by the parties in the presence of witnesses after the terms of
the treaty have been interpreted and explained.[47] Moreover, many
tribes who have never signed treaties (in British Columbia, for example) receive federal money and have had reserves set aside for them.
The rationale for this would seem to be that, even in the absence of a
treaty, these tribes are entitled to benefits equivalent to those of treaty
Indians. Moreover, acceptance of federal money and reserves has not
been regarded as a justification for barring these tribes from bringing
aboriginal land claims.[48]

Neither Steele nor the Court of Appeal referred to any authority that
an Indian tribe can adhere to a treaty merely by accepting the benefits
of it. At the very least, one would expect the judges to have considered
in what circumstances, if any, non-signatories of other kinds of written
agreements, such as international treaties and contracts, can become
parties by accepting benefits under them.[49] For although the Supreme
Court of Canada has said that Indian treaties are unlike other agreements, being *sui generis*, the principles respecting international treaties
and contracts can be helpful by way of analogy when legal precedents
on Indian treaties are lacking.[50]

In my view, the explanation for the ready acceptance by Steele and
the Court of Appeal of adherence to the treaty lies in their attitude to
aboriginal title. We have already noticed Steele's view that, because
aboriginal title was non-proprietary, a treaty surrendering it to the
crown did not need to be formal in nature. As no conveyance of title

was involved, the formalities usually associated with a conveyance of title could be dispensed with. From this it followed that, in the case of adhesion to an existing treaty, there was no requirement that the Indians actually sign a document or even expressly agree to the treaty after the terms had been interpreted and explained to them.

Although the Court of Appeal judges did not comment directly on the legal status of aboriginal title, one can infer that, like Steele, they regarded it to be non-proprietary. Given the value of land rights and the importance of certainty of title, English law has always required strict compliance with formal procedures when title to land is conveyed. In transfers between private parties, at common law there generally had to be a feoffment with livery of seisin.[51] The crown could neither deliver nor accept title by livery, however, as that would be inconvenient and beneath the royal dignity.[52] If a person wanted to transfer title to the crown, that had to be done by a written deed, which at common law had to be enroled as a memorial of a court of record or parliament.[53] Although statutory provisions have largely replaced the common law respecting transfers of title to land, the basic requirement of formality remains. The fact that the Court of Appeal did not even consider what formalities were necessary at the relevant time for land titles generally to be transferred to the crown reveals that it probably regarded the aboriginal "title" of the Temagami Indians as non-proprietary.

This classification of aboriginal title probably explains why neither Steele nor the Court of Appeal bothered to specify precisely *when* the Temagami Indians adhered to the treaty. The Court of Appeal said: "The learned trial judge held that the acts of the Temagami Band in requesting to be added to the annuity list in 1882, the subsequent conduct in receiving payments, requesting and receiving a reserve, amounted to an adhesion to the Robinson-Huron Treaty and that the Temagami Band was therefore bound by its terms. We think he was right in so holding."[54] This may mean that the adhesion was not complete until a reserve had been received,[55] but did that happen when reserve lands were first set aside in 1943, or when the Bear Island Reserve was officially created in 1971? Perhaps it was not strictly necessary for the purposes of the legal action to decide this point, so long as the ad-

196 / Kent McNeil

hesion took place before the action was commenced. But what, then, would be the status of land grants made by the crown in the Land Claim Area prior to 1971? As we now know that aboriginal title is proprietary in nature,[56] pre-adhesion crown grants would be either invalid or subject to the Temagami Indians' aboriginal title,[57] because there is a fundamental common-law rule that the crown cannot derogate from vested property rights by grant.[58] It would thus be vital to know when the adhesion took place to determine which land titles were affected. Steele avoided this problem by expressly holding that aboriginal title can be extinguished by crown grant,[59] a conclusion which is consistent with his apparent classification of aboriginal title as non-proprietary. Although the judges of the Court of Appeal did not deal with the issue of grants, it seems likely that they agreed with Steele in this regard, for otherwise one would expect them to have specified when the adhesion took place.[60]

Before moving on to the Court of Appeal's third ground for rejecting the appeal, one further matter deserves attention. Before that court, counsel for the Temagami Indians had argued that there could be no surrender of aboriginal title by informal adhesion to the treaty because that would violate the Royal Proclamation of 1763. We have seen that the proclamation provided, among other things, that if any Indians should be inclined to dispose of the lands reserved for them, those lands could be purchased only by the crown at a public meeting or assembly of the Indians concerned. The Court of Appeal, while doubting whether this provision applied to the Land Claim Area,[61] decided that it had been repealed in 1774 by the *Quebec Act*.[62] This is surprising, given that the crown followed the public-meeting procedure in the Robinson-Huron Treaty and the eleven numbered treaties which followed. Moreover, on numerous occasions Canadian courts, including the Supreme Court of Canada, have treated the provisions of the proclamation relating to Indian lands as generally still in force.[63] The Court of Appeal apparently relied on section 4 of the *Quebec Act*, which revoked and annulled the proclamation in so far as it related to the province of Quebec, which as defined by the act probably included most, if not all, of the lands claimed by the Temagami Indians. The preamble to that section, however, reveals that the imperial parliament was concerned with problems associated with the application of the proclamation to the *French* inhabitants of Quebec, not with the matter of Indian lands. In my view, to read that section as repealing the requirement of a public meeting for the surrender of aboriginal title is entirely unjustified. But even if the *Quebec Act* did have that effect, it would not necessarily follow, as the Court of Appeal thought, that "at the relevant times there was in existence no positive law prescribing the manner in which aboriginal rights could be ceded to the Crown."[64] Irrespective of whether the proclamation was in force, we have seen that formalities appropriate to a transfer of title to land would be required because aboriginal title is proprietary in nature. Once again, the judges of the Court of Appeal by this statement implicitly revealed that they regarded aboriginal title as non-proprietary, a view which is clearly untenable in light of the decision of the Supreme Court of Canada in *Canadian Pacific Limited* v. *Paul*.[65]

THE ROBINSON-HURON TREATY AS A SOVEREIGN ACT OF EXTINGUISHMENT

The third reason given by the Court of Appeal for dismissing the appeal was that, even if the Temagami Indians did not sign or adhere to it, the Robinson-Huron Treaty was "an expression of the will of the sovereign to extinguish aboriginal rights."[66] In other words, the crown could unilaterally extinguish aboriginal title to an area by means of a treaty, even if the Indians living there never became parties to it.[67] This is the most disturbing and, in my view, the most wrong-headed aspect of the decision.

The holding that the treaty unilaterally extinguished the Temagami Indians' aboriginal title depends on the court's conclusion that their lands were within the treaty area. In the court's view, this was so obvious that it could not "be reasonably argued otherwise."[68] The court based this conclusion on the description of lands contained in the treaty, which it quoted as follows: "the Eastern and Northern Shores of Lake Huron, from Penetanguishene to Sault Ste. Marie, and thence to Batchewanaung Bay, on the Northern Shore of Lake Superior; together with the Islands in the said Lakes, opposite to the Shores thereof, and inland to the Height of land which separates the Territory covered by the charter of the Honorable Hudson Bay Company from Canada; as well as all unconceded lands within the limits of Canada West to which they have any just claim ... "[69]

The court then stated: "The eastern boundary of Canada West was the same boundary as now exists between Ontario and Quebec and includes Lakes Temiskaming, Nipissing and Temagami. This interpretation of the land described in the treaty is confirmed by subsequent events."[70]

Looking at the treaty itself, one sees that the portion quoted by the court is preceded by a list of the names of the Ojibwa signatories "inhabiting and claiming the Eastern and Northern Shores of Lake Huron..." (the text continues as in the above quotation).[71] The actual disposition of lands is in the next paragraph, whereby the named chiefs and principal men, on behalf of their tribes or bands, surrendered to the crown "all their right, title, and interest to, and in the whole of, the territory above described, save and except the reservations set forth in the schedule hereunto annexed."[72]

In my view, there are two serious problems with the Court of Appeal's conclusion respecting the extent of lands surrendered by the treaty. First, the treaty does not say that the *whole territory* described is being surrendered; instead, it says that the named Ojibwa leaders are surrendering all *their rights* to and in the whole of that territory, as well as anywhere else in Canada West (reservations excepted).[73] Accordingly, only the land rights of *those* leaders and *their* tribes or bands were surrendered. On its face, the treaty could not have been intended to extinguish the land rights of Indians who did not sign, whether their lands were inside or outside the territory referred to.

Secondly, the treaty manifestly does not contain a complete description of the territory covered by it. The description begins at Penetanguishene near the south end of Georgian Bay, and then runs north and west, presumably along the shore, through Sault Ste Marie to Batchewanaung Bay (now Batchawana Bay) on Lake Superior. Included are the islands opposite the shore, and the territory inland to the height of land forming the boundary with the territory granted to the Hudson's Bay Company in 1670.[74] One can reach the height of land marking the southern extent of the Hudson watershed by drawing a straight line northward from Batchewana Bay,[75] but any straight line from Penetanguishene to the height of land has to pass through the Severn Sound portion of Georgian Bay. This makes little sense, as it places a portion of the "inland" boundary off-shore.[76] If the treaty-makers intended to establish a boundary from Penetanguishene inland to the height of land, they clearly failed to indicate where that boundary was to be located.

So on what basis did the Court of Appeal conclude that the Land Claim Area is within the treaty area? Apparently the court thought that the eastern boundary of Canada West was also the eastern boundary of the treaty area because "all unconceded lands within the limits of Canada West to which they [the Ojibwa signatories] have any just claim" were included in the surrender.[77] Since these "unconceded lands"[78] might be anywhere in Canada West, however, it is extremely unlikely that the words of the treaty just quoted were intended as a description of the treaty area.[79] Rather, these words must have been inserted to ensure that the Ojibwa chiefs who signed the treaty would not lay claim later to lands elsewhere in Canada West.

In my view, the makers of the treaty did not provide a precise description of the lands surrendered by it because that was not their intention.[80] Instead, they described the general area where the Ojibwa leaders who signed the treaty lived, and relied on the outright surrender of land rights of the Ojibwa parties within that area and, just to be sure, anywhere else in Canada West as well. So the only lands being surrendered were those of the Ojibwa Indians who took part. The lands of Indian tribes who did not sign, wherever located, were not included. That the crown itself so interpreted the treaty is confirmed by the fact that in 1923 His Majesty signed another treaty with certain tribes of Chippewa Indians for a surrender of all their rights to lands on the northeast shore of Georgian Bay from the French River south, and east as far as the Ottawa River, a surrender which included lands on Georgian Bay which were apparently located within the same vaguely defined general area referred to in the Robinson-Huron Treaty.[81]

My conclusion on this issue is that it cannot be said with any certainty that the lands claimed by the Temagami Indians are within the treaty area because the treaty provides no clear description of that area. Moreover, if the Temagami Indians did not sign or adhere to the treaty, even if their lands are within the treaty area their rights could not be extinguished by the treaty because only the land rights of the Ojibwa signatories were dealt with. I have little doubt that this is how the treaty should be interpreted. But if the treaty is found to be ambiguous in these respects, the rule laid down by the Supreme Court of Canada is that ambiguities in treaties should be resolved in favour of the Indians.[82] Moreover, where property rights are concerned there is a general rule that executive and legislative acts should be strictly construed in favour of protecting those rights.[83] If these rules of interpretation are applied to the treaty, any ambiguities respecting the area covered and the application of the treaty to the lands of Indians who were not parties should be resolved in favour of the Temagami Indians. Their aboriginal rights would not be affected by the treaty unless they signed or adhered to it.

But even if we *assume* that the lands claimed by the Temagami Indians are within the treaty area, and that the crown intended to extinguish their rights by the treaty, I think the Court of Appeal's conclusion that the crown can unilaterally extinguish aboriginal title in this way is simply wrong. The judges of that court prefaced their discussion of this issue with a general statement that aboriginal rights, whether at common law alone or recognized by the Royal Proclamation of 1763, "exist at the pleasure of the Crown."[84] They then quoted a portion of the proclamation which declares it to be the crown's "Will and Pleasure, for the present as aforesaid, to reserve under our Sovereignty, Protection, and Dominion, for the use of the said Indians," all lands within a vast, vaguely defined area, which may be referred to as the "Indian territory."[85] Equivalent words — "for the present, and until our further Pleasure be known" — qualify another provision forbidding governors in Britain's older American colonies from granting survey warrants and patents for lands within the Indian territory or anywhere else, "which, not having been ceded to or purchased by Us as aforesaid, are reserved to the said Indians" (significantly, a similar restriction on surveys and patents by the governor of Quebec was not so qualified).[86] The words "for the present" reveal that the crown anticipated that the extent of the lands expressly reserved as Indian territory would not be permanent. The proclamation envisages that the limits of that territory could and would be changed as Indian nations surrendered their lands to the crown, making those lands available for survey and patent.[87]

Yet the *general* recognition and protection which the proclamation accords to Indian land rights are not temporary in nature.[88] The Indian provisions start with a preamble which recognizes in unqualified terms that lands possessed by the Indian nations which have not been ceded to or purchased by the crown are reserved to them as their hunting grounds.[89] The proclamation's prohibitions on purchases and settlement of Indian lands by the crown's European subjects are likewise unqualified in time. Moreover, there are no words such as "for the present" limiting the protective requirement that crown purchases of reserved lands can take place only at a public assembly of Indians who are inclined to dispose of their lands.[90]

Notwithstanding the fact that the words "for the present" relate only to the proclamation's express reservation of lands within the Indian territory and the prohibition of surveys and patents by governors of the old American colonies, in the *St. Catherine's* case Lord Watson relied on those words to conclude that "the tenure of the Indians was a personal and usufructuary right, dependent upon the good will of the Sovereign."[91] He seems to have thought that the words "for the present" qualify the Indian provisions generally, and so have to be taken into account in determining the nature of Indian tenure under the proclamation. But Lord Watson's approach gives those words an impact which is inconsistent with the proclamation's terms. The overall tenor of the Indian provisions reveals a clear intent to acknowledge and protect Indian land rights, not to impose a narrow definition on those rights and subject them to the crown's good will.[92] For the same reason, the conclusion of the Ontario Court of Appeal in *Bear Island* that aboriginal rights which are recognized by the proclamation "exist at the pleasure of the Crown"[93] cannot be sustained.

The words "for the present" may, however, have been included in the proclamation for a purpose beyond that of envisaging that lands within the Indian territory would become available for survey and patent as the Indian nations voluntarily surrendered them to the crown. Perhaps the crown contemplated amending the provisions to which those words relate at some future time. The crown may have meant those words to give notice that it could, for example, unilaterally withdraw lands from the Indian territory if it so desired. If that was the intention (which I doubt), would this reservation of a limited power of amendment have been valid within the territory acquired from France by the Treaty of Paris in 1763?

Because New France was a conquered and ceded territory, the crown would not have had prerogative legislative power there until English law was introduced or a local legislative assembly was promised or created.[94] For this reason, the proclamation's Indian provisions would have been valid in the former French territory, even to the extent that they had legislative effect.[95] Among the proclamation's other provisions, however, is a declaration that English law would apply and legislative assemblies would be set up in the colonies, including Quebec, which were created out of the territories acquired by the Treaty of Paris. Consequently, by its own act the crown lost its general legislative authority there.[96] As defined by the proclamation, the colony of Quebec would have included neither the lands in question in the *St. Catherine's* case nor the lands claimed by the Temagami Indians, but the *Quebec Act*[97] of 1774 extended the colony so that the *St. Catherine's* lands and most, if not all, of the Temagami Land Claim Area would have been within its boundaries.[98] Without a reservation in the proclamation of legislative authority, this extension of Quebec's boundaries would have taken away the power which the crown previously had to legislate with respect to those lands.

In British colonial law, the crown can expressly reserve legislative power to itself when it establishes a legislative assembly in a conquered or ceded territory.[99] As a matter of principle, however, the manner in which this power is exercised should conform with certain norms. If, for example, the crown retained legislative power over property rights generally in a conquered or ceded colony such as Quebec, it could no doubt infringe or extinguish those rights by Order in Council or proclamation.[100] Given the reservation of power, those would be legislative acts, and would take effect as such. If, on the other hand, the crown simply seized private property into its own hands or issued grants of privately owned lands to third parties, surely those actions would not qualify as legislative acts. On the contrary, they would be equivalent to acts of state which the crown cannot commit within its own dominions.[101] In other words, to qualify as legislative acts the actions of the crown would have to abide by the manner and form appropriate to acts of that kind. They could not be arbitrary acts of sovereign power.

If this reasoning is applied to the Royal Proclamation of 1763, the words "for the present" may have reserved legislative power to the crown to amend the parts of the proclamation to which those words relate.[102] Thus the crown by a subsequent proclamation could have lifted the restriction on surveys and patents by the governors of the old American colonies and redefined the extent of the Indian territory.[103] Yet the crown could not take away lands reserved for the Indians, whether within that territory or elsewhere, by granting them to third parties or unilaterally executing a treaty. Since individual grants could not take effect as amendments to the proclamation, at best they would be non-legislative attempts to deviate from the proclamation's terms, and as such would be of no force or effect.[104] As for unilaterally executed treaties, even if authorized and ratified by Orders in Council (as the Robinson-Huron Treaty apparently was[105]), they could not operate as legislative exceptions to the public-assembly procedure set out in the proclamation because the crown did not reserve authority to itself to alter that procedure. Although the restrictions on grants by certain colonial governors and the reservation of the Indian territory were "for the present," no such words qualify the requirement that reserved lands can be purchased only by the crown at an assembly of the Indians concerned. Consequently, the crown could not amend or repeal the public-assembly procedure.[106] *A fortiori*, it could not avoid that procedure by unilaterally executing a treaty.

But even supposing the crown had used its reserved legislative power to amend the proclamation's provisions by lifting the restrictions on grants or diminishing the extent of the Indian territory (which was never done), this would *not* mean that the land rights of Indian nations affected by the amendments would be without legal protection. As we have seen, the proclamation recognizes that *all* unceded Indian lands, whether within the Indian territory or not, are reserved for the Indians' use.[107] More important still, although the Privy Council in the *St. Catherine's* case appears to have regarded the proclamation as the sole basis for Indian title,[108] subsequent decisions have clearly held that aboriginal land rights do not depend on the proclamation for their existence. In *Guerin* v. *The Queen,* decided in 1984, Mr Justice Dickson said that there was an "assumption implicit in *Calder* that Indian title is an independent legal right which, although recognized by the Royal Proclamation of 1763, nonetheless predates it."[109] He found support for this assumption in "the principle that a change in sovereignty over a particular territory does not in general affect the presumptive title of the inhabitants."[110] Applying Dickson's views on this matter to lands within New France which were occupied by Indian nations when that territory was ceded by France to Britain in 1763,[111] we can conclude that the Indians had aboriginal title to those lands and that their title was not affected by the change in sovereignty.[112] Since the effect of the proclamation would have been merely to recognize this pre-existing title, the repeal *in toto* of the proclamation by an act of the imperial parliament would have removed the recognition but would not have impaired the title.

To conclude our discussion of the Royal Proclamation and the *St. Catherine's* case, we have seen that Lord Watson's opinion that Indian title was "dependent upon the good will of the Sovereign" was based on a misleading oversimplification of the proclamation's terms. That in itself is a sufficient reason for rejecting his view on this matter. Moreover, Lord Watson's words must be read in light of his conclusion that the proclamation was the sole source of Indian title. Since the Supreme Court of Canada has gone beyond that conclusion, and decided that aboriginal land rights *predate* the proclamation, any basis for crown authority over those rights has disappeared.[113] Power to infringe or extinguish aboriginal land rights cannot be derived from the power the crown may have retained to amend some of the proclamation's terms. The Supreme Court has said that the aboriginal title which predates the proclamation is proprietary, and in Anglo-Canadian law property rights are not subject to infringement or extinguishment by prerogative act, whether in the form of a grant, treaty, or act of state.[114] Only legislation can interfere with vested rights, and, apart from the possible amending power over parts of the proclamation itself, the crown relinquished legislative authority in the colony of Quebec when it made provision in the proclamation for a legislative assembly.[115]

In the *Bear Island* case, the judges of the Court of Appeal none the less thought there was other authority for their view "that the sovereign power can unilaterally extinguish aboriginal rights."[116] They referred first to the 1973 *Calder* decision, where both Justices Judson and Hall quoted the United States Supreme Court as authority for their opinion that aboriginal title can be extinguished "by treaty, by the sword, by purchase, by the exercise of complete dominion adverse to the right of occupancy, or otherwise."[117] Yet, although Judson appears to have agreed with this view, Hall did not. Referring to the Nishga Indians who asserted their aboriginal title in *Calder*, Hall said: "When the Nishga people came under British sovereignty ... they were entitled to assert, as a legal right, their Indian title. It being a legal right, it could not thereafter be extinguished except by surrender to the Crown or by competent legislative authority, and then only by specific legislation."[118] Since Judson and Hall were each speaking for three members of the Supreme Court, the *Calder* decision left open this issue of how aboriginal title can be extinguished.

In *Bear Island*, the Court of Appeal also relied on *State of Idaho* v. *Coffee*,[119] a 1976 decision of the Supreme Court of Idaho. In that case the Idaho Court held that an Indian treaty ratified by the United States Senate in 1859 extinguished the aboriginal title of the Kootenai Indians to lands within the treaty area, even though they did not sign it. In the majority judgment, Chief Justice McFadden wrote:

> Whether the Indians signing the treaty had the power to give the land away is not relevant. The United States did have the

power to take the land, and when it said it was receiving the land, the effect was that the land was taken. Remembering that the Indian title is only a revocable right of occupancy granted by the United States, it is inferable in any Indian treaty that the government intends to take the land ceded in the treaty. A treaty, when made effectual, becomes the law of the land as much as any legislation. [U.S. Const. Art. 6]. By ratifying the treaty and terms of the treaty by which the United States took possession of the relevant land, the Senate put the force of law into the taking of the land. Thus, Indian title was extinguished on July 16, 1859, when the treaty ratification expressed the congressional intent to take possession of the land.[120]

Agreeing with McFadden, the Court of Appeal in *Bear Island* observed: "The reference to the United States Constitution and the method of ratification in the judgment does not make the general principle any less applicable in this country."[121] But these matters do make a difference. The treaty in question was ratified by the Senate, a legislative body which has specific authority under article II, section 2(2), of the American Constitution to consent to treaties (including Indian treaties), which then have the force of law owing to article VI, section 2. In contrast, the Robinson-Huron Treaty was made by the crown in its executive capacity, acting through the governor general in council. In Anglo-Canadian law, there is a constitutional rule that the crown cannot infringe the rights of third parties by an executive act, such as the signing of a treaty.[122]

There is an even more fundamental reason why the *Coffee* decision is not applicable in Canada. As McFadden said in the passage quoted above, in American law "Indian title is only a revocable right of occupancy granted by the United States." For authority, McFadden relied primarily on *Tee-Hit-Ton Indians* v. *United States*, where Justice Reed's majority judgment referred to the aboriginal interest in land "after the coming of the white man" as "original Indian title or permission from the whites to occupy."[123] Reed continued: "This is not a property right but amounts to a right of occupancy which the sovereign grants and protects against intrusion by third parties but which right of occupancy may be terminated and such lands fully disposed of by the sovereign itself without any legally enforceable obligation to compensate the Indians."[124] The American position that aboriginal title is a non-proprietary right of occupancy derived from the United States as sovereign is in stark contrast to the Canadian position that aboriginal title is a right of property predating the crown's acquisition of sovereignty. The American cases on this matter, including *Coffee*, are therefore inapplicable in Canada.

So on the issue of unilateral extinguishment by treaty, the judges of the Court of Appeal in *Bear Island* were misled by American authority and Lord Watson's interpretation of the Royal Proclamation. Had they realized that aboriginal title in Canada is a proprietary interest which does not depend on the proclamation for its existence, they could have avoided the erroneous conclusion that the crown extinguished the aboriginal title of the Temagami Indians unilaterally by executing the treaty.

CONCLUSION

The 1888 decision of the Privy Council in the *St. Catherine's* case is usually taken as the starting-point for judicial treatment of aboriginal land rights in Canada. Relying on the Royal Proclamation, their Lordships took a restrictive view which effectively placed a judicial straitjacket on the concept of aboriginal title. That restrictive garment remained in place for eighty-five years. The process of removing it began in 1973 when the Supreme Court of Canada in *Calder* acknowledged that the proclamation is not the sole source of aboriginal land rights. This process has continued over the past two decades as the Supreme Court has cautiously untied more of the strait-jacket's laces. While avoiding a precise definition of aboriginal title, the court has made clear that it is a proprietary interest which predates the crown's assertion of sovereignty over Canada and exists independently of any executive or legislative act. As a proprietary interest, aboriginal title stands on the same footing as other proprietary interests, and is therefore entitled to the same respect and protection.

Unfortunately, the Ontario Court of Appeal does not seem to appreciate what the Supreme Court has been doing. The Court of Appeal's decision in the *Bear Island* case is pre-*Calder* in tone — it is rooted in attitudes to aboriginal rights which are no longer viable. By granting leave to appeal, the Supreme Court has accepted the task of reassessing the case. Let us hope that the judges of Canada's highest court will use the opportunity to loosen even further the unjustifiable restraints which the Privy Council placed on aboriginal title over a century ago.

These endnotes contain legal citations that may be unfamiliar to some readers. For their convenience, the citations contained in this paper are as follows:

A.C. = Law Reports, Appeal Cases, 1891– (Britain)

All E.R. = All England Law Reports

App. Cas. = Law Reports, Appeal Cases 1875-90 (Britain)

C.N.L.R. =Canadian Native Law Reporter

Co. R. =Coke's English King's Bench Reports

D.L.R. = Dominion Law Reports (Canada)

Ex. C.R. = Reports of the Exchequer Court of Canada

F. = Federal Reporter (United States)

F.C. = Canada Federal Court Reports

Geo. = King George (statutes)

Holt K.B. = Holt's English King's Bench Reports

Imp. = Imperial (Britain)

L.C.R. = Lower Canada Reports

L.R.P.C. = Law Reports, Privy Council (Britain)

Lofft = Lofft's English King's Bench Reports

N.S.R. = Nova Scotia Reports

N.Z.P.C.C. = New Zealand Privy Council Cases

O.L.R. = Ontario Law Reports

P.= Pacific Reporter (United States)

P. Wms. = Peere Williams' English Chancery and King's Bench Reports

Pet. = Peters' Reports (United States)

Plow. = Plowden's English King's Bench Reports

Q.B. = Law Reports, Queen's Bench (Britain)

R.S.C. = Revised Statutes of Canada

S.C.R. = Canada Supreme Court Reports

St. Tr. = State Trials (Britain)

U.S. = United States Supreme Court Reports

Vict. = Queen Victoria (statutes)

W.L.R. = Weekly Law Reports (Britain)

W.W.R. = Western Weekly Reports (Canada)

1   (1989) 58 D.L.R. (4th) 117, 68 O.R. (2d) 394, [1989] 2 C.N.L.R. 73, hereafter cited to C.N.L.R.

2   (1984) 15 D.L.R. (4th) 321, 49 O.R. (2d) 353, [1985] 1 C.N.L.R. 1, hereafter cited to C.N.L.R.

3   In this paper, "Teme-Augama Anishnabai" (also spelled Teme-Agama Anishnabay) and "Temagami Indians" will be used interchangeably.

4   The background and nature of the legal action are outlined in Steele's judgment, [1985] 1 C.N.L.R. 1, at 7–9. The Royal Proclamation is in R.S.C. 1985, appendix II, No. 1.

5   Steele concluded that the proclamation does not apply to lands *north* of the height of land because, until 1870, they were within Rupert's Land, the territory granted to the Hudson's Bay Company by Charles II in 1670: [1985] 1 C.N.L.R. 1, at 32. However, in the *Ontario Boundaries Case* (Privy Council, 22 July 1884, Report Embodied in Imperial Order in Council, 11 August 1884, reproduced in *The Proceedings before the ... Privy Council ... Respecting the Westerly Boundary of Ontario* (Toronto: Warwick and Sons, 1889), at 416–18), it was decided that the southern boundary of Rupert's Land, at least from 1774 to 1870 in what is now northwestern Ontario, was north of the height of land: see discussion in K. McNeil, *Native Rights and the Boundaries of Rupert's Land and the North-Western Territory* (Saskatoon: University of Saskatchewan Native Law Centre, 1982), especially 26–33. Steele does not seem to have been aware that *St. Catherine's Milling and Lumber Company* v. *The Queen* (1888) 14 App. Cas. 46, one of the principal

authorities cited by him on the application of the Royal Proclamation, in fact involved lands in northwestern Ontario which are *north* of the height of land. Moreover, the application of the proclamation in Rupert's Land is also controversial: see K. M. Narvey, "The Royal Proclamation of 7 October 1763, the Common Law, and Native Rights to Land Within the Territory Granted to the Hudson's Bay Company" (1973–74) 38 *Saskatchewan Law Review* 123, and "Letter to the Editor: The Supreme Court, the Federal Court of Canada, and the Royal Proclamation of 1763 in Rupert's Land" [1980] 2 C.N.L.R. 109; B. Slattery, *The Land Rights of Indigenous Canadian Peoples* (D. Phil. thesis, Oxford University, 1979, reprinted Saskatoon: University of Saskatchewan Native Law Centre, 1979), 211–12, 258–60; G. S. Lester, *The Territorial Rights of the Inuit of the Canadian Northwest Territories*: A Legal Argument (D. Jur. thesis, York University, 1981), 1084–1181; K. McNeil, *Common Law Aboriginal Title* (Oxford: Clarendon Press, 1989), 274–5.

6   [1985] 1 C.N.L.R. 1, at 21; see also 40–77, where the evidence on these issues is reviewed.

7   In the absence of adverse possession, as a general rule title to land cannot be lost by abandonment: see McNeil (1989), *supra*, n. 5, at 63–73. However, in the United States aboriginal title (or original Indian title, as it is more often called) can be lost in this way: see *Mitchel* v. *United States*, 9 Pet. 711 (1835), at 746; *Buttz* v. *Northern Pacific Railroad,* 119 U.S. 55 (1886), at 70; *Northwestern Shoshone Indians* v. *United States*, 324 US 335 (1945), at 339. The explanation for this is that in the United States, unlike in Canada, aboriginal title is not proprietary in nature: see discussion in text accompanying nn. 119–24, *infra.*

8   [1980] 1 F.C. 518, at 557–8, where Mahoney said that plaintiffs claiming aboriginal title must prove: ":1. that they and their ancestors were members of an organized society, 2. that the organized society occupied the specific territory over which they assert the aboriginal title, 3. that the occupation was to the exclusion of other organized societies, 4. that the occupation was an established fact at the time sovereignty was asserted by England."

9   This appears to be the view adopted by Steele: see [1985] 1 C.N.L.R. 1, at 16, where he said that included with the evidence of an organized society "would be proof that there was an organized system of landholding and a system of social rules and customs distinct to the band."

10   In the United States, aboriginal occupation can be by more than one group provided they are on amicable terms: see *Turtle Mountain Band* v. *United States*, 490 F. 2d 935 (1974), at 944; *United States* v. *Pueblo of San Ildefonso*, 513 F. 2d 1383 (1975), at 1394–5; *Strong* v. *United States*, 518 F. 2d 556 (1975), at 561–2, *certiorari* denied 423 U.S. 1015 (1975).

11   On this distinction, see McNeil (1989), *supra*, n. 5, at 179–221, and, on the general failure of Canadian judges to recognize it, 274–90.

[12] In New Zealand and the United States, it has been held that, although aboriginal title cannot be alienated to settlers of European origin, it can be transferred among aboriginal peoples themselves: see *The Queen* v. *Symonds* (1847) [1840–1932] N.Z.P.C.C. 387, *per* Chapman J. at 391; *Sac and Fox Tribe* v. *United States*, 383 F. 2d 991 (1967), at 998–9; *Turtle Mountain Band* v. *United States*, 490 F. 2d 935 (1974), at 941–2.

[13] On the British colonial-law distinction between settled and conquered or ceded territories, and the juridical consequences of classification of a colony as one or the other, see Slattery, *supra*, n. 5, at 10–35, and McNeil (1989), *supra*, n. 5, 108–33.

[14] See [1985] 1 C.N.L.R. 1, at 32, 40.

[15] See *Blankard* v. *Galdy* (1693) Holt K.B. 341; *Privy Council Memorandum* (1722) 2 P. Wms. 75; *Re Southern Rhodesia* [1919] A.C. 211, at 233; *Amodu Tijani* v. *Secretary of State, Southern Nigeria* [1921] 2 A.C. 399, at 407, 410; *Oyekan* v. *Adele* [1957] 2 All E.R. 785, at 788; *Guerin* v. *The Queen* [1984] 2 S.C.R. 335, *per* Dickson J. at 378. Note, however, that the British crown could extinguish real property rights in a conquest by seizing lands by act of state *prior* to accepting the territory into its dominions: see discussion in McNeil (1989), *supra*, n. 5, at 161–79.

[16] [1989] 2 C.N.L.R. 73, at 78.

[17] *Copy of the Robinson Treaty Made in the Year 1850 with the Ojibewa Indians of Lake Huron, Conveying Certain Lands to the Crown, reprinted from the edition of 1939* (Ottawa: Queen's Printer, 1964). Note that I have adopted the spelling of Ojibwa used in the judgments rather than the spelling in the treaty.

[18] *Ibid.*, at 4.

[19] Spelled "Tagawinini" in the treaty: *ibid.*, at 3.

[20] 1985] 1 C.N.L.R. 1, at 16, 95. See also *Calder* v. *Attorney-General of British Columbia* [1973] S.C.R. 313, *per* Hall J. (dissenting) at 404; *Re Paulette* [1973] 6 W.W.R. 97, at 143, reversed on other grounds (1975) 63 D.L.R. (3d) 1, [1977] 2 S.C.R. 628.

[21] 1985] 1 C.N.L.R. l, at 82.

[22] *Ibid.*, at 26–34, especially 33, where Steele underlined a quotation from *Baker Lake* v. *Minister of Indian Affairs* [1980] 1 F.C. 518, at 577, stating that aboriginal title is not a proprietary right. Elsewhere, however, Steele used equivocal language to describe aboriginal title: for example, it is not an " *independent* interest in lands ..., merely a limited dependent interest" (at 78); "aboriginal title, whatever else it may be, is an incorporeal hereditament, a thing capable of being inherited communally by the band" (at 115); "while the personal or aboriginal right or interest of the Indians comes within the

extended definition of 'land' in the *Limitations Act*, it is not such an interest in land that gives a right to file a caution against the Crown's title pursuant to the *Land Titles Act*" (at 118, following a statement at 117 that a caution can be registered only by a person who claims a "proprietary interest" in land). From this, it would seem that Steele regarded aboriginal title as a non–proprietary interest in land, which in this context is probably a contradiction in terms.

23 (1888) 14 App. Cas. 46, at 54.

24 In settled parts of Canada, the common law should have precluded the crown from acquiring any interest in lands occupied by aboriginal peoples at the time of settlement; at best, the crown would have acquired a paramount lordship *over* those lands: see McNeil (1989), *supra*, n. 5, especially 205–21. In the part of Canada which was formerly New France, the crown by conquest and the Treaty of Paris would have acquired title to lands which were previously owned by the French king. For the crown to establish its own title to lands occupied by aboriginal peoples in the former French colony, it would have to prove that the king of France owned those lands at the time Britain acquired sovereignty. As was said by Lord Davey in *Nireaha Tamaki* v. *Baker* [1901] A.C. 561, at 576, "in a constitutional country the assertion of title by the Attorney–General in a Court of Justice can be treated as pleading only, and requires to be supported by evidence"; see also *Bristow* v. *Cormican* (1878) 3 App. Cas. 641, where the House of Lords decided that the crown's title to land (in Ireland, which had been acquired by conquest) cannot be presumed, but must be established by evidence. In the *Bear Island* case, Steele's treatment of this issue was perfunctory. He concluded that, when the French were defeated, "the British Crown did not merely take on what the French Crown had but took total sovereignty": [1985] 1 C.N.L.R. 1, at 23. For him, "total sovereignty" seems to have included title to Indian lands, for on the same page he said: "Notwithstanding the arguments that were advanced by counsel for the defendants, and the lengthy evidence that he introduced, in his final argument he admitted that all rights were in the British Crown and that the only rights that the defendants might have stemmed from the *Royal Proclamation of 1763*. I believe that this is the correct proposition which is supported, not only by the evidence, but by previous court decisions." Unfortunately, Steele did not outline the evidence he was referring to, nor did he specify the court decisions, though one may surmise that the *St. Catherine's* case was foremost in his mind.

25 [1985] 1 C.N.L.R. 1, at 25–6.

26 (1888) 14 App. Cas. 46, at 53–5.

27 *Ibid.*, at 58. Note that Steele referred to this passage, [1985] 1 C.N.L.R. 1, at 108, apparently without comprehending its significance.

28 30 and 31 Vict., c.3 (Imp.).

29 *Attorney-General for Quebec* v. *Attorney-General for Canada* [1921] 1 A.C. 401, at 408; *Guerin* v. *The Queen* [1984] 2 S.C.R. 335, *per* Dickson J. at 382.

30 *Canadian Pacific Limited* v. *Paul* [1988] 2 S.C.R. 654, at 677.

31 The same tendency to rely on circumstantial evidence is apparent in the Court of Appeal's review of this issue: see [1989] 2 C.N.L.R. 73, at 81–3.

32 Protection of property rights, particularly against encroachments by the crown, is fundamental to the common law: see H. Broom, *Constitutional Law Viewed in Relation to Common Law and Exemplified by Cases*, 2nd edition, by G.L. Denman, (London: W. Maxwell and Son, 1885), at 225–33. This is exemplified by the rule that legislation is to be strictly construed in favour of property rights: see *Colet* v. *R.* [1981] 1 S.C.R. 2, at 10.

33 [1985] 1 C.N.L.R. 1, at 84.

34 *Ibid.*, at 85.

35 "Leaving Our White Eyes Behind: The Sentencing of Native Accused" [1989] 3 C.N.L.R. 1.

36 *Ibid.*, at 2.

37 *Ibid.*, at 1.

38 *Stein* v. *The Ship "Kathy K"* [1976] 2 S.C.R. 802, at 808: see [1989] 2 C.N.L.R. 73, at 75–6.

39 [1989] 2 C.N.L.R. 73, at 77, 83.

40 For example., *ibid.*, at 82: "It is difficult to believe that they [the other chiefs present when the treaty was signed] would permit Tawgaiwene to play such an active role if he was not recognized by them as a chief with representation in the treaty area."

41 The Court of Appeal said that this conclusion was based on incomplete records: [1989] 2 C.N.L.R. 73, at 84.

42 [1985] 1 C.N.L.R. 1, at 67–8, 72–3, 89–92; [1989] 2 C.N.L.R. 73, at 84.

43 1985] 1 C.N.L.R. 1, at 88–9.

44 *Ibid.*, at 92.

45 Some of these requests seem to have been based on the Robinson–Huron Treaty, while others were not: *ibid.*, at 93–4. However, Steele concluded that denial of the treaty prior to 1973, when a lawyer was retained, had been "merely a bargaining ploy in the negotiation attempts to obtain the reserve": *ibid.*, at 94.

46 The long delay appears to have been due to the reluctance of the Ontario government to give up lands which it considered to be provincial crown

lands. The Ontario attorney general admitted in his factum presented to the Court of Appeal that "from 1885 until 1939 the government of Ontario was unresponsive and intransigent": [1989] 2 C.N.L.R. 73, at 85.

47 For example, see *The James Bay Treaty: Treaty No. 9 (Made in 1905 and 1906) and Adhesions Made in 1929 and 1930*, reprinted from the edition of 1931 (Ottawa: Queen's Printer, 1964), at 29–31.

48 The federal government is willing to negotiate land-claim settlements with non–treaty Indian tribes for whom reserves were set aside: for instance, see "Map of Comprehensive Native Claims in British Columbia," inside back cover of *Canada, Living Treaties: Lasting Agreements: Report of the Task Force to Review Comprehensive Claims Policy* (Ottawa: Indian and Northern Affairs, 1985). Note, however, that in some instances the tribes did not accept the creation of reserves for them. The Nishga Indians are an example: see *Calder* v. *Attorney–General of British Columbia* [1973] S.C.R. 313, *per* Judson J. at 318.

49 In international law, at least, it seems doubtful that non–signatories can become parties to treaties in this way: see A.B. Keith, ed., *Wheaton's International Law*, 6th edition (London: Stevens and Sons, 1929), vol. 1, at 519–21; J.G. Starke, *Introduction to International Law*, 9th edition (London: Butterworths, 1984), at 421–3; Vienna Convention on the Law of Treaties, 1969 (in force as of 27 January 1980), articles 34–8, in I. Brownlie, ed., *Basic Documents in International Law*, 2nd edition (Oxford: Clarendon Press, 1972), at 246–7.

50 See *Simon* v. *The Queen* [1985] 2 S.C.R. 387, at 404, in particular with regard to the application of principles of international law to Indian treaties.

51 This involved a physical transfer of possession by handing over a clod of earth or a twig, which symbolized the land being conveyed: see A.K.R. Kiralfy, *Potter's Historical Introduction to English Law*, 4th edition (London: Sweet and Maxwell Limited, 1958), at 519–20.

52 *Case of Duchy of Lancaster* (1562) 1 Plow. 212, at 213.

53 See E. Coke, *The First Part of the Institutes of the Laws of England; or a Commentary upon Littleton*, 15th edition (London: E. & R. Brooke, 1794), at 260a; J. Chitty, *A Treatise on the Law of the Prerogatives of the Crown* (London: J. Butterworth and Son, 1820), at 389–91.

54 [1989] 2 C.N.L.R. 73, at 85, referring to Steele's judgment, [1985] 1 C.N.L.R. 1, at 95.

55 Compare [1985] 1 C.N.L.R. 1, at 111, 116, where Steele suggested that the adhesion took place in 1883 (the year when annuity payments began).

56 See text accompanying nn. 22–30, *supra.*

57 For a discussion of the complex issue of the effect of crown grants of lands which are subject to aboriginal title, see McNeil (1989), *supra*, n. 5, at 235–41.

58 Chitty, *supra*, n. 53, at 386. See also *The Queen* v. *Hughes* (1866) LR 1 PC 81, at 87–8; *Bristow* v. *Cormican* (1878) 3 App. Cas. 641; *Drulard* v. *Welsh* (1906) 11 O.L.R. 647, at 656, reversed on other grounds (1907) 14 O.L.R. 54. Note that grants of unceded Indian lands were prohibited by the Royal Proclamation of 1763 as well: see nn. 86–7, 102–6, and text, *infra*.

59 [1985] 1 C.N.L.R. 1, at 81, 103, 109.

60 Moreover, as discussed below the Court of Appeal decided that the crown could extinguish aboriginal title unilaterally by treaty. If the crown could do that, presumably it could accomplish the same thing by grant.

61 In response to this doubt, although this provision may not have initially applied there, it was made applicable to most, if not all, of the Land Claim Area before the Robinson–Huron Treaty was signed: see Slattery, *supra*, n. 5, at 333, and text accompanying nn. 97–8, *infra*.

62 14 Geo. III, c.83 (Imp.): see [1989] 2 C.N.L.R. 73, at 85. Steele reached the same conclusion: [1985] 1 C.N.L.R. 1, at 23.

63 For example, see *The King* v. *McMaster* [1926] Ex. C.R. 68, at 72–4; *Easterbrook* v. *The King* [1931] S.C.R. 210, at 214–15, 217–18; *Calder* v. *Attorney-General of British Columbia* [1973] S.C.R. 313, especially *per* Hall J. (dissenting) at 394–401; *R.* v. *Isaac* (1975) 13 N.S.R. (2d) 460, at 478, 496; *Guerin* v. *The Queen* [1984] 2 S.C.R. 335, *per* Dickson J. at 383. In *R.* v. *Secretary of State for Foreign and Commonwealth Affairs, ex parte Indian Association of Alberta* [1982] Q.B. 892, at 913, Lord Denning of the English Court of Appeal said: "The Proclamation of 1763 governed the position of the Indian peoples for the next 100 years at least. It still governs their position throughout Canada, except in those cases when it has been supplemented or superseded by a treaty with the Indians."

64 [1989] 2 C.N.L.R. 73, at 85.

65 [1988] 2 S.C.R. 654: see text accompanying n.30, *supra.*

66 1989] 2 C.N.L.R. 73, at 86.

67 *Ibid.,* at 78.

68 *Ibid.,* at 86. See also [1985] 1 C.N.L.R. 1, at 86, where Steele reached the same conclusion. However, unlike the Court of Appeal, Steele was careful to exclude the portion of the Land Claim Area lying north of the height of land. He nevertheless denied the Temagami Indians any right to that portion because he said it had never been occupied by them.

69 [1989] 2 C.N.L.R. 73, at 86.

70 *Ibid.* On the subsequent events relied on by the court, see n. 81, *infra.* The boundary referred to was first created when the old colony of Quebec was divided into Upper and Lower Canada by an imperial Order in Council, dated 24 August 1791 (reproduced in McNeil (1982), *supra,* n. 5, at 58–60), and was maintained between Ontario and Quebec by the *Constitution Act, 1867,* 30 and 31 Vict., c.3 (Imp.), s.6.

71 *Supra,* n. 17, at 3.

72 *Ibid.*

73 Contrast Steele's interpretation, [1985] 1 C.N.L.R. 1, at 86.

74 The treaty's drafters apparently assumed that the height of land between the St Lawrence–Great Lakes and Hudson Bay watersheds formed the southern boundary of Rupert's Land in the region, a matter placed in doubt in 1884 by the *Ontario Boundaries Case:* see n. 5, *supra.*

75 This line would then correspond with the eastern limit of the Robinson–Superior Treaty, signed two days before the Robinson–Huron Treaty by the Chiefs of Ojibwa Indians inhabiting the northern shore of Lake Superior from Batchewanaung Bay to Pigeon River and inland to the height of land: see A. Morris, *The Treaties of Canada with the Indians* (Toronto: Belfords, Clarke and Company, 1880, reprinted Toronto: Coles Publishing Company, 1979), at 302, where the Robinson–Superior Treaty is reproduced.

76 Moreover, if the line is drawn due north, which seems to be the most logical direction, it cuts through the Land Claim Area, leaving the eastern portion outside the treaty.

77 See text accompanying nn. 69–70, *supra.*

78 The meaning of "unconceded lands" is ambiguous. It may refer to lands which had not been surrendered by other Indian tribes by earlier treaties, though in that case the word "unceded" would be more appropriate (for example, the Royal Proclamation of 1763 referred to Indian lands which had not been "ceded to or purchased by" the crown: R.S.C. 1985, appendix II, No. 1, at 5). More commonly, the term "unconceded" is used to describe crown lands which have not been divided up or granted: see definition of "concession" in *The Canadian Law Dictionary* (Don Mills, Ontario: Law and Business Publications (Canada) Inc., 1980), and *Black's Law Dictionary,* 5th edition (St. Paul, Minn.: West Publishing Co., 1979).

79 Similar all–inclusive surrenders appear in some subsequent treaties: for instance, see *Treaty No. 4 Between Her Majesty the Queen and the Cree and Saulteaux Tribes of Indians at Qu'Appelle and Fort Ellice,* 1874 (Ottawa: Queen's Printer, 1966), at 6, where a surrender of precisely described lands, in what are now southern Manitoba, Saskatchewan, and Alberta, is followed by these words: "Also all their rights, titles and privileges whatsoever to all

other lands wheresoever situated within Her Majesty's North–West Territories, or any of them." If this had operated as a valid surrender of all Indian lands (rather than just all lands of the Cree and Saulteaux parties to the treaty) within the then North–West Territories, Treaties 5 to 11 would have been largely unnecessary (indeed, Treaties 5 to 11 contain a clause which is even more extensive, including all land rights of the Indian parties anywhere in Canada).

[80] The vague description given may be contrasted with the precisely drawn boundaries in the numbered treaties: for example, see Treaty No. 4, *ibid.*, at 6.

[81] *Copy of the Treaty Made October 31, 1923, Between His Majesty the King and the Chippewa Indians of Christian Island, Georgina Island and Rama* (Ottawa: Queen's Printer, 1967), at 3–4. Although the Court of Appeal said that its interpretation of the Robinson–Huron Treaty as extending east to the Ontario–Quebec boundary (formed in part by the Ottawa River) was confirmed by subsequent events, it did not refer to the 1923 treaty. Instead, it relied in part on its conclusion that, prior to the dispute leading to the litigation, "the Temagami Indians never took the position that their traditional lands were outside the treaty area": [1989] 2 C.N.L.R. 73, at 86. But one may ask how the interpretation of the treaty could depend on the understanding of Indians who, on the court's own assumption in this part of the judgment, were not parties to it. Also, the basis for the Temagami Indians' understanding should be inquired into. Steele, on the other hand, found support in Treaty No. 9 for his view that all of the Land Claim Area lying south of the height of land was within the Robinson–Huron area: [1985] 1 C.N.L.R. 1, at 86. Treaty No. 9 describes the southern limit of the territory covered by it as "the height of land and the northern boundaries of the territory ceded by the Robinson–Superior Treaty of 1850, and the Robinson–Huron Treaty of 1850": *supra*, n. 47, at 19–20. Although this does indicate a crown view that the Robinson–Huron Treaty extended north to the height of land, this is explicit in the treaty itself. However, Treaty No. 9 sheds no light on the crown's view of the eastern extent of the Robinson–Huron Treaty and its application to the aboriginal rights of Indian tribes who are not parties to it.

[82] See the judgments of Dickson C.J.C. in *Nowegijick* v. *The Queen* [1983] 1 S.C.R. 29, at 36 ("treaties and statutes relating to Indians should be liberally construed and doubtful expressions resolved in favour of the Indian"), and *Simon* v. *The Queen* [1985] 2 S.C.R. 387, at 402 ("Indian treaties should be given a fair, large and liberal construction in favour of the Indians").

[83] See n. 32, *supra*. On the proprietary nature of aboriginal land rights, see nn. 22–30 and text, *supra*.

[84] [1989] 2 C.N.L.R. 73, at 86.

85 R.S.C. 1985, Appendix II, No. 1, at 5. The term "Indian territory" has been employed by Professor Slattery to refer to the lands expressly reserved for Indian use by this provision: see B. Slattery, "The Hidden Constitution: Aboriginal Rights in Canada" (1984) 32 *American Journal of Comparative Law* 361, at 369–72. On the proclamation's territorial extent, see the works cited at the end of n. 5, *supra.*

86 R.S.C. 1985, Appendix II, No. 1, at 5. Note that, although at first glance the restriction on surveys and grants by the governor of Quebec appears to be limited to lands beyond that colony's boundaries, the proclamation can, and probably should, be read as prohibiting such interference with *all* Indian lands, wherever located, by all colonial governors, including the governor of Quebec: see Slattery, *supra,* n. 5, at 261–7.

87 See Slattery, *supra,* n. 5, at 220–1.

88 In *R.* v. *Secretary of State for Foreign and Commonwealth Affairs, ex parte Indian Association of Alberta* [1982] Q.B. 892, at 912, Lord Denning said: "To my mind the Royal Proclamation of 1763 was equivalent to an entrenched provision in the constitution of the colonies in North America. It was binding on the Crown 'so long as the sun rises and the river flows.'" See also the other cases cited in n. 63, *supra.*

89 R.S.C. 1985, Appendix II, No. 1, at 5: see discussion in Slattery, *supra* n. 5, at 217–19.

90 R.S.C. 1985, Appendix II, No. 1, at 5–6.

91 (1888) 14 App. Cas. 46, at 54–5.

92 For this and other reasons, the *St. Catherine's* decision is seriously flawed. These matters will be pursued in a critical reassessment of the decision which I am in the process of writing.

93 See text accompanying nn. 84–5, *supra.* Although the Court of Appeal judges did not refer directly to *St. Catherine's,* there can be no doubt that they had that decision in mind, as Steele had relied heavily upon it at trial: see [1985] 1 C.N.L.R. 1, 26–31, 106–11.

94 Although a fundamental rule of British constitutional law prevents the crown from legislating (see *Proclamations Case* (1610) 12 Co. R. 74), the crown had this exceptional power in conquered and ceded territories: see *Calvin's Case* (1608) 7 Co. R. la, at 17b; *Campbell* v. *Hall* (1774) Lofft 655; *Wilcox* v. *Wilcox* (1857) 8 L.C.R. 34, at 81.

95 To the extent the proclamation did not infringe vested rights or alter the law, legislative power probably would not have been necessary for the crown to issue it: see Slattery, *supra,* n. 5 at 292.

96 See *Campbell* v. *Hall* (1774) Lofft 655, at 746–8, regarding Grenada, one of the four colonies created by the proclamation.

97 14 Geo. III, c. 83 (Imp.).

98 Although the *St. Catharine's* and Temagami Indians' lands were within the territory ceded by France in 1763 (see *R.* v. *St. Catharine's Milling and Lumber Company* [1885] 10 O.R. 196, at 204; *Attorney General for Ontario* v. *Bear Island Foundation* [1985] 1 C.N.L.R. 1, at 22–3), the original colony of Quebec was of more limited extent: see R.S.C. 1985, Appendix II, No. 1, at 1–2. On the western and northern boundaries of Quebec under the *Quebec Act*, see discussion of the *Ontario Boundaries Case*, 1884, in McNeil (1982), *supra*, n. 5, at 26–33.

99 See *Abeyenskera* v. *Jayatilake* [1932] A.C. 260; *Sammut* v. *Strickland* [1938] A.C. 678; *Sabally and N'Jie* v. *H.M. Attorney–General* [1964] 3 W.L.R. 732.

100 See *Oyekan* v. *Adele* [1957] 2 All E.R. 785, at 788; *Winfat Enterprise* v. *Attorney–General of Hong Kong* [1985] A.C. 733.

101 See *Entick* v. *Carrington* (1765) 19 St. Tr. 1029; *Johnstone* v. *Pedlar* [1921] 2 A.C. 262; *Attorney–General* v. *Nissan* [1970] A.C. 179. On the rule that the crown cannot derogate from vested rights by grant, see authority in n. 58, *supra.*

102 On the provisions in question, see nn. 85–90 and text, *supra*. Arguably, however, this power was taken away at the latest by the *Constitution Act, 1867*, 30 & 31 Vict., c. 3 (Imp.), s. 91(24), which gave the Canadian parliament exclusive legislative authority over "Indians, and Lands reserved for the Indians" (this argument depends in part on the effect of the *Colonial Laws Validity Act*, 28 & 29 Vict., c.63 (Imp.)). In the *St. Catharine's* case, the Privy Council held that "Lands reserved for the Indians" include lands reserved by the Royal Proclamation: (1888) 14 App. Cas. 46, at 59. However, their Lordships did not consider the effect of s. 91(24) on the crown's power. For a detailed discussion of the modifiability of the proclamation, see Slattery, *supra*, n. 5, at 314–28.

103 Owing to the reservation of power, the crown could do this regardless of whether the amendments would have legislative effect. Note, however, that the extent to which the proclamation's Indian provisions are legislative in nature (and therefore unamendable except by the exercise of legislative authority) is a complex issue which, apart from a brief mention in n. 106, *infra*, cannot be persued here: see n. 95, supra.

104 See *The King* v. *McMaster* [1926] Ex. C.R. 68 at 73; *Brick Cartage Ltd.* v. *The Queen* [1965] Ex. C.R. 102, at 106–7. Compare *R.* v. *Isaac* (1975) 13 N.S.R. (2d) 460, *per* MacKeigan C.J. at 476, 479. For further discussion, See Slattery, *supra*, n. 5, at 303–13.

105 See [1985] 1 C.N.L.R. 1, at 83; [1989] 2 C.N.L.R. 73, at 86.

106 This procedure affected the rights of Indians to sell and settlers to buy Indian lands: see McNeil (1989), *supra* , n. 5, at 221–35. For this reason, legis-

lative power would have been necessary not only to create it, but also to change it.

[107] See nn. 88–9 and text, *supra.*

[108] Referring to the Indians who signed Treaty No. 3 in 1873, Lord Watson said that "their possession, such as it was, can only be ascribed to the general provisions made by the royal proclamation in favour of all Indian tribes then living under the sovereignty and protection of the British Crown": (1888) 14 App. Cas. 46, at 54.

[109] [1984] 2 S.C.R. 335, at 378, referring to *Calder* v. *Attorney-General of British Columbia* [1973] S.C.R. 313 (see especially 375–6, 390, 394). This was affirmed by Justice Wilson, speaking for the Supreme Court of Canada in *Roberts* v. *Canada* [1989] 1. S.C.R. 322, at 340: "As Dickson J. (as he then was) pointed out in *Guerin, supra,* aboriginal title pre–dated colonization by the British and survived British claims of sovereignty."

[110] [1984] 2 S.C.R. 335, at 378. For additional authorities on this principle, see n. 15, *supra.*

[111] Although the *Guerin* case involved reserve lands in British Columbia, a settled colony, in this passage Dickson was referring to aboriginal land rights generally. Moreover, in addition to *Calder,* the authority relied on by him was *Amodu Tijani* v. *Secretary of State, Southern Nigeria* [1921] 2 A.C. 399, a Privy Council decision involving lands in a ceded colony.

[112] For the crown to rebut this presumption of aboriginal title with respect to any particular lands, it would have to prove that those lands were owned by the French king when the Treaty of Paris was signed: see n. 24, *supra.*

[113] Compare Steele's unsupported view to the contrary: [1985] 1 C.N.L.R. 1, at 119.

[114] See authority in nn. 58, 101, *supra,* and n. 122, *infra.*

[115] Recall that from 1774 most, if not all, of the lands claimed by the Temagami Indians would have been within the colony: see nn. 97–8 and text, *supra.*

[116] [1989] 2 C.N.L.R. 73, at 87. By "sovereign power," the court clearly meant the crown rather than the legislature because the Robinson–Huron Treaty had been ratified by the governor general in council, not the legislative assembly, of the province of Canada. Note that the court recognized that section 35 of the *Constitution Act 1982,* enacted as Schedule B to the *Canada Act 1982,* c. 11 (UK), may have changed this, but as the alleged unilateral extinguishment by treaty took place long before, section 35 was inapplicable.

[117] [1989] 2 C.N.L.R. 73, at 87, referring to *Calder* v. *Attorney-General of British Columbia* [1973] S.C.R. 313, at 334–5, 393. The quoted passage is from *United States* v. *Santa Fe Pacific Railroad,* 314 U.S. 339 (1941), at 347.

118 [1973] S.C.R. 313, at 402.

119 556 P. 2d 1185 (1976.)

120 *Ibid.*, at 1191–2.

121 [1989] 2 C.N.L.R. 73, at 88.

122 See *Walker* v. *Baird* [1892] A.C. 491, and the cases cited in n. 101, *supra*. This rule explains why in Canada, unlike in the United States, international treaties which affect vested rights need to be implemented by a statute which makes the required change in the law: see P.W. Hogg, *Constitutional Law of Canada*, 2nd edition (Toronto: Carswell Company Limited, 1985), at 245–6. In *R.* v. *Agawa* [1988] 3 C.N.L.R. 73, another case involving the Robinson–Huron Treaty decided just six months before *Bear Island*, the Ontario Court of Appeal (at 75) said that Indian treaties are like international treaties in this respect.

123 348 US 272 (1955), at 279, cited 556 P. 2d 1185 (1976), at 1190–1.

124 *Ibid.* For a more detailed discussion of *Tee–Hit–Ton Indians* and other American cases on original Indian title, see McNeil (1989), *supra,* n.5, at 244–67.

The controversy over Maple Mountain, the site of a proposed tourist development in 1973, triggered an early alliance between preservationists and the Teme-Augama Anishnabai. *Courtesy: Hap Wilson*

Twelve

Where Justice Lies: Aboriginal Rights and Wrongs in Temagami

Tony Hall

There is an undercurrent of polite brutality in most of the court-room dramas that pit aboriginal groups in argumentative combat with legal officers of the federal and provincial governments in Canada. On the one side sit lawyers for Native communities, communities that by almost any standard have benefited least from Confederation.[1] On the other side sit crown officers whose duty it is to represent the interests of the general population. Most often this responsibility to give legal articulation to the larger society's political will is channeled into ideological assaults against the assertion by aboriginal groups that they hold aboriginal rights.

In making their arguments, crown officials return again and again to a few key ideas: aboriginal people were too primitive before the arrival of Europeans to have a legal system and they therefore lacked a basis to exercise any coherent form of land tenure; because aboriginal people were non-Christians, their laws were automatically superseded by those of the representatives of a Christian monarch; aboriginal people were conquered and thereby lost the right of self-determination; the rights of aboriginal people were created by the imperial crown and these rights can be unilaterally extinguished by officers of the crown;

aboriginal people can exercise their human rights as individual Canadian citizens but not as members of distinct aboriginal collectivities.[2]

In various combinations and permutations, these ideas constitute the essential arsenal of legal theories employed, especially by provincial authorities, to counter the claims of Native people. What links the ideas is a view of humanity that would situate all groups and races along a hierarchy of worth and advancement. A racially inspired paradigm of law is the result, a legal construct supported by legions of Victorian social philosophers who in the nineteenth century went about elaborating a bold edifice of Darwinian theory to justify the apparent ascendancy on the stage of world history of Anglo-Saxons over the perceived lower races of dark-skinned peoples.[3]

Another major theory of legal relations between Native people and newcomers in crown domains holds that as a basic rule aboriginal peoples had the inherent human right not to be dispossessed of their ancestral lands without their consent and without some reasonable compensation. This approach to the law places emphasis on the Royal Proclamation of 1763 and the line of Indian treaties and land-claim agreements that flows from it. All of these constitutional instruments, it is held, demonstrate that the crown rule of law in Canada is founded on recognition, however begrudgingly or insufficiently applied, that aboriginal peoples are fully human and therefore the holders of certain inalienable human rights.

These two approaches to history and law have found clear expression in one of the lengthiest and most contentious land-claim disputes ever to develop in the Canadian courts. The case sets the Teme-Augama Anishnabai, sometimes known as the Bear Island band, against the attorney general of Ontario.[4] The area in dispute, a major portion of Temagami, covers 9,000 square kilometres of prime northeastern Ontario land. In 1973 the chief of the Bear Island band, Gary Potts, together with Bruce Clark, a Haileybury lawyer, successfully filed a legal caution on N'Daki Menan, the Teme-Augama people's ancestral territory (Figure 1). The caution was judicially sanctioned in light of the Supreme Court of Canada's finding in 1973 on the land claim of the Nishga people in British Columbia. Although the Nishga technically lost the case, the finding forced on law officers in Canada the recognition that aboriginal title — that is, the interest of aboriginal people in their ancestral land — is not only an ethical principle but also a legal construct within the crown tradition of common law, legislation, convention, and jurisprudence.[5]

The contention of the several hundred people who make up the Teme-Augama Anishnabai is that their ancestors never ceded away their aboriginal title to their ancestral lands. They maintain that, when the original Indian treaty covering Temagami and adjacent areas was negotiated in Sault Ste Marie in 1850, their leaders were not present to sanction the agreement. As early as 1885 the Temagami Indians convinced the federal government of this fact, a detail of history demonstrated by the reality that the band found itself without a reserve throughout much of the twentieth century. In 1943 the government of Ontario, the claimant of exclusive proprietary interest in the province's crown lands, finally relented from treating the Temagami people essentially as squatters,[6] but it was not until 1971 that the 285-hectare Bear Island site of the Indians' village was finally granted reserve status. Further, as Chief Potts was later to assert in the courts, the establishment of the Bear Island reserve did not speak to the larger question of his people's unceded aboriginal title to their entire homeland.

The land claim of the Teme-Augama Anishnabai threw legal attention on the need for reconsideration of Ontario's intricately evolved legacy of crown-Indian relations through the medium of treaties. Ontario officials, who hold that all provincial lands are subject to the outcome of Indian treaty negotiations, found themselves in a position akin to that of provincial authorities in British Columbia. The vastest part of BC's lands, like much of Yukon, Northwest Territories, northern Quebec, and Labrador, have never been covered by crown treaties with indigenous peoples. Ontario, on the other hand, is the Canadian jurisdiction with both the oldest and newest heritage of Indian treaties. Major treaties were made with Native people of the Ontario area at intervals between 1784 and 1923, a range of history that encompasses many different political regimes of Native-newcomer relations.[7]

THE ROYAL PROCLAMATION OF 1763 AND EARLY INDIAN TREATIES IN HISTORICAL PERSPECTIVE

The constitutional status of the Royal Proclamation of 1763 is one of the major issues in the Temagami land dispute. Indeed the Royal Proclamation, which Lord Denning recently titled the Indian Bill of Rights or the Indian Magna Carta,[8] figures centrally in virtually all the controversies in Canada that hinge on the legal interpretation of Indian treaties and of aboriginal title. King George III, on the advice of his Privy Council, issued the proclamation in order to establish several regimes of colonial government in those portions of North America from which France withdrew its claim after having lost the Seven Years' War. A framework of colonial administration was put in place for Quebec, Grenada, East Florida, and West Florida. As well, a fifth legal regime, the Indian territory, was established south of the Hudson's Bay Company lands and west of the watershed running along the crest of the Appalachian mountains. The Indian territory described by the Royal Proclamation included all of present-day Ontario within the Great Lakes-St Lawrence watershed, including much of Temagami.[9]

The Royal Proclamation was imposed by British imperial authorities as a means to enforce a degree of law and order on the western frontiers of the crown's Thirteen Colonies. The Seven Years' War, concluded by Pontiac's Indian uprising in the Detroit-Michilimackinac area, had confirmed the importance of appeasing Native fighting forces. The affirmation in the Royal Proclamation that the North American interior was reserved to Indian nations for their exclusive use was therefore a reflection of a calculated geopolitical assessment of British imperial self-interest.[10]

While reservation of the continental interior served Indian self-interest and British imperial self-interest, the move infuriated land speculators in the Thirteen Colonies who had their eyes on the speedy commercial exploitation of the rich Ohio valley. When administration of the Indian territory was given to Quebec in 1774, American land speculators, represented by the likes of Benjamin Franklin and George Washington, saw red. It remains to be widely appreciated just how influential in moving forward the agenda of the American rebels was the desire for unobstructed access to Indian lands on the western frontiers of the Thirteen Colonies.[11]

During the American revolution and in the following years, the British Indian Department became a bastion of Tory resistance against the westward thrust of republicanism.[12] British army officers and leading Indian strategists in the Ohio valley-Great Lakes area cooperated strategically in opposing the land-grabbing expansionism of the newly liberated colonials.[13] It was in this atmosphere of collaboration between military allies that crown treaties were negotiated with Indian groups to open new areas for the settlement of United Empire Loyalists and others in the Royal Proclamation lands north of the lower Great Lakes.

Indian groups entered freely into these treaty negotiations, which were conducted in a manner consistent with the terms of the Royal Proclamation. That document had specified: "If at any time any of the said Indians should be inclined to dispose of the said Lands, the same shall be Purchased for Us in our Name, at some public meeting or Assembly of the said Indians to be held for that purpose." A system began to coalesce around the terms of the Royal Proclamation which made the British sovereign the exclusive agent of land transfers between Indians and non-Indian settlers in the continental interior of British North America.[14]

The successful development of the Indian treaty system during the decades following the American revolution was a fundamental factor in the maintenance of crown dominion over territories north of the Great Lakes. The crucial British takeover of the American post of Detroit at the outset of the War of 1812, which resulted largely because of the early mobilization of Tecumseh's Indian fighting forces, is generally taken as the highpoint of strategic cooperation during an era when Indian treaties were but one aspect of a well-established ebb and flow of relations between military allies.[15]

This legacy of military cooperation, a legacy most enduringly entrenched in the early genesis of Canadian Indian treaties, remained a vividly recalled aspect of Ontario's heritage until the early twentieth century, especially among some Tories whose cultivated sense of British imperialism retained a vital anti-republican aspect. In 1887, in the famous *St. Catherine's Milling* case, Canadian Supreme Court Justice Strong cited this chapter of the country's past in a dissenting judicial opinion. In seeking to clarify the meaning of "Lands reserved for the Indians," the phrase in the British North America Act most in contention in this seminal conflict in federal-provincial relations, Mr Justice Strong looked not to technicalities but rather to the broad sweep of history to find the essential underlying spirit of the new Dominion's primary constitutional document. After noting "the great impolity" of the Old Thirteen Colonies' "frequent frontier wars" with the Indians, he explained:

> From the memorable year 1763, when Detroit was besieged and all the Indian tribes were in revolt, down to the date of Confederation, Indian wars and massacres entirely ceased in the British possessions in North America, although powerful Indian nations still continued for some time after the former date to inhabit those territories. That this peaceful conduct of the Indians is in a great degree to be attributed to the recognition of their rights to lands unsurrendered by them, and to the guarantee of their protection in the possession and enjoyment of such lands given by the crown in the Proclamation of October, 1763...is a well known fact of Canadian history which cannot be controverted. The Indian nations from that time became and have since continued to be the firm and faithful allies of the crown and rendered it important military services in two wars — the War of the Revolution and that of 1812.[16]

THE CONVERGENCE OF ARGUMENTS IN THE ONTARIO SUPREME COURT

There was a circus-like atmosphere in the proceedings that made the Ontario Supreme Court the principal forum of conflict between the Temagami Indians and the province's chief legal officers. The marathon trial covered 119 days at intervals over a two-year period beginning in 1982. The testimony fills 68 volumes. Evidence presented by both sides included 3,000 exhibits which fill an entire room at Osgoode Hall in downtown Toronto. Both the crown and the Teme-Augama Anishnabai made ample use of expert witnesses. One of these, James Morrison, who had worked with Chief Potts since 1974 in developing the historical research to support the Indian case, was on the witness stand for a full 28 days. The sheer magnitude of the proceedings soon elevated the case to almost legendary proportions in Ontario legal circles.

The preparation of the Indian case by Chief Potts, Bruce Clark, and their colleagues can be viewed as a reflection of a more broadly based scholarly movement. The energy channeled into this movement amounts to a virtual rethinking of the nature of the country's past with a view to correcting the propensity of a previous generation of Canadian historians to relegate Native people and the role of Native-newcomer relations to the periphery of the story of national development.[17] The direction of this enterprise in historical reconstruction intersects with a similar trend among some legal scholars, especially in the field of constitutional history. The writing of constitutional history, in turn, has drawn deeply on the resources and intellectual energy generated by the political activity accompanying both the prelude to and aftermath of patriation of Canada's constitution in 1982. The eloquence and effectiveness of aboriginal voices in this political activity — activity which overflowed into the prevailing atmosphere of the court-room proceedings — helped to reinforce recognition on several academic fronts of the fundamental importance of crown-Indian relations in the early stages of Canadian constitutional development.

Gary Potts had become Chief of the Bear Island band in 1972, while still in his early twenties.[18] By that time Chief Potts was well prepared for a remarkable career that would see him combine the tasks of scholar, politician, and social activist in his quest to defend his people. As for Bruce Clark, Pott's early partner in his search for justice, [19] he quickly became so completely immersed in the details of the case that he decided to devote his entire professional life to it. He even moved to Bear Island. Following the successful imposition of the legal caution in 1973, Chief Potts and Bruce Clark increasingly spent their time in libraries and archives, and travelling widely, determined to track down the scholars and sources that would provide the pieces they needed for their giant historical jigsaw puzzle. Their research was not confined to

Canada. Clark's files on jurisprudence involving aboriginal people burst with documentation on cases from the United States and throughout the Commonwealth.

As the Temagami case evolved, it attracted the attention of a widening circle of researchers with significant contributions to make. One of the first to become involved was Don Smith, who met Gary Potts in the spring of 1973 at a Native studies conference at Trent University. At the time, Smith was an eager Ph.D. candidate in Canadian history at the University of Toronto. He knew something of the historical background of the land dispute in Temagami as a result of his digging into the life of Grey Owl. Grey Owl, or Archie Belaney, was the famous author, conservationist, and Indian imposter who, during the early twentieth century, had gained much of his knowledge about aboriginal life from living among the Native people of the Temagami district.[20] With Smith's usual generosity, he shared what he knew of the documentation of the Temagami dispute with Chief Potts. The latter was beginning to weave together the basic fabric of the evidence he was gaining from his reading and from the oral testimony he had heard from the elders of his community over his lifetime.

Smith was later asked by Bruce Clark to work on the genealogy of the band. At this stage one of Smith's academic supervisors, the late Dr Ed Rogers of the Royal Ontario Museum, also developed an interest in the case. Rogers would eventually serve as an expert witness for the Teme-Augama Anishnabai during the marathon trial. Other researchers to enter the fray included Craig Macdonald, Thor Conway, and James Morrison. Morrison in particular was to emerge as one of the most effective researchers and tacticians in this pioneering effort to map the emergence of the basic principles of aboriginal rights in the development of Ontario's constitutional landscape.

Morrison's attraction to aboriginal issues drew strength from his friendship with Smith, a contemporary he had first met in a Latin American history course at the University of Toronto. The former's work on the Temagami land claim began when Morrison was employed as a researcher for the Cree and Ojibwa people under the Grand Council of Treaty No.9. In 1978 he began working full time for Chief Potts.

Another important figure in developing the primary documentation in support of the Indian case was Professor Bruce Hodgins of Trent University, the site of much informed discourse in the years ahead on the uses and abuses of Temagami lands. On Bear Island several younger band members, including Mary Laronde, were caught up in the mass of documents and ideas that the chief was assembling. As the court date approached, they too contributed to the articulation of their community's collective position, a position channeled to the courts through Chief Potts's testimony.

Much of the development of the Indian position involved meeting the precedent-setting criteria of a legitimate land claim as laid out in 1980 by Mr Justice Mahoney of the Federal Court in the Baker Lake case.[21] In order to justify its assertions, the band had to show that it was a distinct and organized society in exclusive occupation of the Temagami area at the time when crown dominion was asserted. Similarly, it had to show that it was not connected either by clan or custom to any of the leaders who did sign the treaty in 1850. Finally, the band had to counter the attorney general's contention that its aboriginal rights had "been extinguished by various statutes and physical affirmative acts of Ontario."[22]

These legal demands required the researchers to delve deeply into clan lineages, archaeology, oral tradition, original eye-witness literature describing Indian life, and the extensive primary documentation associated with the history of crown-Indian relations throughout the continent. The need to produce empirical evidence to prove the distinct identity of the Teme-Augama Anishnabai made particularly great demands on the innovativeness of Chief Potts and his colleagues. As part of the wide range of evidence they brought forward, they went to the length of assembling nine canoes of various styles in the court room to demonstrate the unique design of the vessel traditionally used by Native people in Temagami.

The investment of time and energy in the development of the Indian case was easily matched by the work of the province's legal staff. Blenus Wright, the assistant deputy attorney general, directed the preparation of Ontario's case.

There was sympathy among some in Ontario's legal establishment for the task faced by Steele. According to this view, Chief Potts and Bruce Clark failed to confine their arguments to a manageable framework; specifically, they failed to narrow the issues sufficiently to meet the limitations of what can realistically be addressed through the medium of civil litigation. On the other hand, it has been charged that Steele placed an unrealistically burdensome onus of proof on the Teme-Augama Anishnabai. Moreover, it is asserted that he failed to exercise sufficient control over the wide-ranging inquiry and questioning conducted by both Bruce Clark and Blenus Wright.

Steele's finding is a fascinating and important document of broad sociological significance. In rendering explicit so many attitudes that are usually left unarticulated, the judgment suggests much about the dynamics of tension in Canada between Native and non-Native groups in general, and between Native people and the apparatus of the law in particular. Sally Weaver, one of Canada's pre-eminent anthropologists, has termed the finding "antediluvian."[23] Steele's words reveal the persistent force of old evolutionist views that place aboriginal societies near the low end of a hierarchy of peoples. They also reveal a view of the law without the ability to recognize human rights as inherent, flowing from the common attributes of shared humanity, and an attitude that sees Indianness as a static form of human existence fixed firmly in the past — a form of human existence without the inner capacity for adaptation to changing conditions. In short, Steele's judgment gives clear voice to widely-held if largely unconfronted assumptions in society that aboriginal groups are essentially anachronistic holdovers from an earlier era of Canadian history who ultimately should and will disappear in the course of "progress."

The attitudes brought by Steele to the adjudication of the case are revealed with particular clarity in the remark he included in his finding concerning the reliability of the expert witnesses who appeared on behalf of the Teme-Augama Anishnabai. The judge indicated that Craig Macdonald, Thor Conway, and James Morrison "were typical of persons who have worked closely with Indians for so many years that they have lost their objectivity when giving opinion evidence."[24] If non-Indians who have lived with Indians thereby lose their "objectivity," one wonders how Steele views the capacity of Indians themselves for "objectivity." Objectivity, he apparently would have us believe, lies more or less exclusively in the realm of non-Indians who have not lived among Indians.

Steele's controversial finding, given in December 1984, followed by and large the main outlines of the case presented by Blenus Wright. His finding came down against the contentions of the Indians on practically every detail. Much space was devoted to his judicial declaration that the Teme-Augama Anishnabai are a band that has coalesced only in relatively recent times, that the community is but a close offshoot of Ojibwa bands who were represented at the treaty negotiations, and that band members had sanctioned the treaty in any case by accepting the four-dollar annuity payments. Yet Steele also looked far beyond the local details of the case to the broader questions of how aboriginal groups are constitutionally and legally situated in relationship to the principal institutions of the Canadian state. His broad generalizations on these matters therefore have wide significance for the future of all Native people throughout the country. Indeed his finding speaks to some of the most fundamental issues concerning the essential values at the root of our shared citizenship.

Steele held that the aboriginal title asserted in the Royal Proclamation of 1763 is "personal and usufructuary and exists solely at the pleasure of the Crown."[25] He selected this often-quoted phrase from the judgment of Lord Watson in the *St. Catherine's Milling* case,[26] a dispute between the governments of Ontario and Canada over the constitutional meaning of the phrase "Lands reserved for the Indians" in section 91 (24) of the British North American Act of 1867. With some qualifications, Ontario won this pivotal constitutional case in 1888. By arguing for a narrow interpretation of the phrase in question, the provincial government strengthened its claim to control of crown lands within provincial boundaries.

The province gained victory in 1888 partly by denying the Dominion assertion that Indian rights have been consistently and expansively recognized by the crown throughout the history of British colonization in North America. Among the theories marshalled by Ontario officials in making the provincial case against aboriginal rights was the idea that Native people before the arrival of Europeans were too primitive and too unorganized to exercise any kind of binding land tenure over the territories they occupied. And even if they had been able to assert some kind of "primitive" ownership of the soil, this ownership was immediately extinguished when their pagan domains were "discovered" by representatives of the higher laws vested in Christian monarchs.[27]

The Ontario government has never renounced the principles its officials expounded when they originally denied the existence of aboriginal title in the *St. Catherine's Milling* case. In fact the province's legal officers implicitly renewed their recourse to such retrogressive theories of Indianness when they relied so heavily on the *St. Catherine's Milling* judgment in building their case against the Teme-Augama Anishnabai. Rather than questioning the recycling of such obnoxious theories of racial inferiority in contemporary jurisprudence, Steele reinforced the old pattern in his finding.

In Steele's view, the Royal Proclamation created an Indian right where no right had existed before. In other words, Steele saw the proclamation itself as the source of the right rather than as a recognition of a prior right that existed for thousands of years before the arrival of the British in North America. From the proposition that the aboriginal right is created rather than merely confirmed by the crown, Steele deduced the "limited dependent nature" of this right[28] — a right than can be "uni-"unilaterally extinguished"[29] at the crown's "pleasure."

Steele only vaguely addressed the issue of how the British sovereign gained this tremendous life-or-death authority over the collective existence of aboriginal groups. He alluded, however, to the notion of "conquest."[30] The quelling by British soldiers of the brief protest by those Indians following Chief Pontiac in 1763 was mentioned as an event in the constitutional process that rendered aboriginal rights subject to legal annihilation by authority of the crown.[31] Steele's perception of this facet of the country's history contrasts sharply with the view expressed by Justice Strong a century earlier. Whereas Steele saw Indians in Ontario as conquered peoples, Strong characterized them as allies of the crown who had actively resisted the republican conquest of what remained of British North America after 1776.

Steele's decision included a long section where he attempted to explain "the nature" of aboriginal rights.[32] His efforts along these lines bore with particular weight on the new dynamics of jurisprudence that developed with the patriation of the Canadian constitution. Section 35 of the *Constitution Act, 1982* recognizes and affirms "existing Aboriginal and treaty rights," although the phrase is not explicitly defined. Steele's finding started the process of fleshing out the technical meaning of a term which of itself is relatively new to legal language even if it speaks to old concepts that are well elaborated in Canadian constitutional tradition.[33]

Steele found that "the essence of Aboriginal rights is the right of Indians to continue to live on their lands as their forefathers lived."[34] Elsewhere he found that "Aboriginal rights are limited by the wording of the Royal Proclamation"; aboriginal rights consist of "the uses to which Indians put the lands in 1763."[35] These uses were outlined in some detail: fish, game, berries, and, possibly, maple syrup for food; furs for clothing and trade; birchbark, vegetable fibre, and tree gum for canoes; wood for fire and poles for tents; stone for pipes, arrowheads, lances, scrapers, knives, and axes.[36]

Steele could hardly have given more precise legal expression to the theory that sees true Indianness as a way of life fixed forever in the past. What else is to be derived from a finding which deems that aboriginal rights cannot involve the use of any technology acquired by Indians after 1763? Clearly the suggestion is that aboriginal life cannot continue apart from the stereotypical realm of teepees, canoes, snowshoes, and feathered wardrobe; when Indian people act differently from their ancestors — when they use modern technology, for instance — they lose the right to be respected for their Indianness.

Such a view of aboriginal societies is iniquitous. It holds aboriginal groups to rules and expectations unlike those applied to other ethnic and national collectivities. It denies members of aboriginal groups regard as adaptive partners in the wider human family. It would hold aboriginal communities exclusively to the status of folkloric remnants of Canadian heritage without affording them a place of dignity and security in the modern-day world.

By fixing aboriginal rights exclusively to a static place in Canada's past, then, Steele's finding seems aimed at shutting aboriginal societies out of a constructive role in the country's future. In this way the sweep of his judgment extends far indeed. He even ventures beyond the secular sphere, declaring "there was no strong legal or no spiritual attachment to the lands" on the part of the ancestors of the Teme-Augama Anishnabai."[37]

The whole thrust of Steele's judgment is that aboriginal rights constitute tenuous and vulnerable principles of law. As rights that are derived from the authority of the crown, they can be unilaterally eliminated, it is argued, by agents of the crown. In this scheme of interpretation the existence of Indian treaties or the lack of Indian treaties in any given area counts for very little. The judge wrote: "A treaty is not a conveyance of title because title is already in the crown. A treaty is simple acknowledgement that may be formal or informal in nature."[38]

In these few words Steele cast the entire tradition of treaty-making with the Indians in Canada outside the realm of law. Instead he held that the practice should be understood as belonging more to the domain of diplomacy, ritual, and politics. "Where there was no concern about an Indian insurrection, the crown did not enter into treaties," he wrote. "Whenever the Crown felt it could defend its white citizens, it did not provide for treaties with the Indians. Where it had doubt, it did so provide."[39]

Does the outlook revealed in these passages indicate that Steele's attitude towards the law has much in common with those who see in the apparatus of the state little more than a protector of the most powerful members of society? Does Steele hold the legal system in contempt when he claims that government officials who made treaties were bereft of any consideration of justice, law and order, or constitutional tradition? Does he see their credo as rooted primarily in the balance of terror — in the might-is-right school of human affairs? His characterization of treaties not as legal instruments but rather as mere theatre designed to appease Indians would seem to mock Native people for having taken crown representations in the negotiations at face value. Moreover, there is the suggestion that today, as in the past, only the threat of "insurrection" is sufficiently compelling to engage government interest in aboriginal claims.

On the one hand, Steele placed treaties outside the realm of the law, but on the other he named treaties as one of the means for the legal extinguishment of aboriginal rights. Those rights, he concluded, "exist at the pleasure of the Crown and they can be extinguished by treaty, legislation or administrative acts."[40] The "opening of land to settlement" is among the legislative or administrative acts that have the effect, according to Steele, of eliminating the aboriginal interest in territory.[41] Such opening, he argued, involves the making of surveys, the building of railways, roads, and hydro-electric works, the issuing of land patents, and the extension of rights to non-Indians to exploit timber, mineral, and wildlife resources. Since all of these developments have taken place in Temagami, Steele held that the crown — in this case the Crown in Right of the government of Ontario — has effectively extinguished the aboriginal rights of the Teme-Augama Anishnabai regardless of their status with respect to the treaty negotiations of 1850.[42] And he wrote the decision in such a way as to affect throughout Canada the entire legal infrastructure of crown-Indian relations through the medium of treaties.

Steele's wide-ranging interpretation of the law of Indian treaties and aboriginal rights essentially amounts to an account of the history of crown dealings with Native people in Ontario. All down the line his view of these dealings portrays crown authority as essentially hostile to recognition of the fundamental human rights of aboriginal people. The plaintiff, the attorney general of Ontario, succeeded in persuading the judge that constitutional tradition in this country justifies unilateral dispossession of Native people.

The principles of racial inequality that appear to inform the Steele decision may be attributable to the racism that predominated in the minds of the lawmakers during the eighteenth and nineteenth centuries. Steele himself asserted, for instance, that at the time of the Royal Proclamation "Europeans did not consider Indians to be equal to themselves."[43] Elsewhere he wrote of the attitude of colonial officials in the mid-nineteenth century "that the Indian occupation could not be considered as a true and legal habitation, and that Europeans were lawfully entitled to take possession of the land and to settle it with colonies." He added: "Whether or not this was the proper view, it was the view in 1845 of persons in what is now Ontario."[44]

Steele is on firm ground in suggesting that notions of racial inequality were ubiquitous and deep-rooted among colonial officials with responsibility for dealing with Indians. But there is also in the history of crown relations with Indians an imperial appreciation of them as useful allies with a role in helping to shield British North America from acquisition by the United States. While this strategic consideration was ultimately self-serving, it nevertheless resulted in the development of a regime of Indian affairs with an undercurrent of acknowledgment of aboriginal rights. The essential legacy of this acknowledgment is to be found in Indian treaties, agreements which could be regarded as the cutting edge of a process that might yet be cultivated to embrace the developing understanding of the importance of respect for human rights in the institutional structuring of political relations between peoples.

Steele was apparently persuaded by lawyers acting for the government of Ontario to disregard our country's earlier recognition of aboriginal rights. Instead he appears to have been persuaded to see Ontario law as flowing out of the racism that is also undeniably an aspect of the crown's historic dealings with Indians. This apparent legitimization of old racist principles through contemporary jurisprudence raises profound issues for society — issues suggested forcefully by James Youngblood Henderson in his commentary on "The Doctrine of aboriginal Rights in Western Legal Tradition." Although Henderson wrote his article before Steele came forward with his decision on the Temagami land dispute, the following passage could have been written with that judgment in mind:

> Instead of facing the role of law in society, weak judges rely on legal precedents and the history of imperial racism. The courts become the caretakers of the racism of the late nineteenth and

twentieth centuries. Such cowardice incurs an enormous cost. When governments act in a disorderly and lawless way, their courts save face by classifying oppression as justice or confiscation as a political question. Their decisions do not pretend to have any generality or stability, nor can they sensibly speak of fixed entitlements and duties. As a result, aboriginal people are deprived of the rule of law.

The historical fascination of Anglo-American society with terror — combined with the systematic use of violence unlimited by law as a device of social control — has laid the foundation for the destruction of all political and property rights in modern society. In its approach to the rights of native people the law becomes tyranny at worst and ineffective apologist at best. The Canadian government may call it law but it is racism. It is not founded on principles that recognize the supremacy of God and the rule of law.[45]

MORE CONTROVERSY AND LITIGATION

The partnership between Bruce Clark and Chief Potts broke up shortly following the handing down of the Ontario Supreme Court's judgment. Clark's handling of the case remains controversial. Not only did he lose the trust of his Indian clients but some charge that his argumentative zealousness was a major factor in stimulating Steele to write perhaps the most sweepingly hostile judicial opinion ever directed against Native people in Canada. In a strictly technical sense, the loss was monumental. On the other hand, perhaps over the long run the legal strategy of Chief Potts and Bruce Clark has forced out of the courts a finding so stunningly and explicitly anti-Indian that this increasingly apparent weakness in our judicial system can at last be squarely addressed. Indeed the problem goes far beyond the judiciary. By the end of the 1980s the many inquiries into the relationship between Native people and the apparatus of the law in Canada have made it even yet more clear that racist attitudes on the part of some officials have too often perverted the course of justice in this country.

Renounced by Native and non-Native colleagues alike, Bruce Clark has kept up the struggle, refining his major arguments in graduate school.[46] He continues to maintain that the Royal Proclamation of 1763 constitutes explicit imperial legislation at the constitutional foundation of Canada that has never been erased. If, as Steele finds, officials in the government of Ontario were capable of overriding the proclamation by unilaterally extinguishing the Indian right to remain "unmolested" in unceded Indian territory, it would not have been necessary to patriate the Canadian constitution in 1982. Before 1982 governments in Canada, whose powers were ultimately derived from the higher jurisdiction of the British imperial authority, did not have the legal capacity to supersede the rights of Indians as affirmed by King George in his famous proclamation.

The Teme-Augama Anishnabai appealed the Ontario Supreme Court's decision. As he approaches his third decade as the principal protagonist in this case, Chief Potts continues to vow that he will take his people's grievances as far as he must to receive justice, even if that involves going beyond Canada to international courts.

The decision of the Ontario Court of Appeal was rendered in the spring of 1989. In upholding the Supreme Court of Ontario judgment, the Court of Appeal was as hostile to the Native position as Steele had been. Indeed perhaps the Appeal Court's decision was even worse from a Native point of view. The Appeal Court judges devoted considerable space to their opinion that the Teme-Augama Anishnabai were represented at the treaty negotiations of 1850. The recorded acceptance by a Teme-Augama Anishnabai leader, Peter Nebenegwune, of $25 from the treaty commissioners was cited as evidence of their adhesion. And the Appeal Court judges made much of the role of a treaty participant by the name of Tawgaiwene who was found to have connections with the Native people in the Temagami area.[47]

In a few words the appeal judges found that "the relevant procedural aspects of the Royal Proclamation were repealed by the Quebec Act (1774)."[48] The anti-Indian argument concerning the Quebec Act, imperial legislation which attached the Indian territory to Quebec for administrative purposes, was first articulated by lawyers for Ontario in the St. Catherine's Milling case. They did not convince the Judicial Committee of the Privy Council. Writing for them in 1888 Lord Watson decided that "there has been no change since the year 1763 in the character of the interest which its Indian inhabitants had in the lands."[49] But the Appeal Court judges simply ignored this decision, which has been used so often against the claims of Indians. All that the judges indicated was that the "relevant procedural aspects" of the Royal Proclamation that have been "repealed" involve the necessity of "some public Meeting or Assembly" for the purchase of Indian rights to land.

If there is one underlying theme that seems to animate the decision both of Mr Justice Steele and the Ontario Court of Appeal, it is the elaboration of a doctrine for the extinguishment of aboriginal rights. The appeal judges added a new dimension to the lower court's doctrine of extinguishment in the concluding portions of their decision. They cited with approval a lengthy passage from the finding in the case of *Idaho versus Coffee*. In 1976 the Idaho Supreme Court held that it did not matter whether or not a band of Kootenai people were represented in the Indian treaty negotiations covering their ancestral lands. The court declared: "Whether the Indians signing the treaty had the power to give the land away is not relevant. The United States did have the power to take the land, and when it said it was receiving the land, the effect was that the land was taken."[50]

The resort to this finding as a precedent for the interpretation of Canadian Indian treaties smacks at the sensibilities of one schooled in the history of crown-Indian relations. The Royal Proclamation of 1763 marked a major dividing of the ways between those Euro-Americans whose leaders soon rejected the British imperial connection and those who did not.[51] The military alliances between the crown and Indians, as sometimes expressed in Indian treaties, became a significant strategic and geopolitical feature of government in that portion of the continent that remained under British rule. On the other hand, wars of conquest directed at different Indian groups, interspersed with the making and breaking of dozens of Indian treaties, were a major characteristic of the United States' westward-moving frontier during the decades following the American revolution.[52]

It seems inappropriate, to say the least, for the Ontario Appeal Court to fall back on the well-known American tradition of lawlessness surrounding Indian treaties as justification for its judicial assault on Indian treaties and aboriginal rights in Canada. But that is precisely what happened in the province at the very heart of the outward-reaching web of treaties which once were so instrumental in supporting the crown's land claim to large portions of the continent *vis-à-vis* the pretensions of Manifest Destiny in the United States. That such a finding was possible in the Ontario courts, then, speaks to issues that go beyond the injustice of one group towards another. The decision hints of a subversive undermining of well-established constitutional principles fundamental to the setting off of the northern portion of North America as a distinct society from the United States.

CONCLUSIONS

It was officials acting for the federal government who brought the Idaho case to the Appeal Court's attention. This intervention by federal law officers raises significant constitutional questions. Since the passing in 1867 of the British North America Act, which stipulated that "Indians and lands reserved for the Indians" fall within the legislative field of the Dominion parliament, it has come to be understood that the federal authority bears the largest part of the responsibility to uphold crown obligations to protect Indian interests against encroachment by other jurisdictions.[53] In his arguments for Ontario in the *St. Catherine's Milling* case, Edward Blake described this Dominion responsibility as one of "protector and vindicator of the Indian rights."[54] In 1984 the Supreme Court of Canada gave renewed vigour to the principle in its finding on the Guerin case involving the land rights of the Musqueam Indians of British Columbia. This major decision indicated that the federal government has a legally enforceable fiduciary duty to safeguard those aboriginal interests in land and resources which are entrusted to its care.[55] In this light, the federal government's intervention against the interests of the Teme-Augama Anishnabai runs counter to its constitutional role as guardian of Indian rights. Indeed a strong case could be made that, by intervening in this way, the federal government has abandoned its fiduciary obligations to Native people.

Moreover, the major thrust of Mr Justice Steele's whole finding, which is founded on the notion that the source of aboriginal rights lies in the crown, appears to have been completely undermined by the opening passage of the Supreme Court's decision in the Guerin case. There the Supreme Court declared: "The Indians' interest in their land is a pre-existing legal right not created by the Royal Proclamation of 1763, by s. 18 (1) of the Indian Act, or by any other executive order or legislative provision. The nature of the Indians' interest is best characterized by its inalienability, coupled with the fact that the Crown is under an obligation to deal with the land on the Indians' behalf when the interest is surrendered."[56] In an addendum to his decision, Mr Justice Steele argued that the author of the Guerin decision, Supreme Court Justice Brian Dickson, was wrong if the implication of his finding was that the crown could not unilaterally extinguish Indian title. This rather strange dismissal of the higher court's finding was based further on Steele's suggestion that the Guerin case has application only to British Columbia.[57] The Ontario Appeal Court failed to address directly this especially dubious feature of Steele's decision.

The responsibility for the federal intervention in the Temagami land dispute, of course, lies ultimately with federal politicians. A similar reality holds true for the government of Ontario. It is the provincial attorney general who bears major responsibility for the arguments developed against the Teme-Augama Anishnabai. A significant intent of this paper has been to demonstrate how fully these provincial arguments run against any enlightened conception of a just regime that respects human rights and abhors racism. Is it overblown rhetoric to suggest that there is a drift towards tyranny in the political assertion of power to extinguish unilaterally the rights of people? Is it unduly alarmist to fear the genocidal or ethnocidal implications of this tendency?

The distance between the provincial government's political policies and the contents of its legal arguments against the Teme-Augama Anishnabai points to the dangers which accompany the employment of adversarial litigation in its present format as a means to address issues involving such basic human rights. New and innovative forums of arbitration are required to adjudicate how the rights and responsibilities of aboriginal groups are to be balanced against the interests of others, especially in disputes involving jurisdiction over land. The day should have passed long ago when it was even thinkable for the chief legal officer of a province or of Canada to oppose aboriginal assertions by making recourse to such discredited old theories of racial hierarchy. It does a grave injustice to the wider citizenry to present such arguments on its behalf. It is a mode of dealing with disputes which ultimately chips away at the very credibility of government as an effective instrument in the protection of the fundamental rights and freedoms of groups and individuals.

What makes Mr Justice Steele's finding such a remarkable document of social history is the extent to which he was won over to the extreme kinds of adversarial positions advanced by Ontario's law officers. Unfortunately, it is difficult not to see in the court's judgment parallels with other instances of marked judicial bias against Native people that came to light in the late 1980s. Both the Manitoba aboriginal Justice Inquiry and the royal commission which investigated the wrongful conviction for murder of Micmac Donald Marshall Jr point to a bias in the enforcement of Canada's criminal code among Native people.[58] Steele's rigid doctrine of extinguishment seems to reflect a similar application of civil law to the collective human rights of Native people.

To put the matter plainly, it is difficult to avoid the conclusion that the treatment afforded Indians by the Ontario courts was different in kind from that which could be anticipated by almost any other group. Imagine, for instance, the political consequences that would flow from a judicial finding that Roman Catholic rights, Jewish rights, or French-language rights can be unilaterally extinguished. What major religious, ethnic, or linguistic collectivity other than aboriginal people would be expected to rest calm in the face of such a decision? What other group would be expected to remain patient with a judicial system that threatened its identity and collective survival with such a potent legal weapon?

The passage of this important aboriginal-rights case through the Ontario courts was accompanied, especially during the late 1980s, by an increasingly tough struggle between environmentalists and those with an interest in logging what remains of the old-growth forest in Temagami. The primary focus of the confrontations was along the construction site which marked out the extension of the Red Squirrel road into one of the most majestic of the province's remaining wilderness areas. At intervals the Teme-Augama Anishnabai and the Temagami Wilderness Society raised a series of blockades to prevent or slow work on the Red Squirrel road. Over three hundred people were arrested over a period of several months in the fall and early winter of 1989, a show of civil disobedience which by Ontario standards is quite significant. Certainly some of those charged, Indians and non-Indians, based at least part of their decision to break the law on their assessment of the quality of justice handed down by Mr Justice Steele and the Ontario Court of Appeal.

The road nevertheless was completed on schedule, a corresponding demonstration of political will on the part of the Ontario government. Clearly the intent was to stress forcefully that the entrenched way of doing things was not to be put off track by the assertiveness of Indians or by the advocates of wilderness preservation. When pushed to reveal its true priorities, the Liberal government of Premier David Peterson showed itself as unrelenting in the use of police, dynamite, and bulldozers as it was with the use of ideological explosives in the court to remove any barrier which obstructed the realization of a particular vision of economic advancement.

This convergence of aboriginal issues with environmental concerns is part of a world-wide phenomenon. Often times patterns of history, geography, and economics have combined to cast indigenous societies — the peoples with the deepest cultural roots in the ecology of particular places — in roles where they provide the inspirational guidance that is helping to mobilize environmentalism as such an influential political force. Often times these aboriginal groups, whether in the Himalayas of India or in the rainforests of Brazil or in the old-growth stands of Temagami, become in effect the last remaining human barriers standing before the bulldozers in the market-driven assault on what remains of the world's rapidly diminishing treasure of relatively undisturbed forest life.

In 1987 the Brundtland report, the highly esteemed statement by the World Commission on Environment and Development, stressed the importance of respecting the integrity of indigenous societies as an essential component in the formulation of national strategies aimed at sustainable economic development. The commissioners noted:

> These [aboriginal] communities are the repositories of vast accumulations of traditional knowledge and experience that links humanity with its ancient origins. Their disappearance is a loss for the larger society, which could learn a great deal from their traditional skills in sustainably managing very complex ecological systems. It is a terrible irony that as formal development reaches more deeply into rain forests, deserts, and other isolated environments, it tends to destroy the only cultures that have proved able to thrive in these environments.
>
> The starting point for a just and humane policy for such groups is the recognition and protection of their traditional rights to land and other resources that sustain their way of life — rights they may define in terms that do not fit into standard legal systems. These groups' own institutions to regulate rights and obligations are crucial for maintaining the harmony with nature and the environmental awareness characteristic of the traditional way of life. Hence the recognition of traditional rights must go hand in hand with measures to protect the local institutions that enforce responsibility in resource use. And this recognition must also give local communities a decisive voice in the decisions about resource use in the area ....
>
> In terms of sheer numbers, these isolated, vulnerable groups are small. But their marginalization is a symptom of a style of development that tends to neglect both human and environmental considerations. Hence a more careful and sensitive consideration of their interest is a touchstone of sustainable development policy.[59]

Perhaps the most telling manifestation of environmental degradation is the escalating rate at which species are becoming extinct on this planet. Plants and animals are diminishing in variety as pollution and the rapaciousness of the rush to transform nature into capital undermine the genetic building blocks of life itself. The organized effort to protect what remains of the old-growth forest in Temagami is a small but significant part of the world-wide movement to curtail further impoverishment of the earth's genetic resources. Old-growth forests are complex ecosystems that are major storehouses of genetic diversity. When these forests are cut down, their genetic resources are massively lessened, even if replanting takes place. Tree plantations modelled along agricultural lines are more the domain of monocultures. The genetic pluralism in the mass of life forms associated with the old-growth forest is replaced by the genetic uniformity of the tree farm.

Just as human beings are responsible for a diminishment in the diversity of many life forms, so we are experiencing — with the market-driven expansion of mass society — a corresponding loss of cultural and linguistic pluralism among ourselves. Recognition of the connection between the impoverishment of genetic diversity and of the limiting of cultural pluralism is essential to understanding the linkage between environmentalism and the movement to protect and celebrate aboriginality. Alternatively, this connection presents a broader context in which to assess the principle asserted by Mr Justice Steele and others that because nation states have the power they have the right to extinguish the collective existence of aboriginal communities. It makes clear that continuing down this road has suicidal implications for everyone.

Enlightened formulation and interpretation of national constitutions represent an important means of striving to achieve a degree of ecological harmony in relationships between indigenous groups and others in the so-called New World. Such affirmations of equality between peoples and respect for those societies with the deepest roots in the land could both mirror and inspire the broader environmental initiative to halt the assault on life in its full, wonderful complexity of myriad forms.[60] Accordingly, the convergence of forces with a competitive will to exercise power over the use of Temagami lands presents an historic opportunity to develop the discourse we need on a range of crucial issues.

As this is being written, the Teme-Augama Anishnabai are preparing to bring their case before the Supreme Court of Canada. Let there be no delusions about the significance of the principles in question in this effort to arbitrate where justice lies.

EPILOGUE

Public concern in Ontario for the fate of Temagami was especially evident during the 1990 Earth Day festivities throughout the province. The following day, 23 April, the government of Ontario announced the creation of a joint-stewardship council to exercise jurisdiction over a 440-square-kilometre section of Temagami, or about one-quarter of the region covered by old-growth forest. Half of the council's membership is to be appointed by the Teme-Augama Anishnabai and half by the government of Ontario.[61]

The creation of this council represents a significant break with tradition for the Ontario government. Rather than gearing the province's legal strategies towards the extinguishment of aboriginal rights, the Peterson administration attempted a political innovation to create a new channel for the exercise of aboriginal rights. Rather than treating aboriginal people as awkward remnants of a past era of human development, the stewardship council implicitly recognizes in aboriginal society a rich source of insight and expertise that should be afforded due authority in the making of land-use decisions. This important innovation will almost certainly become a significant model in working towards more enlightened regimes of ordering the ecological relationships between human beings and the other living entities who draw sustenance from our Mother Earth.

While the creation of the stewardship council holds much promise, the initiative remains relatively limited in scope. The decision, for instance, still leaves the largest part of Temagami's old-growth forest firmly under the authority of the Ministry of Natural Resources. And the existence of the stewardship council does nothing in itself to resolve the dispute over land title, which remains at the heart of the legal clash between the Teme-Augama Anishnabai and the government of Ontario.

That dispute continues its way towards judgment by the Supreme Court of Canada.

On the other hand, the creation of the joint-stewardship council begins to set in place one of the fixtures that could be incorporated into the "treaty of co-existence" sought by Chief Potts on behalf of the Teme-Augama Anishnabai. Ultimately, the pursuit of this land claim through the courts is intended to create the political requirements for the negotiation of such a treaty, a treaty whose realization no doubt would breath new life into the entire constitutional tradition of crown relations with Indians as rooted in the Royal Proclamation of 1763. With the breath of new life would come a revitalized sense of integrity and purpose in a government founded on promises that were to last as long as the sun shines, as long as the grass grows, and as long as the rivers flow.

[1] James S. Frideres, *Native People in Canada: Contemporary Conflicts*, 3rd edition (Scarborough: Prentice–Hall, 1988), 138–206; Andrew J. Siggner, "The Socio–Demographic Conditions of Registered Indians," in J. Rick Ponting, ed., *Arduous Journey: Canadian Indians and Decolonization* (Toronto: McClelland and Stewart, 1986), 57–83.

[2] See Russell Lawrence Barsh, "Behind Land Claims: Rationalizing Dispossession in Anglo–American Law," *Law and Anthropology: Internationales Jahrbuch fur Rechtsanthropologie* 1, 1986, 15–50.

[3] See Christine Bolt, *Victorian Attitudes to Race* (Toronto: University of Toronto Press, 1971); Marvin Harris, *The Rise of Anthropological Theory: a History of Theories of Culture* (New York: Thomas Y. Crowell, 1968), 80–215; Robert F. Berkhofer, *The White Man's Indian* (New York: Vintage, 1979), 49–61; Bruce G. Trigger, "Giants and Pygmies: The Professionalization of Canadian Archaeology," in Glyn Daniel, ed., *Towards a History of Archaeology* (London: Thames and Hudson, 1981).

[4] See James Cullingham, "Home and Native Land," *Saturday Night* vol. 98, no. 4, April 1983, 7–11; Bruce W. Hodgins and Jamie Benidickson, *The Temagami Experience: Recreation, Resources, and Aboriginal Rights in the Northern Ontario Wilderness* (Toronto: University of Toronto Press, 1989), 267–89.

5   See Thomas Berger, "The Nishga Indians and Aboriginal Rights," in Berger, ed., *Fragile Freedoms: Human Rights and Dissent in Canada* (Toronto: Clarke Irwin, 1982), 219–54.

6   See Bruce W. Hodgins, "The Temagami Indians and Canadian Federalism: 1867–1943," *Laurentian University Review*, vol. 11, no. 2, (February 1979), 71–100.

7   See Tony Hall, "Indian Treaties," in *The Canadian Encyclopedia* (2nd edition), vol. 2, 1056–59.

8   Royal Courts of Justice, *The Queen* v. *The Secretary of State for Foreign and Commonwealth Affairs ex parte The Indian Association of Alberta, Union of New Brunswick Indians, Union of Nova Scotian Indians, 28 January 1982*, xerox, 7–8.

9   The Royal Proclamation is published in its entirety in Ian A.L. Getty and Antoine Lussier, eds., *As Long as the Sun Shines and Water Flows: A Reader in Canadian Native Studies* (Vancouver: University of British Columbia Press, 1983), 29–36.

10 See Brian Slattery, "The Hidden Constitution: Aboriginal Rights in Canada," in Menno Boldt and J. Anthony Long, eds., *The Quest for Justice: Aboriginal Peoples and Aboriginal Rights* (Toronto: University of Toronto Press, 1985), 114–38.

11 See Clarence Walworth Alvord, *The Mississippi Valley in British Politics: A Study in Trade, Land Speculation and Experiments in Imperialism Culminating in the American Revolution* (Cleveland: Arthur H. Clark, 1917); Jack M. Sosin, *Whitehall and the Wilderness: The Middle West in British Colonial Policy, 1760–1775* (Lincoln: The University of Nebraska Press, 1961); Francis Jennings, *Empire of Fortune: Crowns, Colonies and Tribes in the Seven Years' War in America* (New York: W.W. Norton, 1988).

12 See Robert S. Allen, "The British Indian Department and the Frontier in North America, 1755–1830," Canadian Historical Sites, *Occasional Papers in Archaeology and History*, no. 14, (Ottawa: 1975), 5–125

13 See A.L. Burt, *The United States, Great Britain and British North America from the Revolution to the Establishment of Peace after the War of 1812* (New Haven: Yale University Press, 1940); Colin G. Calloway, *Crown and Calumet: British–Indian Relations, 1783–1815* (Norman: University of Oklahoma Press, 1987).

14 See Robert J. Surtees, "Indian Land Cessions in Ontario, 1763–1862: The Evolution of a System," Ph.D. thesis, Carleton University, 1982; Ian Johnson, "The Early Mississauga Treaty Process, 1781–1819," in Historical Perspective, Ph.D. thesis, University of Toronto, 1986.

15 See G.F.G. Stanley, "The Indians and the War of 1812" in Morris Zaslow, ed.,

The Defended Border: Upper Canada and the War of 1812 (Toronto: Macmillan, 1964), 174–88; Colin Calloway, *Crown and Calumet*, 193–222; Robert S. Allen, "His Majesty's Indian Allies: Native Peoples, the British Crown and the War of 1812," *Michigan Historical Review*, vol. 14, no. 2, (fall 1988), 1–24.

16 *Reports of the Supreme Court of Canada,* vol. 13 (Ottawa, 1887), 609–10.

17 See James W. St. G. Walker, "The Indian in Canadian Historical Writing," Canadian Historical Association, *Historical Papers*, 1971, 21–50; Bruce G. Trigger, "The Historians' Indian: Native Americans in Canadian Historical Writing from Charlevoix to the Present," *Canadian Historical Review*, vol. 67, no. 3, (September, 1986), 315–342.

18 I have drawn this account of the early stages of the case primarily from discussions with James Morrison.

19 The relationship between Chief Potts and Bruce Clark is discussed in some detail in John Lorinc, "If God is on Vacation," *This Magazine*, vol. 23, no. 4, (November, 1989), 22–7.

20 See Donald B. Smith, *From the Land of Shadows: The Making of Grey Owl* (Saskatoon: Western Producer Prairie Books, 1990).

21 *Hamlet of Baker Lake et al.* v. *Minister of Indian Affairs and Northern Development,* 1980. The case is discussed in Bradford W. Morse, ed., *Aboriginal Peoples and the Law: Indian, Metis and Inuit Rights in Canada* (Ottawa: Carleton University Press, 1985), 81–4.

22 *Attorney-General for Ontario* v. *Bear Island Foundation et al., Potts et al.* v. *Attorney-General for Ontario,* 11 December 1984 in *Ontario Reports*, 2nd series, vol. 49, 1985, 366 (hereafter cited as *OR*).

23 She used the phrase in a conversation with Bruce Hodgins at a Native-studies conference at Trent University in 1985.

24 *OR*, 390.

25 *Ibid.*, 381.

26 *Appeal Cases before the House of Lords and the Judicial Committee of the Privy Council,* vol. 14 (London, 1889), 54.

27 Tony Hall, "*The St. Catherine's Milling and Lumber Company* v. *The Queen*: Indian Land Rights as a Factor in Federal–Provincial Relations in Nineteenth–Century Canada," paper presented in 1988 at a conference at the University of Manitoba. The paper will be published by the University of Manitoba Press in conference proceedings entitled *Aboriginal Resource Use in Canada*, Jean Friesen and Kerry Abel, eds..

28 *OR*, 381.

29 *Ibid.*, 436.

30 *Ibid.*, 381.

31 *Ibid*, 375. On Pontiac's uprising see Howard H. Peckham, *Pontiac and the Indian Uprising* (Chicago: University of Chicago Press, 1947). On the implications of how Britain's conquest of the French affected Indian land title in North America see W.J. Eccles, "Sovereignty-Association, 1500–1783," *Canadian Historical Review*, vol. 65, no. 4 (December, 1984), 475–510.

32 *OR*, 386–92.

33 See Thomas Flanagan, "From Indian Title to Aboriginal Rights," in Louis A. Knafla, ed., *Law and Justice in a New Land: Essays in Western Canadian Legal History* (Toronto: Carswell, 1986), 81–100.

34 *OR*, 386–7.

35 *Ibid.*, 391.

36 *Ibid.*, 387–93.

37 *Ibid.*, 410.

38 *Ibid.*, 441.

39 *Ibid.*, 378–9.

40 *Ibid.*, 466.

43 *Ibid.*, 440.

42 *Ibid.*, 457–66.

43 *Ibid.*, 386.

44 *Ibid.*, 384.

45 James Youngblood Henderson, "The Doctrine of Aboriginal Rights in Western Legal Tradition," in Boldt and Long, eds., *Quest for Justice*, 220.

46 Bruce Clark's M.A. thesis, written for the University of Western Ontario, is published as *Indian Title in Canada* (Toronto: Carswell, 1987). His Ph.D. thesis, entitled, "The Right of Indian Self–Government in Canada," was written for the University of Aberdeen.

47 *The Attorney General for Ontario* v. *The Bear Island Foundation et al.*, 27 February 1989, xerox copy of Appeal Court's finding, 14–25 (hereafter cited as AC).

48 *Ibid.*, 29.

49 *Appeal Cases before the House of Lords and the Judicial Committee of the Privy Council*, vol. 14, 54.

50 AC, 34.

51 *Empire of Fortune* (see note 11). In Francis Jennings's concluding volume of his monumental Covenant Chain series, he stresses that the Royal Proclamation of 1763 marks a major watershed in North American history. The proclamation created the essential framework for the clash of interests that eventually exploded in the American revolution.

52 See Richard Slotkin, *Regeneration Through Violence: The Mythology of the American Frontier, 1600–1860* (Middletown: Wesleyan University Press, 1983); Richard Drinnon, *Facing West: The Metaphysics of Indian–Hating and Empire Building* (New York: Meridian, 1980).

53 Bradford Morse, "Government Obligations, Aboriginal Peoples and Section 91(24) of the Constitution Act, 1867," in David C. Hawkes, ed., *Aboriginal Peoples and Government Responsibility: Exploring Federal and Provincial Roles* (Ottawa: Carleton University Press, 1989), 59–91.

54 *The Ontario Lands Case, Arguments of Mr. Blake Q.C. Before the Privy Council* (Toronto: Press of the Budget, 1988), 18.

55 On the Guerin case see R. H. Bartlett, "You Can't Trust the Crown: The Fiduciary Obligation of the Crown to the Indians: *Guerin* v. *The Queen*," *Saskatchewan Law Review*, vol. 49, 1984–85, 367.

56 *Guerin* v. *The Queen, Supreme Court of Canada Reports*, 1984, 335.

57 *OR*, 480–2.

58 See Tony Hall, "What are We? Chopped Liver? Aboriginal Affairs in the Constitutional Politics of Canada in the 1980's," in Michael D. Behiels, ed., *The Meech Lake Primer: Conflicting Views of the 1987 Constitutional Accord* (Ottawa: University of Ottawa Press, 1989), 447–8.

59 World Commission on Environment and Development, *Our Common Future* (Oxford: Oxford University Press, 1987), 114–6.

60 On the connection between aboriginal issues and environmentalism, see Christopher Vecsey and Robert W. Venables, eds., *American Indian Environments: Ecological Issues in Native American History* (Syracuse: Syracuse University Press, 1980).

61 *Globe and Mail*, 24 April 1990.

FIGURE 1

**TEMAGAMI AREA
BEAR ISLAND
INDIAN BAND
LAND CLAIM
BOUNDARY &
CAUTION**

Bear Island Indian Band
Land Claim Boundary

Caution Boundary

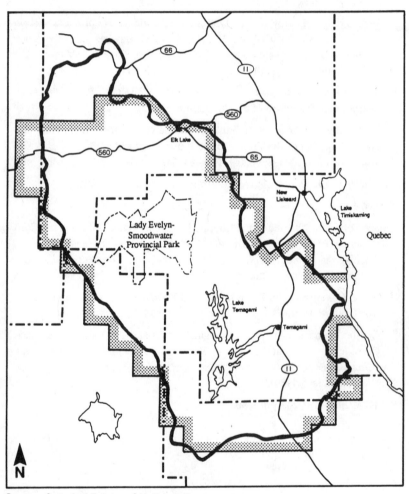

Source: Ontario Ministry of National Resources

"Ancient Pine" by Hap Wilson. (© Copyright 1990 Hap Wilson.)

Printed in Canada